"Jonathan's rare combination of academic's insight and practitioner's experience has enabled him to create a series of important business innovations that have really worked."

—ROY SHAPIRO,
Philip Caldwell Professor of Business Administration
and former senior associate dean,
Harvard Business School

"Byrnes wastes no time in getting straight to the point. This fast-paced book is rich with concisely expressed ideas and concrete advice."

—DAVID MAISTER,
author of *Managing the Professional Service Firm*
and *True Professionalism*

"Jonathan Byrnes has just advanced the field of management in one evolutionary volume. If profitability is your goal, you can't afford not to read this book." —ROBERT KRAFT, President, FOX Music

"Jonathan has showed our company that some of the most powerful ideas don't cost a lot of money or require complex implementations. The concepts of understanding profitability and mining your company for your own best practice are very real and actionable by all levels of the organization." —ERIK GERSHWIND,
EVP and COO, MSC Industrial Direct

"This is a book for our times. With businesses under ever-increasing pressure to perform, Jonathan Byrnes distills twenty years of experience teaching corporate executives at MIT to identify key 'profit levers' to help enhance a company's profitability. *Islands of Profit in a Sea of Red Ink* is an insightful, intelligently written book. A must-read for any manager."

—BROOKS NEWMARK,
member of parliament for Braintree

"This is a very important book for managers at companies of all sizes. Jonathan Byrnes has done a masterly job explaining the fifth 'P,' Profitability, and how significant it is. This book should be read by both students and managers." —DON ROSENFIELD,
senior lecturer, Sloan School of Management,
and director, Leaders for Global Operations Program, MIT

# ISLANDS OF PROFIT IN A SEA OF RED INK

# ISLANDS OF PROFIT IN A SEA OF RED INK

## Why 40% of Your Business is Unprofitable, and How to Fix It

### JONATHAN L.S. BYRNES

PORTFOLIO / PENGUIN

PORTFOLIO PENGUIN
Published by the Penguin Group
Penguin Group (USA) Inc., 375 Hudson Street,
New York, New York 10014, U.S.A.
Penguin Group (Canada), 90 Eglinton Avenue East, Suite 700,
Toronto, Ontario, Canada M4P 2Y3
(a division of Pearson Penguin Canada Inc.)
Penguin Books Ltd, 80 Strand, London WC2R 0RL, England
Penguin Ireland, 25 St. Stephen's Green, Dublin 2, Ireland
(a division of Penguin Books Ltd)
Penguin Books Australia Ltd, 250 Camberwell Road, Camberwell,
Victoria 3124, Australia
(a division of Pearson Australia Group Pty Ltd)
Penguin Books India Pvt Ltd, 11 Community Centre, Panchsheel Park,
New Delhi – 110 017, India
Penguin Group (NZ), 67 Apollo Drive, Rosedale, North Shore 0632,
New Zealand (a division of Pearson New Zealand Ltd)
Penguin Books (South Africa) (Pty) Ltd, 24 Sturdee Avenue,
Rosebank, Johannesburg 2196, South Africa

Penguin Books Ltd, Registered Offices:
80 Strand, London WC2R 0RL, England

First published in 2010 by Portfolio Penguin,
a member of Penguin Group (USA) Inc.

1  3  5  7  9  10  8  6  4  2

Charts by the author

LIBRARY OF CONGRESS CATALOGING IN PUBLICATION DATA
Byrnes, Jonathan L. S.
Islands of profit in a sea of red ink : why 40% of your business is unprofitable,
and how to fix it / Jonathan L.S. Byrnes.
p. cm.
Includes index.
ISBN 978-1-59184-349-8
1.  Corporate profits.   2.  Industrial management.   3.  Cost effectiveness.   I.  Title.
HG4028.P7B97 2010
658.15'54—dc22
2010017340

Printed in the United States of America
Set in Whitman
Designed by Pauline Neuwirth, Neuwirth & Associates, Inc. (AMP)

*This book is dedicated to my family:*
*the happiness of my life.*

# CONTENTS

## SECTION 2. SELLING FOR PROFIT

# SECTION 3. OPERATING FOR PROFIT

# SECTION 4. LEADING FOR PROFIT

# INTRODUCTION

**ISLANDS OF PROFIT** in a sea of red ink. The fundamental premise of this book is an astonishing proposition: nearly 40 percent of every company is unprofitable by any measure, and 20 to 30 percent is so profitable that it is providing all the reported earnings and cross-subsidizing the losses. The rest of the company is only marginal.

I first discovered this about twenty years ago in work that I did with one of the premier companies in the laboratory supply industry. Since that time, I found the same pattern in my research and consulting with leading companies in industries as diverse as hospital supplies, telecommunications, and steel. And these were not laggards; they were among the highest-performing firms in business.

In these projects, I created a systematic process for analyzing a company's profitability, and I developed a number of "profit levers" for turning unprofitable business into good business, and good business into great business.

## Two puzzling questions

This work raised a couple of very puzzling questions: Why is this occurring now in so many companies across all industries? Why is it difficult for managers to get their arms around this huge opportunity, and to act on it?

When I explored these two issues with a number of insightful managers, it became clear that the answer is rooted in a major, historical transition that business is going through today: a change from the prior Age of Mass Markets to a new era in business, the Age of Precision Markets (more on this later). The underlying problem is that most of the management processes and control information in business were developed in the prior era, and are no longer appropriate.

This is the cause of the high level of embedded unprofitability in industry after industry. It means that effective managers today not only have to understand how to profit from this huge new opportunity, they also have to recognize the sources of resistance, and be adept at managing constructive, paradigmatic change.

## HBS *Working Knowledge*

A few years ago, Sean Silverthorne, the editor of Harvard Business School's *Working Knowledge* e-newsletter, suggested that I write a monthly column on this subject. Over the course of four years, I wrote a series of columns that covered these topics.

I remember when I wrote my first column, "Who's Managing Profitability?" which forms the basis for the first chapter of this book. *Working Knowledge* has a readership of tens of thousands of managers all over the world, and the premise of the column was that in most companies, *no one* is managing profitability effectively. I held my breath when the column went out over the Internet on a Monday morning, wondering what the reaction would be.

The reaction was immediate and decisive. My in-box was flooded with dozens of e-mails from managers agreeing with my conclusions.

I wrote nearly fifty columns on profitability management. In each one I explained how to systematically improve a core business process in a practical, hands-on way. I wrote the columns to be high-impact guidelines for action, designed to be read quickly on the Internet—lots of meat without much fat, most with a very precise to-do list at the end.

Most of my columns were widely reprinted in other publications. Many are used in university courses and training programs. Each of these columns was read by and vetted against the experience of thousands of managers. To this day, no one has disagreed with my conclusions and recommendations.

■ ■ ■

# Overview of this book

A number of managers have asked me to develop my *Working Knowledge* columns and some of my other writings into a book. The book that you have in hand is the result of these requests.

I've kept the action-oriented format, and I've organized the chapters into four topics:

▶ Thinking for Profit
▶ Selling for Profit
▶ Operating for Profit
▶ Leading for Profit

This book is about how to make more money from an existing business without costly new initiatives. Its chapters tell you how to systematically improve your business, land the best customers, build your managers' capabilities, and secure your future through thoughtful, effective management. These improvements will not cost you money; in fact, almost all of them will generate profits and cash from the start.

This is a handbook for all the managers in your company, whether you're a global conglomerate or a local shop with five employees. Regardless of the size of your business, it will guide you in moving your business up to its full potential.

At the end of each chapter, I've included a section called "Things to Think About," which highlights the chapter's critical points and suggests how to put them into action. In my courses at MIT, I conclude each class session this way to help my students consolidate their understanding and relate it to their careers. Many have said that this is one of the most valuable parts of my teaching. Several have told me that they keep a typed version of these comments close at hand for reference.

This book follows a logical sequence that enables you to understand the new opportunities, identify the most productive courses of action, and lead the creation of a high-performing management team. I designed the format to help you thumb through to, or return to, the topics that interest you, and easily share these ideas with your colleagues and associates. You should follow your interests, but reading the whole book in order will give you the complete picture you need to manage effectively in today's new era of business.

# New era in business

Why are these huge opportunities present in so many companies today? The answer lies in the sea change that's taking place in business, which I explain in chapter 3, "The Age of Precision Markets."

Today, business is going through a transition from one era to another, from an era of mass markets to an era I call the Age of Precision Markets. In the old era, companies distributed their products as widely as possible using arm's-length customer relationships. Their goal was mass production and mass distribution. In the mass-market era, broad management measures like aggregate revenues and costs were adequate for maximizing profitability. Almost all the management systems and processes in companies today are implicitly geared to meet this legacy objective.

In the new era, however, companies increasingly form different relationships with different sets of customers. These relationships range from arm's length to highly integrated, and include almost everything in between. Today, leading companies are reducing the ranks of their suppliers by 40 to 60 percent or more, creating enormous new opportunities for their most capable suppliers to dramatically increase profits and market share.

The successful business today creates huge competitive advantage and high sustained profitability by developing innovative customer relationships and new types of customer value, and by aligning its internal processes. However, this is a two-edged sword: if customers are matched with the right relationships, and the new value is compelling, sales and profits can increase . . . but if these matches are not done well, profitability plunges.

In this new world, the broad metrics and management approaches of the past no longer enable managers to maximize their companies' profitability. This is the underlying reason for the problematic profitability patterns I've seen so often. It creates an enormous new set of opportunities for the manager who wants to take up the challenge to manage in a new way.

The chapters in this book chronicle this transition and tell you how to create the successful business of the future—what to do, how to do it, what difficulties you'll probably encounter, and how to overcome them. My objective, the reason I wrote this book, is to give you the road map, perspective, and tools that you need to be a highly effective manager in this new era of business.

## Your own best practices

Think about this. Imagine that someone took a comprehensive video of everything that went on in your company over the course of a year, and then edited it carefully to pull out your own best practices. When you view the edited film, I'm certain you'd see the best company in the world.

The problem, however, lies on the cutting-room floor: all the rest of your company's activities that don't live up to your own best practice. When you look at your company's actual performance—net profits, market share, customer relations, operations efficiency—you're looking at a blend of your own best practices and everything else that doesn't meet this standard.

How important is this? It creates the profitability pattern that is the core of this book: islands of profit in a sea of red ink.

When my first *Working Knowledge* column appeared on the Internet, several thoughtful managers sent me notes sharing their experiences.

One CEO wrote to say that he saw this pattern in his company. His biggest concern was how vulnerable he would be if a competitor focused on picking off his most profitable customers.

A senior vice president of sales wrote, "I guess I have two ways to get a 30 percent profit increase: boost my sales by 40 percent, adding a lot of new low-margin business, or focus on managing the day-to-day details of the business. It's a pretty easy choice."

These executives' reactions sum up what this book is about. There is an enormous amount of money to be made by improving the business you already have in hand. For some managers, it's easier to spend money on glossy new initiatives than to systematically improve the business. But when your business is tuned up to its full potential, you can drive it like a Ferrari. It's hugely fun and immensely satisfying to manage. It's also very rewarding.

## Who should read this book

This book is designed to be a handbook of profitability management, one that a top manager in either a large or small company can give to every manager in his or her organization. However, in my experience corresponding with readers, particular sets of managers are especially interested in certain material. Here's a quick guide.

**TOP MANAGERS (CEOs, vice presidents, and general managers).** These managers need to read the book from cover to cover in order to develop effective profitability management programs and guide their subordinate managers. Most top managers have been particularly interested in the material in sections 1 and 4. In particular, chapters 1, 2, 3, 4, 9, 10, 16, 17, 19, 25, 26, 31, 32, 33, and 36 have generated a lot of top management e-mails. Chapters 31 and 32 are especially critical for this group.

**CFOs**. This whole book is extremely relevant for a CFO. If a CFO wants to read selectively, I suggest starting with chapter 9, then continuing with chapters 1, 2, 3, 6, 7, 8, 10, 12, 14, 19, 20, 21, 24, 25, 27, 32, and 34.

**Department heads (director-level managers).** These managers are the heart of all successful profitability management programs. They need to understand the overall concepts, and must coordinate with their counterpart department heads. For all these individuals, sections 1 and 4 are critical. In addition, they should do a "deep dive" in their respective areas of responsibility, and also develop a general understanding of their counterparts' respective areas of management. Above all, department heads must develop a very clear understanding and practical appreciation for chapters 28, 31, and 32, which explain change management and organizational effectiveness.

**Front-line managers.** A front-line manager should focus on developing and managing the profit levers in his or her area of responsibility. Sections 2 and 3 provide deep knowledge in this area. Beyond this, the overall understanding of profitability management that section 1 provides, and the broad overview of leadership that section 4 provides (especially chapter 36), will give a front-line manager an important leg up on career advancement.

**Small business owners/managers and entrepreneurs.** The name of the game for these managers is to go as far as possible with as few resources as possible. These individuals should focus strongly on section 1, especially chapters 2, 5, 6, 9, and 10. In addition, the chapters in sections 2 and 3 offer a number of concrete ways to maximize asset productivity and cash flow. Chapters 11, 12, 13, 15, 16, 18, 19, 21, 22, and 23 are especially relevant. In section 4, chapters 27, 29, 30, and 35 are very important to this group.

## Major profitability and market share increases

All the chapters in this book are based on work that I've done directly with great companies and creative managers over a period of more than twenty years. In most of these consulting projects, I have worked directly with the top-level executives of leading companies to create new strategic initiatives and new ways of doing business that have transformed their companies and industries. I have been very fortunate that I've been given the scope to "challenge everything" and look for innovative ways to make things better. This book is the direct result of these experiences.

In addition to my corporate work, I'm a teacher. I have taught graduate students and executives at MIT for nearly twenty years. Thousands of my former students are putting these ideas into practice every day, and letting me know about their successes.

I hope that this material helps you transform your company, and I look forward to hearing about your experiences.

# THINKING
# FOR PROFIT

# INTRODUCTION

**WHO'S MANAGING PROFITABILITY?** In nearly all companies, the answer is that *no one is*. And most managers aren't even aware that this is a problem.

The first step toward solving this problem is to get your managers to start thinking about profitability in a systematic, productive way. Once they have a practical framework, they can coordinate with one another to systematically increase your company's profitability. This section tells you how to do it.

Section 1 covers strategy, profitability maximization, and business alignment. It explains the nature and source of embedded unprofitability, the size of the potential gain, why it happens in so many companies, and how to analyze the problem. This section also tells you how to define and prioritize practical initiatives to increase your company's profitability. It gives several specific examples, and describes why profitability management is especially important in difficult economic times.

## Why is there so much embedded unprofitability?

**Chapter 1, Who's Managing Profitability?** describes the situation of most companies, in which large portions of the business are unprofitable by any measure, and a few islands of high profitability are providing all the reported net profits and cross-subsidizing the unprofitable business. The chapter explains the root causes and outlines three essential elements for successfully managing profitability.

**Chapter 2, "Revenues are Good, Costs are Bad" and Other Business Myths,** highlights a number of common misconceptions in business that create this surprisingly large drag on earnings.

**Chapter 3, The Age of Precision Markets,** provides a historical perspective. In almost all companies, the fundamental management systems and processes were developed for the earlier Age of Mass Markets. These management systems are no longer appropriate, and this is the core reason for the embedded unprofitability in company after company.

## What can a manager do about it?

**Chapter 4, Three Pillars of Strategy,** explains how to create a strategic foundation for your company's success, and how to align all of your company's activities for maximum profitability.

**Chapter 5, Which Customers Don't Fit?** probes the relationship between account selection and business-model development. When you do this well, profits skyrocket. The chapter gives an example of a national trucking company that made this a cornerstone of its success.

**Chapter 6, The Hunt for Profits,** details a step-by-step process for analyzing the profitability of each of your accounts, products, and services, and for defining action-initiatives to increase your profitability to its fullest potential. This process can be accomplished in a few months using standard desktop tools.

## Are there examples of companies that have done this successfully?

**Chapter 7, Dell Manages Profitability, Not Inventory,** describes how Dell maximizes its profitability by carefully managing and aligning all aspects of its business on a monthly, weekly, and daily basis.

**Chapter 8, Precision Retailing,** explains how to use the process of profitability management in the context of a major retail chain.

## What is the CFO's Role?

**Chapter 9, New CFO Role: Chief Profitability Officer,** examines the role of CFOs in most companies, and describes the need for the CFO—

and all other finance managers—to take a central role in profitability management.

## Why is this important in difficult times?

**Chapter 10, Recession Opportunities,** explains why difficult economic times present managers with a rare opportunity to drive changes that dramatically increase their profitability, their market share, and their long-term competitive advantage.

*The most important issue facing most managers is how to make more money from their existing business without starting costly new initiatives. Here's how to do it.*

# 1

## WHO'S MANAGING PROFITABILITY?

▼

**THE MOST IMPORTANT** issue facing most managers is how to make more money from their existing business without starting costly new initiatives.

In my research and work with companies in a wide range of industries, I have found that 30 to 40 percent of each company's business—by any measure (accounts, products, transactions)—is *unprofitable*.

This sounds amazing, but it's true. In each case, a few islands of high profitability offset the damage done by all that red ink.

I first identified this phenomenon several years ago, when I advised the CEO of a large, successful lab supply distributor. Instead of simply developing a big new initiative to increase the company's profitability, we decided to look systematically at where—and *why*—it was profitable. Which customers, which products, and which situations were responsible for their profits?

We knew that every company could be improved, but we were floored by what we found. The company's biggest opportunities for profit improvement were already in hand. The key to success was not to find new things to do, but instead to systematically increase the profitability of what it was already doing.

Here's what we found:

- ▶ **Accounts.** 33 percent of the company's accounts were unprofitable, ranging from a low of 29 percent in one region to a high of 42 percent in another.
- ▶ **Order lines.** 35 percent of all order lines were unprofitable. Again, this varied by region, from a low of 23 percent in one region to a high of 50 percent in another.
- ▶ **Vendors.** 40 percent of the product lines clustered by vendor were unprofitable, and an additional 38 percent were marginal, including several major vendor lines.
- ▶ **Sales channels.** Telesales achieved much better gross margins (41 percent) than other channels (36 percent for field sales accounts, 30 percent for large accounts), even controlling for other factors. But surprisingly, there was a wide range of regional employment of telesales—ranging from 3 percent to as high as 32 percent.
- ▶ **Products.** Against all expectations, fast-moving stocked products had higher gross margins (36 percent) than slower-moving ones (34 percent), and both surpassed nonstock special and custom orders (29 percent). These differences had a large, magnified impact on the company's *net profits*.

The picture that emerged: the overall profit improvement opportunity exceeded 30 percent. These potential gains stemmed from simple changes to the current business mix that could be rapidly implemented. No capital expenditures were required. And this tracked with my later findings in more than a dozen other industries ranging from steel to retail to telecom.

Believe it or not, this company had been viewed as a solid performer in its industry—on budget and just as good as its competitors. In fact, this is the core of the problem. On budget and just as good as the competition is simply not good enough.

## Who manages profits?

Why does this happen so often? In most companies, everyone pays attention to profits, but few companies have a process to systematically *manage profitability* on a day-to-day basis. (By the way, this means creating real profit increases, not manipulating the numbers to create the appearance of earnings.)

The executive team has a profit plan, each department head owns an important element of that plan, and progress is watched closely. Yet even if each manager meets objectives, the company is still a lot less profitable than it should be. The reason? In most companies, no one is responsible for managing the *interaction* of these elements to increase profitability to its full potential.

> On budget and just as good as the competition
>
> is simply not good enough.

▼

I remember sitting in on a monthly operating review meeting several years ago. The company's president sat at the head of the broad mahogany table, fixed his eyes on each VP in turn, and each responded, "I made my numbers this month." At the end, he sighed and said, "That's great—I'm the only one in the room who didn't make his numbers!"

What happened? Let's look at a few specific situations that happened during that month. The VP of sales grew the top line and met his quota. But the additional sales came from new customers who ordered frequently in small amounts. The gross margins on these orders did not cover the distribution cost. Other customers ordered products that were out of stock locally and had to be shipped in from other regions—even though the customers would have been happy to substitute a similar in-stock product had the question been asked or had a substitution program been in place.

Two things are important in these situations. First, both the sales VP and operations VP were right on budget—the sales VP really did grow revenues, and the operations VP made her numbers because her budget was based on an average cost that assumed that these inefficiencies were simply part of the system. Remember that even though they made their numbers, they lost the opportunity to grow profits. Second, these accounts and orders could have been made much more profitable through some very simple tweaks, which would have benefited the customers as well as the company. These tweaks required only careful thought and management—not a lot of capital.

In a very different industry, telecom, the same profitability issues arise. For example, a really sharp planning manager at one of the "Baby Bells" did a great piece of analysis. He looked at customer profitability and found that the high-volume customers, the ones everyone pursued, were either very profitable or very unprofitable.

He looked carefully at the very unprofitable customers, and found that they fell into one of two categories: they were either early technology adopters or "complainers." Both of these groups of customers used an inordinate amount of customer service support. Everyone agreed that the early adopters were critical to the company's market development, and the company considered supporting them a good investment. The complainers, however, were just a sea anchor on profit growth.

## The solution

Instead of simply eliminating the complainers, the planning manager saw a better way: he decided to make them profitable. The company devised some simple instructional brochures with frequently asked questions, and access to automated help lines, to aid the complainers—many of whom had a legitimate need for instructional assistance—changing many of these from "bad" to "good" customers.

Yet, in the absence of this straightforward analysis, the telecom company had indiscriminately placed its emphasis for sales growth on all high-volume customers. This policy made sense years ago in the earlier mass market era of simple services, when there were large economies of scale and little need for customer support. But it makes no sense today. In this situation, the telecom company's sales VP met her growth quota, and the customer service VP met his average cost targets. But the opportunity for major profit improvement remained very well hidden. As before, these customers were not necessarily "bad" customers. They were *unmanaged customers*—just like the customers of the lab supply company.

> In most companies, no one is responsible for managing
> the interaction of these elements to increase profitability
> to its full potential.

▼

A few years ago, horizontal process management was all the rage. This is a very useful way to coordinate business processes (making products, selling products, collecting revenues) that cross multiple functional department boundaries. I remember looking at a lot of very busy slides showing the product-supply process, the order process, the product-development process, the cash-cycle process, and on and on.

What was always missing was the profitability management process—unseen and unmanaged.

## Managing profitability

How can you manage profitability effectively in your company? In the chapters that follow, I'll explain and illustrate the three key elements: profit mapping, profit levers, and a profit management process. Here are some of the key questions we will answer:

**Profit mapping.** How can I analyze account, product, and order profitability without spending years building an activity-based costing system (a very complicated process of assigning all of a company's costs to its business activities)? How accurate do I have to be? How can I see where my company is "underwater" and where the islands of high profitability are?

**Profit levers.** What are the key profit levers in managing accounts, products, and operations? How can I change "bad" accounts into "good" accounts?

**Profit management process.** How can I prioritize our profit improvement opportunities? Which initiatives have the fastest payoff? How can I get my colleagues to work with me to improve profits when they are already making their numbers? Who should take the lead?

With these three building blocks in place, you will be able to maximize your company's profitability and achieve its full potential.

## Central elements

The three key elements of profitability management described above are central to the theme of this book, reversing embedded unprofitability. They are woven throughout the whole book and illustrated in every section.

■  ■  ■

## THINGS TO THINK ABOUT

**1.** Nearly every company is 30 to 40 percent unprofitable by any measure.

**2.** In almost every company, 20 to 30 percent of the business is highly profitable, and a large proportion of this profitability is going to cross-subsidize the unprofitable part of the business. The rest of the company is marginal.

**3.** Most current business metrics and control systems (budgets, etc.) do not even show the problem, or the opportunity for improvement.

**4.** Most of the unprofitable and marginal business can be turned around using the three key elements of profitability management: profit mapping, profit levers, and a profitability management process. Think about what it would do for your company—and your career prospects—if you took the lead in turning this around in your business.

## What's Next

The next chapters of this section give you a broad overview of why the problem of embedded unprofitability arose at this point in time, and what you can do about it. They also tell you how several successful companies have made stunning improvements in their profitability using the principles explained in this book.

*The key to a company achieving its full potential
is precise thinking and business discipline on the part
of every manager. Start by clearing out all that
bad business mythology.*

# 2

# "REVENUES ARE GOOD, COSTS ARE BAD" AND OTHER BUSINESS MYTHS

▼

**PRECISE THINKING AND** business discipline are essential for profitability and business success. Yet for too many managers in too many companies, "self-evident truths"—in truth, vague generalities—get in the way. Here are ten of the worst such business myths, each of which is fully addressed later in the book.

## 1. Revenues are good, costs are bad

This is the biggest myth of all. The truth is that some revenues are very profitable and some are very unprofitable. If you use profit mapping to look carefully at the net profitability of virtually any company, 20 to 30 percent is profitable, 30 to 40 percent is unprofitable, and the remainder is marginal. Islands of profit in a sea of red ink.

By focusing on average, or aggregate, profitability, you lose this essential fact, along with the opportunity to radically increase profitability at very little cost using sharply targeted measures. Because most sales compensation systems are based simply on revenues—and not all sales dollars are equally profitable (many are not profitable at all)—most companies are doomed to carry significant embedded unprofitability.

What about costs? If all revenues are viewed as equally desirable, it follows that all costs are uniformly bad. Thus, most cost reduction programs are broad and across the board. In fact, the very profitable portion of your business can and should support the extra expenditures needed to lock in and grow that segment of your business. But this is usually precluded because the unprofitable business absorbs unwarranted resources.

The worst danger is that competitors can identify and pick off your best business by focusing their resources very selectively.

## 2. We should give our customers what they want

This myth goes to the heart of how you define your business. You should give your customers what they *need*, which is often different from what they *want*. What your customers want is usually defined by their current way of doing business; what they need moves them forward and enables them to change and improve their business.

Your ability to move a customer to a new and better way of doing business will make you an essential strategic partner, not just a substitutable vendor. This is how you leapfrog your competitors, raise your sales and profits in your key accounts, and lock in lasting strategic advantage. You can discover real customer needs, and new ways to create value, by spending time with your customers and employing powerful tools like channel mapping (a process for assembling and analyzing an economic model of your extended supply chain, described in later chapters).

Often, a customer will not immediately see its real needs, and both lower-level purchasing people and your own sales reps can resist change if they feel that they are losing control when other managers get involved in the relationship. There are, however, effective measures that you can employ to sell and manage the change within the customer, including showcase projects that provide a working demonstration of both feasibility and benefits.

## 3. Sales reps should sell, operations should fulfill orders

In transactional account relationships, where you are responding to one-off customer needs, this distinction holds true. But with your best customers, operations plays a critical role, both in the initial sale and on an ongoing basis. Important companies in industry after industry are reducing their supplier bases (number of suppliers) by 40 to 60 percent. The suppliers that remain get huge market-share increases, while others see big losses. The key factor that allows a supplier to remain is the ability to increase the customer's profitability on the supplier's products by employing vendor-managed inventory, product codesign, and other intercompany operating innovations. Here, the operations team is critical to successful account retention and revenue growth.

## 4. All customers should get the same great service

In most companies, if you try to give all customers the same great service, service declines and costs spin out of control. When this happens, management has trouble rebalancing the supply chain: the objectives swing back and forth between cost and service like a pendulum. One quarter, management focuses on reducing inventories because costs are too high; the next quarter, they push for increased inventories because "the customers are screaming."

The answer is service differentiation, a process in which you set different order cycles (the time between your receipt of a customer order and the customer's receipt of the products) for different customers and products. Typically, customers are divided into core and non-core categories, according to sales volume, profitability, and loyalty. Products are similarly divided into core and non-core categories, according to sales volume, profitability, criticality, and substitutability.

You should give your customers what they need, which

is often different from what they want.

▼

When you break your customers into these four groups, it turns out that each group can best be served by a different supply chain, each with finely tuned service and cost characteristics. This allows you to reduce your costs, even while raising your service levels. The key is to make different but appropriate order-cycle promises to different customers for different products, and to always keep the promises you make.

## 5. Supply chain integration is a great goal

I recall meeting with the vice president of operations of a large consumer products company. He showed me a presentation depicting the stages of supply chain evolution. The stages progressed from primitive arm's-length customer relationships to sophisticated, fully integrated channels in which key suppliers and their key customers developed very tightly coordinated supply chains. The clear implication was that the latter was the ideal to which all supply chains should aspire.

This is ridiculous. The proper degree of supply chain integration should reflect a variety of factors, including channel economics (cost structure of the combined customer-supplier product flow), customer willingness and ability to innovate, loyalty, and customer-supplier strategic alignment. For example, if you created a simple two-by-two matrix with customer importance on one axis, and customer willingness and ability to innovate on the other, you would find that the correct degree of supply chain integration depends on the quadrant the customer is in. Companies have finite resources, and, while potentially very profitable, supply chain integration is a very intense relationship. Companies must be very selective, and tailor the degree of supply chain integration to the account relationship.

## 6. If everyone does his or her job well, the company will prosper

In a stable situation, in which customer needs are known and unchanging and markets are relatively homogeneous, a company can set policies for each functional area that managers can carry out for a period of time without much change. This was the situation that most companies faced in the Age of Mass Markets, decades ago.

But the world has changed enormously. Today, companies face increasingly heterogeneous markets, and they form very different relationships with different customers. In this situation, which I call the Age of Precision Markets, what one manager does has a huge impact on other managers, and managers need to have overlapping responsibilities.

For example, if a supply chain manager works hard to bring a product's inventory costs down by 20 percent, and the product is unprofitable, should the manager feel successful? The answer depends on how the manager defines his or her job. In the prior era, when operations merely fulfilled orders booked by the sales reps, the supply chain manager would be a hero. But today, in leading companies, his or her "job" extends far beyond traditional cost control to encompass asset productivity, which involves both costs and revenues. Both the supply chain manager and the sales and marketing managers should feel joint responsibility for the profitability of each piece of the company. Unless they act together, the interactions between their functions will almost inevitably lead to high levels of embedded unprofitability.

You have to define the "job" properly in each situation in order to have any chance that someone might do it well, and this definition is a rapidly moving target. In most companies, this is one of the most important underlying problems degrading performance. The best execution will fail if the managers are not executing what needs to be done.

## 7. If you are promoted, you should keep doing what brought you success

This is the natural inclination of many managers. But it is exactly the wrong thing to do when you are promoted. In many companies, managers at all levels manage "a level too low." They micromanage their subordinates, who often have their old jobs. Rather than teaching the subordinates and focusing on helping them improve their work processes, they force them to spend an inordinate amount of time preparing for a "grilling" on their operating performance.

This causes two problems. First, the subordinates lose the opportunity to learn and grow. Second, the manager fails to accomplish the key components of his or her new job.

Simply put, first-line managers should operate the company. Directors should coach the managers and spend an equal amount of time working with their counterpart directors in other functional areas to ensure that each piece of the business is productive and profitable. Vice presidents should coach the directors and spend the majority of their time defining and developing the company as it will need to be in three to five years. When everyone focuses only on the day-to-day, the opportunity cost from embedded unprofitability and failure to position the company for the future is enormous.

■ ■ ■

*Leading companies are great because no matter how good they are, they are desperate to get better.*

▼

## 8. Business cases can drive significant change

The business case process is a key component of the resource allocation process in most companies. If a manager wants to create a new initiative, he or she assembles a request for resources, with projected benefits and costs. If the likely return is high enough, the initiative will be funded.

Business cases work well in well-understood situations where both costs and benefits can be predicted with a reasonable degree of certainty. The problem is that many of the most important strategic initiatives move a company into uncharted territory. These investments require a very different decision process, one that involves funding market experimentation without a clearly defined stream of returns.

I recall working with a number of leading technology companies in the early days of PCs, cell phones, and the Internet. All of these now-huge markets were relatively small and undefined at the time. Investments to probe these markets and learn how to accelerate their development had great difficulty passing muster in the rigorous, traditional business case processes. Instead, in many cases, new competitors captured enormous market share from these incumbents.

## 9. Big changes can't be made without a crisis

Large-scale change in advance of a crisis is one of the most challenging problems a top manager can face. Resetting the fundamental way a company does business requires a completely different management process from day-to-day business improvement. Many initiatives to radically raise profits require major change.

Methods for managing large-scale change effectively can be derived from successful companies' experiences and from observing change management in fields as seemingly unrelated as the development of scientific theory.

Successful change management before a crisis has four cornerstones.

First, the top manager must present clear evidence that without change, crisis will occur. Second, he or she must develop a clear picture of what success looks like, because a company will only move toward a concrete, detailed, believable new way of doing business that solves the old problems and creates new advantage. Strategic investments, like limited-scale showcases that discover and demonstrate new ways of doing business, can be extremely effective. Third, the top manager must be relentless and unwavering in advocating the need for change and the effectiveness of the new way of doing business. Fourth, like climbing a large mountain, the organization needs a set of base camps in the change process. These make change digestible, allow managers to acclimate to new ways of doing things, and enable different parts of the organization to catch up with one another.

Even in this context, large-scale change is not at all linear. The organization will probably resist change for a time, then suddenly lurch forward as a critical mass of managers change their attitudes and influence one another. Then it will remain stationary for a time, then lurch forward again. This is why well-thought-out base camps are so important for managing large-scale change.

## 10. Don't change a good thing

"If it ain't broke, don't fix it" is management at its worst. Leading companies are great because no matter how good they are, they are desperate to get better. Lagging companies are most often complacent and self-satisfied, and that's why they stay behind. When great managers have a lead, they step on the gas.

Successful management is reinforcing. Leading companies are not just looking for change but also for their managers to get acclimated to constant change and to become expert at managing progressive change. This environment attracts creative, disciplined managers, and together it creates a virtuous cycle. The more they change, the more they can change, and the more they do change.

Can a lagging company become a leader? Certainly, but this requires considerable leadership from the top management team, and a well-defined, disciplined program for large-scale change in advance of a crisis. Note that this is not continuous improvement, but rather disruptive, discontinuous change.

## Beyond mythology

Every company has enormous potential waiting to be unleashed: a potential for enhanced profitability, for accelerated growth, for renewing change. The key to achieving this potential is precise thinking and business discipline on the part of every manager, particularly those at the top.

These ten business myths are not really wrong; they are merely imprecise enough to be misleading. And this is what creates so much unrealized potential in company after company.

By moving beyond business mythology, you can develop a systematic program of relentless profitability improvement.

---

### THINGS TO THINK ABOUT

**1.** It is amazing how much hard work becomes unproductive or even counterproductive because a manager hasn't thought carefully enough about the assumptions and objectives of a project or initiative. In more than twenty years of working with former students and managers throughout a range of industries, I've seen this again and again.

**2.** Many of the most important assumptions behind business initiatives give the illusion of obvious correctness, when in fact they lead to wrong conclusions and actions. This is one of the themes of my teaching at MIT. It is especially critical to take the time to define precisely the right question when you begin to work on a project.

**3.** You can train yourself to get things right at the beginning of a major project by thinking hard about the business myths in this chapter, and relating them to situations in your company. This quickly becomes a way of seeing your business more clearly. It gives you the ability to be much more productive.

**4.** How important is this problem? The business myths outlined in this chapter lead to the 30 to 40 percent profit improvement opportunity that is the theme of this book. It really pays to take the time to see things clearly.

## What's Next

How did these myths arise? Why do so many companies have so much embedded unprofitability? The next chapter tells you how we are moving from one era of business to another. This transition is changing all the rules of the game.

*The changes we are experiencing in business are as profound as those when mass markets were first developed. Welcome to the Age of Precision Markets.*

## 3

# THE AGE OF PRECISION MARKETS

▼

**WE ARE ENTERING** a new era in business.

The changes we are beginning to experience are as profound and disruptive as those that occurred when roads were first paved, local markets began to join together, and mass markets were first developed. I call this new era the Age of Precision Markets.

In his landmark book, *New and Improved: The Story of Mass Marketing in America*, Richard Tedlow traces the transition about a century ago from localized, unformed markets to mass markets. He describes how companies like Sears aggregated demand, standardized supply, and drove down the costs of production and distribution.

Toward the middle of the twentieth century, mass markets had developed to the point where their submarkets, or segments, were large enough to support efficient-scale production and market development. These segments were defined by demographics and psychographics (e.g., children's aspirin, jogging shoes). In response, mass-marketing companies adapted or differentiated their products to fit these markets in a sort of "theme and variations" strategy. (For simplicity's sake, I refer to both the earlier mass markets and these large segmented markets as mass markets.)

The rise of mass markets created huge benefits for society, and also formed the dominant paradigm of how companies are managed today.

All that is changing, and this book will guide you in making the transition and managing successfully in this new era.

Today, the locus of value creation is shifting from product innovation to customer relationship innovation centered on account management and supply chain management.

This shift is accelerating quickly. Most companies today live partly in both worlds, and their managers are struggling with this transition. This is equally true for both product companies and service companies.

General Foods in its heyday characterized the mass-market paradigm. The company turned product innovation into a science, and distributed its goods to broad, homogeneous markets, and market segments, in a largely standard way. The rise of Dell from a second-tier company to a leading PC producer represents the emerging new era of precision markets. In this critical period, the company developed a way to carefully select its customers and individualize every transaction to "sell what it has," changing its pricing literally minute by minute.

The watershed event in this market shift was the new relationship that P&G and Wal-Mart developed about ten years ago. Before this, P&G was a classic mass marketer like General Foods. With Wal-Mart, however, P&G changed its strategy. Instead of serving Wal-Mart in a standard, arm's-length way, P&G focused on creating intercompany supply chain processes, like vendor-managed inventory, that radically increased Wal-Mart's profitability on P&G products. This increased profitability drove P&G's sales to Wal-Mart, and its own profitability, through the ceiling. As one key P&G vice president put it, "Wal-Mart's chief financial officer became our prime customer."

At the same time, P&G withdrew from distributing directly to many smaller accounts, choosing instead to set up master distributors. No longer did "one size fit all."

## Offensive terminal point

The "offensive terminal point" is a key concept in military strategy. It refers to how deeply a military force can penetrate its enemy's front lines. The more an army concentrates its forces in a narrow front, the deeper it is able to penetrate the battlefield.

In its days as a classic mass marketer, P&G's customer engagement front was very broad, and therefore its offensive terminal point (intercompany supply chain) was very shallow. As a precision marketer in this new era, however, P&G carefully manages its customer relationships to develop a very deep offensive terminal point with a few customers like Wal-Mart, a more standard arm's-length relationship with others, and no direct relationship at all in some cases.

It is this process of choosing and managing the development of different relationships with different customers that characterizes the Age of Precision Markets.

## Fundamental market shift

Five key factors are driving this fundamental market shift:

▶ Mature, sophisticated customers like Wal-Mart, seeking to increase their profitability, are exerting pressure on suppliers.
▶ Increased competition is filling the ecological niches in industry after industry.
▶ Sophisticated information technology capabilities are being deployed inside and between channel partners.
▶ Sophisticated supply chain management capabilities are being developed in many channels.
▶ Strong offshore competitors are forcing domestic incumbents to find new ways to compete through service innovation.

The shift from mass markets to precision markets manifests along several dimensions. It is a shift (1) from product-driven competition to customer-driven competition, (2) from product innovation to account management and supply chain innovation (including related services), (3) from broad-market targeting to precision account targeting, and (4) from functional department separateness with periodic budgetary and planning alignment to functional integration with overlapping responsibilities and ongoing alignment.

The locus of value creation is shifting from product

innovation to customer relationship innovation centered

on account management and supply chain management.

▼

# Old management paradigm

The problems with managing for mass markets in this emerging Age of Precision Markets are evident in almost every company today: a few islands of high profitability in a sea of marginal business.

The classic management paradigm of the mass marketer is the source of this problem. Products are relatively standardized within a market or segment, and all customers are treated more or less the same. Managers in various functional departments like sales, marketing, and supply chain management are largely separate, linked primarily through the company's planning and budgeting cycles. Performance information is collected along departmental lines, such as account and product revenue, category contribution, and distribution cost. All sales dollars look equally attractive.

In this context, microlevel information on real account profitability, product profitability, order profitability, and supply chain productivity (return on invested capital) is neither collected nor analyzed. Consequently, in virtually every company, a very large portion of the business is unprofitable by any measure. Often, a small fraction of the business provides well over 100 percent of the reported profits, and an amazingly large portion of these aggregate profits are consumed in cross-subsidizing the company's embedded unprofitability—the losses incurred in the unprofitable parts of the business.

# The "Fifth P"

At the core of marketing in the Age of Mass Markets is a four-factor classification of marketing decision variables that everyone learns in first-year marketing courses, the "Four Ps." These Ps are *product, place, promotion,* and *price.*

What's missing? *Profitability,* which I call the "Fifth P."

The Four-P mentality is responsible for the crazy-quilt pattern of profitability in every business today. It is simply assumed that if the Four Ps are set correctly, maximum profitability will be the by-product. This assumption is completely wrong.

In the Age of Precision Markets, both sales and profits will be driven to a large extent by direct microlevel profitability maximization, both within companies and between suppliers and customers, using the techniques I explain in this book.

The Fifth P represents management imperatives like selecting accounts that fit your operating capabilities, differentiating your company through your ability to increase your customers' return on invested capital, and developing services, like vendor-managed inventory, that both reduce costs and increase sales for you and your customers.

What's at stake? Major gains in profitability and market share.

Today, most customers are reducing their supplier ranks by 40 to 60 percent or more, and a company's ability to improve customer internal profitability determines whether it will get this market share increase or whether its competitors will.

## Managing change

Here's the critical question: if everyone agrees that their companies have this problematic profitability pattern, why do so few companies do something about it?

The answer is that, at a tacit level, the mass-market management paradigm is the dominant management paradigm today. It is "the way we do business." As long as this paradigm is in place, managers will be blocked from creating meaningful, company-wide change.

I remember when I wrote my column "The Challenges of Paradigmatic Change," which formed the basis for chapter 26 of this book. In it, I argued that many worthy change initiatives hit the wall of "the way we do business." This, I suggested, meant that even great initiatives will flounder if they conflict with the underlying management paradigm, and that the most effective way to get constructive change is to make the paradigm explicit and to show that a better one can replace it.

Within hours of publication, I received a flood of positive e-mails from readers, many sharing their experiences. No one disagreed. Clearly, it had struck a nerve.

## New management paradigm

The new management paradigm for the Age of Precision Markets requires that managers be highly skilled at three things: account management, supply chain management, and change management.

They must be able to survey their customers and markets, and develop a road map for different relationships with different accounts and market segments. Armed with this road map, managers in different functional areas must be adept at working together to select and develop appropriate relationships with appropriate accounts.

Managers across a company must achieve a high degree of aligned focus, and have great change-management skills, both within their own companies and with customers. Interdepartmental coordination must be ongoing, fluid, and characterized by overlapping capabilities and responsibilities.

> Precision markets offer a new way of thinking
>
> about a business, where marketing is just one of
>
> the main components.

Every functional area must broaden its responsibility and increase its interdepartmental coordination. For example, sales reps and account managers must proactively use supply chain innovations to develop account relationships and increase penetration. Marketing managers must develop customer relationship migration paths (a step-by-step planned progression from selling a new customer an early set of products and services, to later selling a broader package, to finally selling a full set) in order to deepen their business and increase their profitability in target accounts, and they must recast their market segmentation criteria (used to cluster sets of similar customers) to incorporate factors such as account potential, operating fit, and readiness to change. Supply chain managers have to shift from reactive cost control to proactive supply chain productivity, which entails teaming with colleagues to maximize the earning power of their assets.

Precision markets offer a new way of thinking about a business, where marketing is just one of the main components.

This change is profound. It requires open-minded, creative managers, and new coordinative processes. All this without dropping the ball on internal efficiency.

Can it be done? Managers in leading companies are doing it today.

■ ■ ■

# Which is the business?

As companies develop more deep, interlocking relationships with their most important accounts, and deploy well-honed profit levers more selectively, the question always arises: is this something we are doing in addition to the business, or is this the business?

When this happens, and it will, you will be standing face-to-face with a paradigm shift.

Some managers will find reasons to resist the change: too much complexity to see a pathway, too many moving parts to manage, too much risk of failure, too hard to get people to change, too much going on elsewhere to get to it. These managers will fail.

Other managers will step up to the new management paradigm and team with their counterparts to innovate and excel, both internally and across their extended supply chain. If you choose to be one of these managers, you can move into the Age of Precision Markets with confidence and success.

---

### THINGS TO THINK ABOUT

**1.** We are entering a new era in business—shifting from a mass-market-based business system to one in which managers carefully craft specific sets of customer relationships and precisely match them with specific sets of customers. This shift is the underlying reason why nearly every company is characterized by islands of profit in a sea of red ink.

**2.** Virtually all of our business processes and measures were developed in the earlier era. Consequently, we need a new way of managing to be successful in the future. This book explains this new way to manage and tells you how to create the new processes.

**3.** Leading companies today have already secured 30 to 40 percent increases in sales and profits by shifting to this new way of managing. Think about the impact on the careers of the managers who took the lead.

**4.** The new way of managing is neither more difficult nor more time-consuming than the old. But it requires a different way of thinking about your business. This creates enormous new leadership opportunities for energetic, creative managers.

**5.** Remember—the Fifth P is for *profitability*!

---

## What's Next

The first two chapters of this section give an overview of the new opportunity for profitability management. This chapter describes why it arose now—both as a problem and as a once-in-a-lifetime opportunity for managers today. The next chapter explains how you can build a solid strategic foundation for profitability management—a foundation that is rooted in real customer value, strategic focus, and competitive differentiation.

*Strategy is critical to every company's success.*
*Here's a short list of essential elements that all*
*managers must get right.*

# 4

## THREE PILLARS
## OF STRATEGY

▼

**"EVERYBODY COMPLAINS ABOUT** the weather, but nobody does anything about it," observed Charles Dudley Warner, the nineteenth-century essayist and friend of Mark Twain. In many companies, the same could be said about strategy.

When I raise the issue of strategy in executive programs at MIT, two things quickly become apparent: everyone participates in strategy development, and many managers do not have a clear understanding of what strategy is and why it's so important.

Strategy is the foundation on which all profitability initiatives are built. If the strategic foundation is sound and well conceived, managers have an opportunity to develop very effective initiatives that produce strong, consistent profits. But if the foundation is faulty, even the best-framed initiatives will fail.

In my experience, three core principles capture the essence of strategy:

1. It's all about customer value.
2. Strategy is defined by what you say no to.
3. You have to be best at something.

If you get these right, chances are strong that you'll succeed.

# It's all about customer value

Considering the cliché that companies exist to serve their customers, it's amazing how many company strategies almost take their customers for granted, focusing almost exclusively on themselves.

All too often, there is a tacit assumption that customer needs are static and well defined, and the essential business problem, therefore, is to optimize the process for filling these needs.

This assumption is one of the core errors of business strategy. The starting point in strategy development must be the creation of value for customers by deeply understanding their real underlying business needs and developing innovative ways to meet them.

Customer innovations very often yield high profitability

and competitive advantage for a long time.

▼

Customer needs are a moving target. This may be the most important and overlooked element of strategy in most companies. You can almost always create a radical improvement in your positioning and prospects by shifting your strategic focus from optimally meeting existing customer needs to partnering with your customers to identify and fulfill new needs.

This is what GE's aircraft engine business did when it shifted from selling engines, parts, and services on a separate basis to selling "power by the hour," an all-in offering at a unified price. This produced great benefits for the airlines, which could better align their costs and revenues.

By shifting the domain of value creation to within the customer, GE's aircraft engine group redefined its business, radically improved its competitive positioning, and greatly increased its sustained profitability. More value, more opportunity for value capture.

What's more, customer innovations very often yield high profitability and competitive advantage for a long time. Successful customer innovations require both deep customer knowledge and the ability to create change within key customers. This change management ability creates enormous barriers to entry through customer knowledge and customer trust. Competitors may be able to replicate product innovations, but they usually can't supplant a competitor embedded with a key customer in a deep, productive relationship featuring interlinked business processes.

Remember that customer needs are often very different from customer wants. This is why you can't just interview customers to get a meaningful answer.

## Strategy is defined by what you say no to

Over the past two decades, I have reviewed many company strategies. The explicit objective of many of them is to create a set of initiatives that will capture all customers, and potential customers, in every nook and cranny of the market. Within the company, various managers are responsible for these customers, and each of these managers has an inexorably increasing revenue quota.

This system is unrealistic and counterproductive. The reason strategy is so important is that it enables a company's management team to do two things extremely well: (1) focus the company on a "sweet spot" in the market, and (2) align all the functional areas of the company to reach and own that part of the market. Enormously effective companies have both focus and alignment. The essence of a great company is achieving maximum "pounds per square inch" of market power. If you think about the great companies of our era—from Southwest Airlines to UPS to Four Seasons Hotels—they do this extremely well.

It's impossible to achieve focus and alignment when a company tries to be everything to everyone. Many managers are instinctively drawn to this counterproductive objective because they do not want to say no to potential business. Ironically, it is this attitude that condemns a company to substandard performance.

A manager can develop a winning strategy only if he or she is willing and able to define crisply and clearly what is out of bounds.

> Enormously effective companies have both
>
> focus and alignment.

▼

Think about your sales compensation system. What does it tell your sales reps to maximize? Revenue dollars? Probably. Gross margin? Maybe. If all sales dollars are equally desirable, you don't have a strategy.

Ironically, the number one way to increase operations or supply chain productivity is not just to optimize the fulfillment of the current business inflow. Instead, it is to discipline the sales system to bring in business that fits the operation and supply chain. Doing this yields 30 to 50 percent productivity increases, rather than the 10 to 15 percent gains that come from simply optimizing existing processes.

And the fastest and most powerful way to increase sales is to partner with your best customers and radically improve their profitability through innovative intercompany operations.

Again, the key to success is focus and alignment: having the clarity and courage to make choices by defining a strategy that has an explicit target and a meaningful set of out-of-bounds conditions that the whole organization understands.

In this way, strategy acts like a laser, bringing the whole company into phase, and enabling the company to burn a hole right through its target market.

## You have to be best at something

The third pillar of strategy may seem so obvious that it is hardly worth mentioning. Yet surprisingly few companies have taken to heart that "you have to be best at something."

Everyone knows that if you are not best at something, someone better will beat you. So why does this happen to so many companies?

The answer lies in the preceding paragraphs of this chapter. Many managers are so reluctant to let go of any business opportunity, they cannot make the choices necessary to create a focused strategy. They cannot say no.

Instead, they dissipate their go-to-market resources (resources used to engage a company's customers, including a company's sales force, advertising, promotion, and supply chain integration) across too broad a customer/product/service base, and fail to achieve meaningful traction in any one area. Because the incoming business stream is so diverse, they cannot focus their operations and supply chain to achieve the major gains in productivity and accelerated sales that come from aligning sales and operations.

It all comes back to the core reasons for strategy: focus and alignment.

Companies that fall into the trap of trying to be everything to everyone almost by definition cannot be best at something. This leads to a vicious cycle.

Surprisingly few companies have taken to heart that "you have to be best at something."

▼

When a more-focused competitor takes business away in one area, the company tries to increase its capabilities in that area to recapture the business. A short time later, another focused competitor takes business away in another area, and again the company expends its resources trying to stem the tide.

Soon, the company is so busy defending itself against an array of more focused competitors that it has spent all of its resources to little avail. Time and time again, the sales force is exhorted to sell their way out of trouble, and the operations managers are forced to constrict their operations to the point where they lose important capabilities. In the endgame, the company's market share, profitability, and resources evaporate, and its managers are left wondering what happened to them.

By failing to focus and align the company, these managers forfeited the opportunity to be best at something, and thereby created a situation in which their company was systematically overtaken by more focused competitors.

## Effective strategy

Consider Wal-Mart's strategy evolution. Initially, Wal-Mart's strategy centered on locating stores in relatively small cities and towns of around 50,000 to 100,000 residents in the U.S. South and Midwest. In each location, Wal-Mart could provide enough value as a volume discounter to supplant the mom-and-pop businesses without enough business left over to support a second, competing discounter.

In these locations, Wal-Mart could be best at providing a clear and unique customer value: it offered "everyday low prices," which was extremely important to the folks in smaller cities and towns where income typically was lower. At the same time, Wal-Mart's managers clearly understood which locations didn't fit. The company carefully avoided larger cities and instead focused its resources on the markets where it had a clear advantage.

After Wal-Mart developed a critical mass of stores, it entered a second phase, in which it focused its attention on utilizing its large and growing volume of business to develop an extremely efficient supply chain. This enabled Wal-Mart to drive down its costs even more, and to offer its customers even lower prices for quality merchandise.

With this newly developed supply-chain cost advantage, Wal-Mart could underprice other retailers, while innovating new ways to be best at providing the best customer value and convenience. This dynamic allowed the company to supplant other discounters and expand its footprint into a host of new locations.

In a third phase, Wal-Mart's enormous volume made it the partner of choice for major suppliers. This led to a set of highly efficient supplier operating partnerships, which greatly lowered Wal-Mart's costs and increased its flexibility even more. Through this process, Wal-Mart widened its lead over the competition and reaped enormous profits.

## THINGS TO THINK ABOUT

**1.** It's all about customer value. Many chapters in this book, especially those in sections 2 and 3, tell you how to push the frontier of customer value creation. Remember, the more customer value you create, the more opportunity you will have for value capture through higher prices and increased share of wallet.

**2.** The two reasons for strategy: (1) to focus your company on the sweet spot in the market, and (2) to align your company's functional departments to achieve this objective. This is how you achieve "maximum pounds per square inch" of market power.

**3.** It's hard to focus and align your company when your sales compensation systems tells your sales reps that all revenue dollars are equally desirable. This is one of the biggest problems in most companies today—and one of the biggest levers for asset productivity and profit improvement.

**4.** You have to be best at something. If not, someone better will beat you. This means that you have to say no to business that doesn't fit. You need clarity of thought and the courage of your convictions. Great companies have a very crisp definition of what business fits—and what does not—and have a tightly aligned business model congruent with their strategic focus.

**5.** The same principles hold true for you as you build your business career. Think about it.

## What's Next

So far, we have viewed the problem of embedded un-profitability and the opportunity to reverse it, and understood why it arose today. We also have learned how to build a solid strategic foundation for profitability management. The next chapter explains how a well-known national trucking company successfully developed a powerful profitability management system that transformed its customer relationships and turbo-charged its performance.

*Asking yourself which customers, products, and services don't fit your business model can quickly reveal whether your company is managing profitability effectively, and whether your key managers' actions are aligned. How to start? Get an earful from your managers.*

# 5

# WHICH CUSTOMERS DON'T FIT?

▼

**TRY THIS TODAY.** Sit down for thirty minutes with the managers who run your company's major departments (sales, operations, etc.), and ask each one to write down the names of five significant companies that shouldn't be customers, five products that shouldn't be carried, and five services that shouldn't be provided.

Surprisingly, in many companies, the managers' lists would be so different that an outsider would think they were from different companies.

Why? Because most companies don't manage profitability on a day-to-day basis—coordinating sales and operations to maximize profits to the fullest potential. Consequently, they have a few islands of high profitability, but lots of unprofitable accounts, products, and transactions.

As the CEO of a health-care company said, "We see the same thing in our company. I worry about the risk of having so much riding on such a small portion of the business."

The questions of which customers, products, and services don't fit are penetrating diagnostics. They tell you quickly whether your company is managing profitability effectively, and whether your key managers' actions are aligned.

The questions of which customers, products, and services don't fit are penetrating diagnostics.

▼

The question of fit really has two parts: *what fits?* and *fits what?* A company has to get both right to manage profitability effectively, and they are closely related.

A manager answering *what fits?* needs to think about customers, products, and transactions in a methodical way. To answer *fits what?* the manager must focus on the company's business model (internal business processes and the way the company engages the market), shaping it to maximize the company's profit potential.

These two questions are answered through a process involving the three key profit management elements: profit mapping, profit levers, and a profit management process.

*Profit mapping* shows which accounts, products, and transactions fit the business model (and are profitable). *Profit levers* are elements of a company's business model that can be adjusted to improve profitability, selecting and penetrating more "good" customers, and turning "bad" customers into "good" customers. And a *profit management process* is the organizational procedure a company can use to align its day-to-day business activities with its business model.

## A company that got it right

Let's look at how one national trucking company got it right. Three years ago, this company did not have a good process to manage profitability. Today, it has more than doubled its profit margins. As one key manager put it, "Now our sales reps know exactly what to sell."

**Profit mapping.** In the first step, a small group of key sales and operations managers, called the Yield Management Team, thought hard about what was driving their costs.

The Yield Management Team was a small group of managers responsible for pricing trucking services. In a very creative move, the head of the team decided to go beyond his traditional, narrow mandate and look more broadly at all the elements leading to the company's profitability. Through this process, he created a revolutionary new approach to the business that produced major profitability increases. It also led to his promotion to head of the business unit. (You might think about how your company could benefit from this approach.)

They had an insight—the sales department had been selling individual point-to-point movements, but the real cost driver was the whole route, including backhauls. (In a traditional trucking company, a sales rep might sell a truckload movement from, say, Chicago to St. Louis—called the primary or point-to-point movement—and leave the company with the problem of trying to sell the return trip from St. Louis to Chicago, which is called the backhaul.) So a sales rep might charge a price for the primary movement that appeared to make a profit, but the company would lose money if the backhaul price was too low.

They developed a set of cost models for their routes. They also saw that each cost model divided into three components: fixed costs (daily cost of a truck), variable costs (mileage), and special costs (handling, etc.).

Next, they put together a database of all their transactions over a six-month period. They applied the cost models to the transactions to see which customers, services, and routes were profitable and which were not.

They found a few islands of customers that were very profitable—20 to 30 percent margins. They were shocked to find that fully 40 percent of the business was unprofitable—islands of profit in a sea of red ink.

**Profit levers.** While the Yield Management Team was analyzing profitability, the company pushed hard for a general cost reduction—but this was not nearly enough. To increase profitability, they had to engage several profit levers.

> Profit levers are elements of a company's business
> model that can be adjusted to improve profitability.

▼

First, the team moved aggressively to secure the highly profitable customers by ensuring that they received flawless service, including first priority on capacity.

The next lever was pricing—and it wasn't simply a matter of a price increase. In the past, when the company had sold a point-to-point movement to a customer, the sales reps had to scramble to sell backhaul movements at low rates. If the customer canceled the pickup, the company had to scramble to find a new headhaul. This was very reactive and inefficient.

Under the new regime, the team did two things. First, they decided to charge rates with fixed and variable components. The customer who ordered a truck had to pay a fixed daily charge whether it used the truck or not, while the customer's mileage charge reflected actual use. Second, they incorporated forecast accuracy in pricing. The customer had to forecast its needs a month in advance, and pay an additional charge if the usage was greater than 110 percent of forecast (causing uncovered backhauls) or less than 94 percent of forecast (causing uncovered headhauls).

This changed the customer/company relationship to one of shared risks and rewards, and created a strong incentive for joint planning. Now the trucking company could presell the whole route, receiving a much better price, and could get much better equipment utilization. In return, the company awarded the customer priority on capacity—crucial at peak times of the year—and passed on some of the savings as a price *decrease*.

In a series of meetings, the team sold the concept to the key customers. Most of the best customers saw the need for a stable supplier, and understood the wisdom of focusing on joint cost reduction. To further reduce costs, the company scheduled monthly safety meetings with these customers, and agreed to reduce prices even more if safety targets were met.

Also, the trucking company sought to increase its integration with these key customers (providing coordinated services that took the place of tasks the customer formerly did itself), offering services such as loading and inventory processing—further reducing customer costs while building competitive differentiation and switching costs.

Most important, according to a key team manager, the company "stopped saying yes to everyone." With the new bottom-line focus, the team took hard stances. They walked away from customers who were not willing to participate in joint cost reductions and risk/reward sharing. As it turned out, many of these customers came back and accepted the new pricing terms because the company offered the opportunity for them to reduce costs and lock in capacity.

**Profitability management process.** The profitability management process featured three key components.

**First.** The Yield Management Team continued periodic reviews of account and service profitability, ensuring that profitability management was permanently built into the company.

**Second.** The company strengthened day-to-day profitability management at the account level. Previously, account management was primarily a sales task. Now a high-level sales team sets the relationship and pricing, and operations personnel manage the day-to-day account relationship.

Sales became so productive that the company was able to *reduce* its sales force by 50 percent over time.

**Third.** The company used training to drive bottom-line awareness down to the grassroots level. The goal was to ensure that the front-line sales and operations people understood the profit levers, and that they managed the details of the account relationship to achieve its full profit potential.

The training sessions were held in five-member groups. They were very interactive, with lots of "What would you do if . . . ?" examples and quizzes. In the first wave, the company trained the dispatchers and customer service reps; in the second wave, they trained the support groups, such as billing.

One manager on the Yield Management Team described the change. "At first, the customers thought I was the bad guy. Now it's very rewarding. The hard feelings went away. Before, customer meetings were about price increases; now they're about cost reductions. We start every meeting with a business review of cost takeouts, and only adjust prices if necessary."

## What changed?

What changed here? These managers had the clarity to answer the two key questions *what fits?* and *fits what?* They did this through a three-step process. First, they analyzed which customers and services were profitable and which were not, and *why*. Second, they changed the company's business model to realign the way prices were developed and quoted with their customer relationships, focusing on joint cost reductions (and selective price decreases) to benefit both parties. Third, they modified account selection and account management to drive the new efficiencies through every service, in every account, every day.

> They changed the company's business model to realign the pricing mechanism and customer relationship, focusing on joint cost reductions to benefit both parties.

▼

In other words, they managed profitability on a day-to-day basis, driving profits up to the fullest potential: no big investments, just clarity and great management.

**1.** There is tremendous power in developing a program of profitability management. This national trucking company doubled its profitability by building a very successful program around the three key elements: profit mapping, profit levers, and a profitability management process.

**2.** The company used profit mapping to understand both where it was making money and *why* these islands were profitable. It developed a creative set of profit levers focused on partnering with customers for mutual cost reduction. The result was the "holy grail" of customer relationships: lower prices *and* higher profits.

**3.** The company stopped saying yes to everyone, and focused its business on the set of customers who were willing and able to partner to drive down costs for mutual benefit. The best customers welcomed the program. Some customers left—then many of them returned.

**4.** The manager in charge developed a relatively straightforward training program for employees at the grassroots level to teach them the new behavior.

**5.** This profitability management process was very creative and effective, but relatively simple and fast to develop. Mostly, it took a creative manager with the energy to innovate. By the way, this individual was promoted in a very short period of time, and now is a vice president.

## What's Next

This chapter describes how a national trucking company combined the three essential elements of profitability management into a very successful program of business improvement. The next chapter explains how you can quickly figure out where your islands of profit are in your sea of red ink. It also gives you practical tips and pitfalls in identifying and prioritizing your action plan.

*A profit map is a shrewd way to conceptualize the relation-ships among your customers, products, services, and trans-actions. Here are the five steps to creating your plan.*

# 6

## THE HUNT FOR PROFITS

▼

**THE HUNT FOR** profits begins in your own backyard. The theme of this book is that in most companies, 20 to 30 percent of the business provides most of the profits, while 30 to 40 percent of the customers, products, and transactions lose money. The key question is how to identify which is which.

### Profit map

A profit map is the core analytical tool that you can employ to identify and fix your embedded unprofitability. It enables you to cluster your customers, products, services, and transactions by profitability, to assess and prioritize your key profit levers, and to crystallize this into a high-impact action plan.

The essential starting point for successful profit mapping is to decide to analyze profitability at *70 percent accuracy.* This decision will make or break your analysis. Some companies spend a huge amount of time and money setting up an activity-based costing system that is much too detailed. In meeting after meeting, managers argue over cost allocations that will not change an action. All too often, the measurement becomes the project. After endless debates, the projects lose momentum before they are translated into actions that hit the bottom line.

In practice, the most important results will be very clear from rapid, intelligent analysis using best available knowledge and reasonable rules of thumb. Once a profitability picture emerges, it makes sense to improve the accuracy only where better information will change an important action. After all, most effective managers have learned to focus on the few high-leverage initiatives that will really affect the bottom line. In the next round of analysis, you can move on to the next set of improvements.

How long does it take to create and analyze a profit map? In most companies with reasonable data availability, a small team of two or three managers using a PC can accomplish this in two or three months. The process has five steps.

## Five-step process

**Profitability database.** First, construct a profitability database. This requires two things: (1) a representative set of transactions (customer purchase order lines, like "three blue sponges, product # 3572, @ $6.30"); and (2) a set of costs to apply to the transactions. In essence, you are creating an "income statement" for each order line. When you do this, you can create a very powerful, detailed analysis of your company. You can see your company's profitability customer by customer and product by product. You can even see the relative profitability of particular products in different customers, and vice versa. Importantly, you can easily project the impact of changing your mix of customers and products, and you can see the impact of changing your costs in a set of highly targeted initiatives.

In order to create a database of transactions, just select a time period that is representative, perhaps three or four months, and load the set of transactions into a database program using standard desktop tools. Each transaction should carry information identifying the customer and the product as well as the revenue and cost of the product (yielding the transaction's gross margin).

Common-sense cost functions (systematic ways to allocate costs to order lines, described below) are not hard to develop. In developing cost functions, it is generally best to allocate costs using an easy-to-measure variable. For example, allocating operations costs by transaction or order line usually works well, as each line requires order taking and picking. Inventory carrying costs can be handled by rules of thumb, such as holding A items for two weeks, B items for four weeks, and C items for eight weeks. Transportation costs can be allocated through simple decision rules based on customer location (region, near-to or far-from a distribution center). Where a sales call is needed to take an order, that portion of the selling expense can be allocated by orders. Other costs can be similarly allocated with reasonable accuracy.

It's important to allocate all costs, including general overhead, for two reasons: (1) this enforces the discipline of viewing the whole cost of the business when determining whether to keep or change a major component; and (2) this ties the analysis directly to the company's financial statements, giving you credibility and accurate projections.

Some managers argue that it is a good idea to accept business that contributes, even marginally, to covering overhead. However, when you take on a lot of business that contributes only marginally to overhead, in almost all cases it will absorb a significant amount of sales and operations resources that otherwise would have been devoted to increasing your "good" business. And it will remain and grow into the embedded unprofitability that drags down earnings in company after company. If the underlying reason for taking marginal business is to fill unused capacity, you need a sunset policy to stop taking the marginal business once capacity is filled, and to remove it when full-freight business is available. Not many companies have the information and discipline to do this.

By applying the common-sense costs to each transaction, you will develop a database of individual transactions, each with its own revenues, gross profit, and net profit. At this point, it is easy to analyze the details of your company's profitability. In fact, it is a lot like being a detective—finding the profitable parts, hunting down the embedded unprofitability, and figuring out how to change things in the most practical, effective way.

The most important results will be very clear from rapid,
intelligent analysis using best available knowledge and
reasonable rules of thumb.

▼

For example, you can quickly use the database to project the impact of changing your account and product mix, as well as changing the cost of key elements of your operations and sales process. The former shows the effect of focusing the company on high-profit products and market segments, while the latter shows the effect of altering your business model to change "bad" customers into "good" customers.

Some managers make the mistake of trying to figure out their company's profitability by simply allocating broad categories of cost to broad segments of their business in a top-down manner, rather than creating a database of individual transactions. There are two serious problems with this approach. First, managers throughout the company will rightly question the accuracy. Second, the results will be so broad that it will be almost impossible to create a highly targeted, effective action plan. Importantly, it is no harder to do the analysis correctly.

**Model a customer.** In the second step, choose a few individual customers and products that are reasonably representative. For each, develop a profitability profile by clustering their transactions in your database. Try choosing a large and small customer from each of a few key market segments, and a fast-moving and slow-moving product from each of a few key product families. Ideally, you will have about six to twelve representative situations to examine closely.

For each customer, look methodically at the profit drivers—revenues, margins, and costs—for different products. Try different business model configurations such as changing the order cycle, sales process, or service interval. Look at the pricing, both price levels and price mechanisms. Altering the product mix and developing substitution programs also can provide valuable levers for profit improvement. Bear in mind that your profit map will enable you to target specific initiatives to specific sets of customers and products, releasing your company from the need to resort to broad "one-size-fits-all" policies. (The preceding chapter offers an example of how a national trucking company did this; to see how a successful distributor did this, look at chapter 12, "Profit-Focused Selling.")

The sidebar gives an example of a profit map for a sample of four customers.

---

▶ **EXAMPLE PROFIT MAP OF A SAMPLE OF FOUR CUSTOMERS**

Here is an example profit map of four focus customers. This is derived from an actual company using slightly disguised data. Figure 1 shows an overview of the sample, with summaries of each customer. Figures 2, 3, 4 and 5 show the details for each customer.

In this example, the revenues, gross profit (GP, consisting of revenues less product cost), and net profit (GP less supply chain and selling costs, but before

| | SUMMARY OF 4 CUSTOMERS | % of Sales | CUSTOMER A | % of Sales | CUSTOMER B | % of Sales | CUSTOMER C | % of Sales | CUSTOMER D | % of Sales |
|---|---|---|---|---|---|---|---|---|---|---|
| Total Dollars (Sales) | $ 26,276,445 | 100% | $ 15,384,933 | 100% | $ 689,944 | 100% | $ 2,275,739 | 100% | $ 7,925,829 | 100% |
| No. SKUs (Products) | 11,646 | | 5,823 | | 737 | | 977 | | 4,109 | |
| No. Lines | 148,190 | | 74,095 | | 2,499 | | 60,306 | | 11,290 | |
| Avg. Inventory | $ 15,698,014 | | $ 7,849,007 | | $ 377,020 | | $ 499,668 | | $ 6,972,319 | |
| Volume (units) | 1,857,186 | | 928,593 | | 17,785 | | 871,323 | | 39,485 | |
| Est. Gross Profit | $ 4,138,054 | 16% | $ 2,427,804 | 16% | $ 94,056 | 14% | $ 714,637 | 31% | $ 901,557 | 11% |
| Units / Line | 13 | | 13 | | 7 | | 14 | | 3 | |
| $ / Unit | $ 14 | | $ 17 | | $ 39 | | $ 3 | | $ 201 | |
| $ / Line | $ 177 | | $ 208 | | $ 276 | | $ 38 | | $ 702 | |
| GP / Line | $ 28 | | $ 33 | | $ 38 | | $ 12 | | $ 80 | |
| GP / Inventory $ | $ 0.26 | | $ 0.31 | | $ 0.25 | | $ 1.43 | | $ 0.13 | |
| Estimated Net Profit[1] | $ 153,262 | 1% | $ 435,408 | 3% | $ 10,014 | 1% | $ (23,679) | -1% | $ (268,481) | -3% |

[1] Net of supply chain costs and selling costs, but before corporate overhead allocations.

Figure 1

allocation of company overheads) are shown. Also shown are some of the key elements of the supply chain cost structure in order to give you a feel for the power of profit mapping at a more detailed level. (Similar details could have been shown for the key elements of the selling cost structure as well.)

In Figure 6-A, we see that the sample of four customers produces a total of $153,000 in net profits, but the net profitability of each of the four customers is very different from one another. Customer A is a very large customer that is quite profitable; Customer B is a small customer that is slightly profitable; Customer C is a mid-sized customer that is slightly unprofitable; and Customer D is a large customer that is very unprofitable. We can quickly see that the $153,000 in overall net profits is comprised of some very profitable business and some very unprofitable business.

Figure 2 shows a more detailed breakdown of the business that this company is doing with Customer A. Here, the company's overall sales to Customer A is divided into four quadrants, each reflecting the nature of the products sold: Quadrant A consists of high-volume products with a low price; Quadrant B consists of low-volume products with a low price; Quadrant C consists of high-volume products with a high price; and Quadrant D consists of low-volume products with a high price. (Because this analysis is built from a database of all of the company's transactions, or order lines, it would be easy to look at the products sold to Customer A along other dimensions, like product families or products purchased steadily versus occasionally.)

It is striking that even though Customer A is quite profitable overall, contributing more than $435,000 in net profits, the more detailed quadrant-by-quadrant view shows that two of the quadrants provide about $1,325,000 in net profits, while the other two quadrants show a net profit loss of about $890,000. Think about the huge opportunities to improve profitability, even in a very large, profitable account—this is very typical.

Let's take a closer look at Quadrant A (low-price, high-volume products sold to Customer A). This quadrant is a huge winner. (I'll bet there are a surprising number of money-losing products even in this quadrant.) It comprises about 27 percent of the company's product sales to Customer A, but contributes 43 percent of the gross profit, and a massive 217 percent of the overall net profit. The GP per order line is a stunning $1,144, while the cost to pick, pack, and ship each order line is probably about $10 to $15 (this cost has to be covered by the GP). The GP generated by each dollar of inventory is $1.59, showing very strong asset productivity. (Here, the inventory measure is a 70 percent accurate measure of the inventory specifically supporting this particular sales mix—not just an average for the company—estimated using the techniques described in this chapter.) Remember that this quadrant

## PRICE

|  | | LOW | | | HIGH | |
|---|---|---|---|---|---|---|

|  | QUADRANT A |  | % OF SALES | QUADRANT C |  | % OF SALES |
|---|---|---|---|---|---|---|
| **HIGH** | Total Dollars (Sales) | $ 4,105,542 | 100% | Total Dollars (Sales) | $ 1,340,170 | 100% |
|  | No. Skus (Products) | 347 |  | No. Skus (Products) | 4 |  |
|  | No. Lines | 921 |  | No. Lines | 31 |  |
|  | Avg. Inventory | $ 662,032 |  | Avg. Inventory | $ 243,162 |  |
|  | Volume (Units) | 52,045 |  | Volume (Units) | 755 |  |
|  | Est. Gross Profit | $ 1,054,068 | 26% | Est. Gross Profit | $ 416,756 | 31% |
|  | Units / Line | 57 |  | Units / Line | 24 |  |
|  | $ / Unit | $ 79 |  | $ / Unit | $ 1,775 |  |
|  | $ / Line | $ 4,458 |  | $ / Line | $ 43,231 |  |
|  | Gross Profit (GP) / Line | $ 1,144 |  | Gross Profit (Gp) / Line | $ 13,444 |  |
|  | Gp / Inventory $ | $ 1.59 |  | Gp / Inventory $ | $ 1.71 |  |
|  | Estimated Net Profit [1] | $ 944,632 | 23% | Estimated Net Profit [1] | $ 379,941 | 28% |

|  | QUADRANT B |  | % OF SALES | QUADRANT D |  | % OF SALES |
|---|---|---|---|---|---|---|
| **LOW** | Total Dollars (Sales) | $ 4,437,794 | 100% | Total Dollars (Sales) | $ 5,501,427 | 100% |
|  | No. SKUs (Products) | 4,363 |  | No. Skus (Products) | 1,109 |  |
|  | No. Lines | 69,396 |  | No. Lines | 3,747 |  |
|  | Avg. Inventory | $ 2,664,159 |  | Avg. Inventory | $ 4,279,664 |  |
|  | Volume (Units) | 869,267 |  | Volume (Units) | 6,526 |  |
|  | Est. Gross Profit | $ 332,348 | 7% | Est. Gross Profit | $ 624,632 | 11% |
|  | Units / Line | 13 |  | Units / Line | 2 |  |
|  | $ / Unit | $ 5 |  | $ / Unit | $ 843 |  |
|  | $ / Line | $ 64 |  | $ / Line | $ 1,468 |  |
|  | Gross Profit (Gp) / Line | $ 5 |  | Gross Profit (Gp) / Line | $ 107 |  |
|  | Gp / Inventory $ | $ 0.12 |  | Gp / Inventory $ | $ 0.15 |  |
|  | Estimated Net Profit [1] | $ (830,632) | -19% | Estimated Net Profit [1] | $ (58,533) | -1% |

[1] Net of supply chain costs and selling costs, but before corporate overhead allocations.

Figure 2

includes only low-priced products. It's a safe guess that this quadrant is characterized by very steady multiunit orders that are very predictable, and thus require little safety stock (just-in-case inventory)—low-price products with extremely low supply chain costs and selling costs, thus yielding a lot of net profits.

Contrast this with Quadrant B (low-price, low-volume products sold to Customer A). This quadrant is a big drag on earnings, with a net loss of about $830,000. The more detailed view of the supply chain cost structure in this quadrant is completely different from that of Quadrant A. Quadrant B accounts for well over $4 million in sales to Customer A, or 29 percent of Customer A's purchases from this company. Here, Customer A is buying a lot of low-priced products that are very rarely bought. These products generate a relatively low gross profit, and the supply chain costs are extremely high. For example, the GP per order line is $4.79 (compared to $1,144 in Quadrant A); at $10 to $15 to pick, pack, and ship each order line, it is clear that each line is underwater. While each dollar of inventory in Quadrant A generated $1.59 of GP, each dollar of inventory in Quadrant B generated only $0.12 of GP—because these products were low-volume, the inventory was very high relative to sales.

Quadrant C is comprised of high-price, high-volume products. This quadrant represents only 9 percent of the company's sales to Customer A, but contributes a whopping $380,000 in net profits on only thirty-one order lines. Here, the GP per order line is an incredible $13,444, and $1.71 in GP was generated by each inventory dollar. Clearly this quadrant is a big winner.

Quadrant D, the high-price, low-volume products, tells yet another story. This quadrant represents more than $5.5 million in sales, but generates a modest net loss of about $60,000. Why is this happening? The GP per line is a healthy $167, which more than covers the cost to pick, pack, and ship each line. However, the GP generated by each dollar of inventory is only $0.15. Here, the company has to carry a lot of very expensive inventory to accommodate unexpected orders.

Looking at Customer A overall, many managers would see a profitable key account and be very satisfied. But looking at the much more detailed profit map, an astute manager would find his or her mind racing with possibilities for changing the cost structure and profit picture. Could we change the order pattern and predictability in order to lower inventory, especially in Quadrant D? Could we change the pricing of the products in Quadrant B? Could we provide second-day service rather than next-day delivery for the Quadrant B and especially Quadrant D products, as this would enable us to bring them in from a regional warehouse with more customers drawing from the same inventory? By posing questions like this, managers thinking carefully about their profit maps can very easily develop ideas for sharply focused initiatives that will have a fast, major impact on their company's profitability. And most of these initiatives will actually generate cash almost immediately. Bear in mind that this analysis focused on only the supply chain cost factors; a similar, and equally telling, analysis could be done to improve the sales cost picture.

**PRICE**

| | LOW | | | HIGH | | |
|---|---|---|---|---|---|---|
| **QUADRANT A** | | | **% OF SALES** | **QUADRANT C** | | **% OF SALES** |
| Total Dollars (Sales) | $ | 21,003 | 100% | Total Dollars (Sales) | $ 142,488 | 100% |
| No. Skus (Products) | | 63 | | No. Skus (Products) | 2 | |
| No. Lines | | 195 | | No. Lines | 29 | |
| Avg. Inventory | $ | 66,613 | | Avg. Inventory | $ 15,333 | |
| Volume (Units) | | 9,983 | | Volume (Units) | 734 | |
| Est. Gross Profit | $ | 5,573 | 27% | Est. Gross Profit | $ 14,668 | 10% |
| Units / Line | | 51 | | Units / Line | 25 | |
| $ / Unit | $ | 2 | | $ / Unit | $ 194 | |
| $ / Line | $ | 108 | | $ / Line | $ 4,913 | |
| Gross Profit (GP) / Line | $ | 29 | | Gross Profit (Gp) / Line | $ 506 | |
| Gp / Inventory $ | $ | 0.08 | | Gp / Inventory $ | $ 0.96 | |
| Estimated Net Profit [1] | $ | 6,564 | -31% | Estimated Net Profit [1] | $ 12,049 | 8% |
| **QUADRANT D** | | | **% OF SALES** | **QUADRANT D** | | **% OF SALES** |
| Total Dollars (Sales) | $ | 122,314 | 100% | Total Dollars (Sales) | $ 404,139 | 100% |
| No. SKUs (Products) | | 526 | | No. Skus (Products) | 146 | |
| No. Lines | | 1,710 | | No. Lines | 585 | |
| Avg. Inventory | $ | 172,967 | | Avg. Inventory | $ 122,107 | |
| Volume (Units) | | 5,891 | | Volume (Units) | 1,177 | |
| Est. Gross Profit | $ | 45,600 | 37% | Est. Gross Profit | $ 28,215 | 7% |
| Units / Line | | 3 | | Units / Line | 2 | |
| $ / Unit | $ | 21 | | $ / Unit | $ 343 | |
| $ / Line | $ | 72 | | $ / Line | $ 715 | |
| Gross Profit (Gp) / Line | $ | 27 | | Gross Profit (Gp) / Line | $ 50 | |
| Gp / Inventory $ | $ | 0.26 | | Gp / Inventory $ | $ 0.23 | |
| Estimated Net Profit [1] | $ | 846 | 1% | Estimated Net Profit [1] | $ 3,684 | 1% |

*Left axis: VOLUME (HIGH / LOW)*

[1] Net of supply chain costs and selling costs, but before corporate overhead allocations.

Figure 3

Figures 3, 4 and 5 show the detailed, quadrant-by-quadrant profit maps of three other customers. These customers all have a mix of good business and bad business. Even Customer D, which at first glance seems to be a real candidate for being handed over to a competitor, has a large critical mass of good business, and on close examination may well be capable of becoming a top contributor. This is the power of profitability management.

PRICE

|  | LOW | | | HIGH | | |
|---|---|---|---|---|---|---|
| **QUADRANT A** | | | % OF SALES | **QUADRANT C** | | % OF SALES |
| Total Dollars (Sales) | $ | 12,981 | 100% | Total Dollars (Sales) | $ – | 100% |
| No. Skus (Products) | | 4 | | No. Skus (Products) | – | |
| No. Lines | | 28 | | No. Lines | – | |
| Avg. Inventory | $ | 131,354 | | Avg. Inventory | $ – | |
| Volume (Units) | | 22,332 | | Volume (Units) | – | |
| Est. Gross Profit | $ | 7,011 | 54% | Est. Gross Profit | $ – | 0% |
| Units / Line | | 798 | | Units / Line | – | |
| $ / Unit | $ | 1 | | $ / Unit | $ – | |
| $ / Line | $ | 464 | | $ / Line | $ – | |
| Gross Profit (GP) / Line | $ | 250 | | Gross Profit (Gp) / Line | $ – | |
| Gp / Inventory $ | $ | 0.05 | | Gp / Inventory $ | $ – | |
| Estimated Net Profit [1] | $ | (13.000) | -100% | Estimated Net Profit [1] | $ – | 0% |
| **QUADRANT B** | | | % OF SALES | **QUADRANT D** | | % OF SALES |
| Total Dollars (Sales) | $ | 1,749,943 | 100% | Total Dollars (Sales) | $ 512,815 | 100% |
| No. SKUs (Products) | | 829 | | No. Skus (Products) | 144 | |
| No. Lines | | 58,990 | | No. Lines | 1,288 | |
| Avg. Inventory | $ | 283,919 | | Avg. Inventory | $ 84,395 | |
| Volume (Units) | | 846,142 | | Volume (Units) | 2,849 | |
| Est. Gross Profit | $ | 583,456 | 33% | Est. Gross Profit | $ 124,170 | 24% |
| Units / Line | | 14 | | Units / Line | 2 | |
| $ / Unit | $ | 2 | | $ / Unit | $ 180 | |
| $ / Line | $ | 30 | | $ / Line | $ 398 | |
| Gross Profit (Gp) / Line | $ | 10 | | Gross Profit (Gp) / Line | $ 96 | |
| Gp / Inventory $ | $ | 2.06 | | Gp / Inventory $ | $ 1.47 | |
| Estimated Net Profit [1] | $ | (108,022) | -6% | Estimated Net Profit [1] | $ 97,343 | 19% |

VOLUME — HIGH / LOW

[1] Net of supply chain costs and selling costs, but before corporate overhead allocations.

Figure 4

| CUSTOMER D | | | | | | |
|---|---|---|---|---|---|---|
| **PRICE** | | | | | | |
| **LOW** | | | | **HIGH** | | |

| QUADRANT A | | % OF SALES | | QUADRANT C | | % OF SALES |
|---|---|---|---|---|---|---|
| Total Dollars (Sales) | $ 650,273 | 100% | | Total Dollars (Sales) | $ 125,546 | 100% |
| No. Skus (Products) | 280 | | | No. Skus (Products) | 2 | |
| No. Lines | 698 | | | No. Lines | 2 | |
| Avg. Inventory | $ 464,065 | | | Avg. Inventory | $ 227,829 | |
| Volume (Units) | 19,730 | | | Volume (Units) | 21 | |
| Est. Gross Profit | $ 112,144 | 17% | | Est. Gross Profit | $ 83,235 | 66% |
| Units / Line | 28 | | | Units / Line | 11 | |
| $ / Unit | $ 33 | | | $ / Unit | $ 5,978 | |
| $ / Line | $ 932 | | | $ / Line | $ 62,773 | |
| Gross Profit (GP) / Line | $ 161 | | | Gross Profit (Gp) / Line | $ 41,618 | |
| Gp / Inventory $ | $ 0.24 | | | Gp / Inventory $ | $ 0.37 | |
| Estimated Net Profit [1] | $ 34,856 | 5% | | Estimated Net Profit [1] | $ 49,039 | 39% |

| QUADRANT B | | % OF SALES | | QUADRANT D | | % OF SALES |
|---|---|---|---|---|---|---|
| Total Dollars (Sales) | $ 2,565,537 | 100% | | Total Dollars (Sales) | $4,584,473 | 100% |
| No. SKUs (Products) | 3,008 | | | No. Skus (Products) | 819 | |
| No. Lines | 8,696 | | | No. Lines | 1,894 | |
| Avg. Inventory | $ 2,207,273 | | | Avg. Inventory | $4,073,152 | |
| Volume (Units) | 17,234 | | | Volume (Units) | 2,500 | |
| Est. Gross Profit | $ 68,091 | 3% | | Est. Gross Profit | $ 638,087 | 14% |
| Units / Line | 2 | | | Units / Line | 1 | |
| $ / Unit | $ 149 | | | $ / Unit | $ 1,834 | |
| $ / Line | $ 295 | | | $ / Line | $ 2,421 | |
| Gross Profit (Gp) / Line | $ 0 | | | Gross Profit (Gp) / Line | $ 337 | |
| Gp / Inventory $ | $ 0.03 | | | Gp / Inventory $ | $ 0.16 | |
| Estimated Net Profit [1] | $ (358,656) | -14% | | Estimated Net Profit [1] | $ 6,280 | 0% |

Left axis: VOLUME — HIGH / LOW

[1] Net of supply chain costs and selling costs, but before corporate overhead allocations.

Figure 5

Here, you are looking for profit levers, which many of the subsequent chapters of this book address. Once you have found effective profit levers, check several other similar customers to make sure you can generalize your findings.

Modeling the effects of key profit levers on representative customers is especially effective for three reasons: (1) it will be intuitively clear which elements of the business model (e.g., sales process) can be changed and what the effect will be; (2) you can actually call the customers to see what their reactions to the potential changes would be; and (3) it will be easier to explain the changes using concrete examples when you present the initiative to your colleagues.

**Project to the whole business.** Third, take another look at the whole business. Because you modeled representative customers and products in the previous step, you can project your findings onto the corresponding segments of your business. This will allow you to see where the big pools of profits and losses are, and what the profit impact would be of making the changes you found effective in your modeling. When you factor in the difficulty and timing of the changes, you have the essential components of an action plan.

**Create an action plan.** In the fourth step, identify the few high-payoff actions that your company can take relatively quickly. I think of this as the view-to-effort ratio. When our kids were young, we used to take them hiking in New Hampshire. They complained about the uphill walk, but liked the resulting vista. So we used to rate hikes by view-to-effort ratio. This is a very helpful concept in managing change.

> To be truly effective, you need to create a cross-functional team that understands how the business operates.

▼

First and foremost, move quickly to secure the high-profit segment of your business. As soon as you have done this, focus your resources on getting more of this business. Only then, institute a process to improve the profitability of the marginal part of the business.

What about the unprofitable customers? Here's what the CEO of a major service company said about exiting unprofitable business segments or customers:

Before exiting, give them a chance to pay higher prices or modify the profit levers. We did exactly that. We knew our profitability was eroding. Through analysis, we found a business segment where we were losing money. Profit analysis allowed us to determine what changes would be required to generate acceptable returns. The underlying issue was not pricing—it was order pattern, order size, and delivery requirements. Before exiting the segment, we told our customers what we needed in order to continue servicing them. To our pleasure, they agreed to make the changes, and we saw a quantum improvement in profitability in six months!

After working to improve the remaining unprofitable parts of your business, you can begin to phase out the parts that you can't improve. The way to do this is to raise your prices to a profitable level. Some in the company will resist, but keep your eye on the huge upside to refocusing 20 to 40 percent of your sales force and operations assets on aggressively growing your high-profit business. When the higher-paying business begins to roll in, the resistance to dropping unprofitable customers will quickly fall away.

**Institutionalize profit mapping.** Finally, institutionalize the process. Repeat the analysis every six months. Once you have set up the analysis, subsequent rounds will go very quickly. The process itself will build teamwork, and it will become a new way for all your managers to look at the business. In parallel, build profit mapping into your new account qualification process. As your profitability improves, new opportunities will constantly be created. The better you get, the better you can get.

## From financial information to action

The service company CEO mentioned above reflected on his profit-mapping experience: "Financial systems often do not have the information that you need. If they did, the problems would have been solved long ago. To be truly effective, you need to create a cross-functional team that understands how the business operates. This will allow the conversion of financial information into management information which, through analysis, will lead to action."

**1.** It takes two or three managers a few months to figure out where your islands of profit are, and how to create major improvements in your company's profitability. Shouldn't you be one of these managers?

**2.** An important key to success in this process—as in most business analysis—is to operate at 70 percent accuracy. This will give you the answers you need to move forward, and it will keep you from getting bogged down in endless arguments about minutiae that won't change an action. Once you have identified a direction, you can sharpen your pencil to tune it up.

**3.** In your analysis, work with a database of transactions. It will give you the answers you need in enough detail to develop highly focused policies and initiatives. The top-down approach won't give you useful answers, and it is no harder to do the analysis correctly than to do it wrong.

**4.** Model a few actual representative customers and products. That way, you can take your colleagues to visit the customers, and see why they are doing what they are doing. You can also explore how receptive they will be to the changes you suggest. Remember: most changes that will improve your company's profitability will improve your customers' profitability as well.

**5.** Once you have accomplished the first round of profit mapping, repeat the process every six to twelve months. After the first round, it will be relatively easy, and you will continually find new ways to improve your company's profitability.

## What's Next

This chapter explains how to use profit mapping to find your islands of profit, and gives you a process to develop a prioritized action plan. The next two chapters offer two more examples of situations where companies effectively managed to improve their profitability. After that, the last two chapters of this section explain the CFO's role in the process, and outline why difficult times present unusually ripe opportunities to act aggressively.

*Dell Computer was a second-tier PC provider—until it learned the secrets of just-in-time inventory. Here's an inside look at how Dell learned to manage profitability.*

7

# DELL MANAGES PROFITABILITY, NOT INVENTORY

▼

**IN 1994 DELL** was a struggling second-tier PC maker. Like other PC makers, it ordered its components in advance and carried a large amount of component inventory. If its forecasts were wrong, the company had major write-downs. Then Dell began to implement a new business model. Its operations had always featured a build-to-order process with direct sales to customers, but it took a series of ingenious steps to eliminate its inventories. The results were spectacular, and hurtled Dell into the ranks of leading PC producers.

Over a four-year period, Dell's revenues grew from $2 billion to $16 billion, a 50 percent annual growth rate. The company's earnings per share increased by 62 percent per year, and its stock price increased by more than 17,000 percent in a little more than eight years. By 1998 Dell's return on invested capital was 217 percent, and the company had $1.8 billion in cash.

## Dell's transformation

Profitability management, coordinating a company's day-to-day activities through careful forethought and great management, was at the core of Dell's transformation in this critical period. The company created a tightly aligned business model that enabled it to manage away the need for its component inventories. Not only was capital not needed but the change generated enormous amounts of cash that Dell used to fuel its growth.

> Dell created a tightly aligned business model
>
> that enabled it to manage away the need for its
>
> component inventories.

▼

At the heart of Dell's profitability management was a seemingly impossible dilemma: the company had adopted a build-to-order system, yet it had to commit to purchase key components sixty days in advance. How did Dell manage this?

The answer lay in its tightly aligned business model, which had several key elements.

**Account selection.** Dell purposely selected customers with relatively predictable purchasing patterns and low service costs. The company developed a core competence in targeting customers, and kept a massive database for this purpose. A large portion of Dell's business stemmed from long-term corporate accounts with predictable needs closely tied to their budget cycles. Dell developed customer-specific intranet Web sites with predetermined custom specifications and budgets. The remainder of its business involved individual consumers. In order to obtain stable demand in this segment, Dell used higher price points and the latest technology products to target repeat buyers who had regular upgrade purchase patterns, required little technical support, and paid by credit card.

**Demand management.** "Sell what you have" was the phrase that Dell developed for the crucial function of matching incoming demand to predetermined supply. This occurred at several levels.

At a *monthly* MSP/MPP (master sales plan/master production plan) meeting led by CEO Michael Dell, top-level managers agreed on a five-quarter rolling forecast, with a strong focus on "the current quarter plus one." In this meeting, Dell's functional department leaders reviewed their product plans and forecasts, the sales inroads that competitors were making in various product lines, and the company's production plans and bottlenecks. Based on this review, they revised the company's sales targets and production plans to reflect Dell's evolving situation, and they made sure that both sales and production remained in close alignment. At the meeting, the sales commission plan was set to equal the production plan. Through this process, Dell synchronized the company every thirty days.

At a *weekly* Lead-Time Meeting, senior sales, marketing, and supply chain executives collectively interpreted demand trends and supply issues to determine where component overages or underages were likely to develop. The meeting focused on a common variable: lead time for product delivery to customers. At this meeting, the group focused on managing product lead times to ensure that customers would not cancel sales, and that Dell would not be stuck with unsold components.

If a product lead time was climbing, purchasing could expedite component deliveries or shift to alternative sources of supply, or sales could try to induce customers to buy substitute products. If component overages were accumulating, sales could provide incentives for order takers to steer customers toward the makeable set of products, or could bundle products with an attractive umbrella price. The order takers could tell from their screens which configurations were available, and dynamic incentives induced them to steer point-of-sale demand toward these.

When in doubt, Dell managers overforecast on

high-end products.

▼

Dell's pricing also reflected real-time demand management, and varied considerably from week to week. While its competitors' prices were stable with periodic adjustments, Dell's prices varied as the company modified its prices to push products where component inventory was building beyond prescribed levels.

The weekly Lead-Time Meetings had a very strong impact on Dell's culture. Once the sales executives agreed on a set of products to be made, they owned the task of ensuring that these products would be sold. The product lead times were posted daily for all to see, and this drove the daily profitability management process.

Dell's core philosophy of actively managing demand in real time, or "sell what you have," rather than making what you want to sell, was a critical driver of the company's successful profitability management. Without this critical element, Dell's business model would not have been effective.

**Product lifecycle management.** Because Dell's customers were largely high-end repeat buyers who rapidly adopted new technology, Marketing could focus on managing product lifecycle transitions. The company's direct marketing provided real-time customer feedback, which gave Dell the rapid rounds of learning essential to product development and crisp lifecycle timing. Dell became expert at curtailing the end-of-life tail of its six-to-nine-month product cycle.

**Supplier management.** Although Dell's manufacturing system featured a combination of build-product-to-order and buy-component-to-plan processes, the company worked closely with its suppliers to introduce more flexibility into its system. It concentrated its supplier base into fifty to one hundred suppliers accounting for 80 percent of its purchases. Supplier selection was based only 30 percent on cost, with the other 70 percent on quality, service, and flexibility.

**Forecasting.** Dell's forecast accuracy was about 70 to 75 percent, due to its careful account selection. Demand management, in turn, closed the forecast gap. When in doubt, Dell managers overforecast on high-end products because it was easier to sell up, and high-end products had a longer shelf life.

**Liquidity management.** Direct sales were explicitly targeted at high-end customers who paid with a credit card. These sales had a four-day cash-conversion cycle (converting customer billings into cash receipts), while Dell took forty-five days to pay its vendors. This generated a huge amount of liquidity that helped finance Dell's rapid growth and limited its external financing needs. This cash engine enabled Dell to earn its extraordinarily high returns.

Dell used the freed-up cash to fuel its growth, chiefly in

major corporate accounts.

▼

## Genesis of Dell's process

How did Dell create its tight profitability management process? The answer is very telling.

The seeds of Dell's success were sown in its failures of an earlier time. In 1994 it produced a set of portable computers that had serious quality problems. Sales plummeted and Dell faced a serious cash shortfall. At the same time, the company realized that it had to accelerate its growth in order to move from the list of declining Tier 2 manufacturers (Commodore, Zeos, etc.) to the group of prospering Tier 1 producers (IBM, Compaq, etc.), and this required even more cash.

Dell's executives met to decide how to generate the funds to keep the company alive. They decided to dramatically reduce inventories. The heads of manufacturing and marketing were charged with devising a way to run the business without component inventories. At first they resisted. Then they developed a way to meet this goal.

The new Dell business model developed in phases over a period of time. The first set of objectives focused on lowering inventory by 50 percent, improving lead time by 50 percent, reducing assembly costs by 30 percent, and reducing obsolete inventory by 75 percent.

As Dell phased in the new system, component inventory dropped from seventy days to thirty-to-forty days, then to twenty days, then to nearly zero. At the same time, the sales force was trained to "sell what you have." As the new profitability management system emerged and proved viable, Dell moved aggressively to refine it and to bring the other functional activities into tight alignment.

Dell used the freed-up cash to fuel its growth, chiefly in major corporate accounts. These accounts were originally hard for the company to penetrate because it was generally buying from resellers. In order to win this business, Dell had to convince the accounts that its products were high-quality, and that it could meet their service and delivery requirements.

Many major companies initially thought that Dell's build-to-order model could not meet their delivery requirements. Once Dell demonstrated that it could build to specific customer orders and meet delivery and quality requirements, growth followed. This dynamic enabled the company to catapult to first-tier status.

Two surprises greeted the Dell executives who were creating this new process.

First, as inventory dropped, lead-time performance improved. Dell was not simply carrying a large inventory of component parts against forecasted sales, but was rather aligning inventory and sales, managing profitability on a daily, weekly, and monthly basis.

Second, as inventory disappeared, the company's returns grew disproportionately. Not only did Dell avoid carrying costs and obsolete stock but, importantly, it was saving enormous amounts of money because the component prices were dropping 3 percent per month.

# Profitability, not inventory

The inventory of a product in a company is determined by the variance in the customer demand for the product (steady or erratic orders), and the variance in the replenishment of the product by suppliers; unless these variances are reduced, inventory can only be moved around, not eliminated. I think of this as the "waterbed effect." When you sit on a waterbed, it sinks in one place and bulges in another. The water is redistributed but the amount stays the same.

Through its use of profitability management, Dell matched supply and demand on a daily, weekly, and monthly basis. It sharply reduced the variance, and the need for inventories simply disappeared.

In most companies, inventory substitutes for profitability management, tying up valuable capital and preventing the company from focusing on day-to-day business alignment. Managers face a choice between managing inventory and managing away the need for it. Those who choose the latter option turbocharge their company's profitability, and create lasting competitive advantage in the process.

---

### THINGS TO THINK ABOUT

**1.** Dell used the key principles of profitability management to change its strategic and competitive positioning—catapulting the company from second-tier manufacturer to premier PC maker.

**2.** Dell's profit levers ranged from account selection to demand management to product lifecycle management to supplier management. Dell's managers combined these into a tightly integrated package perfectly aligned with its strategy. This gave Dell "maximum pounds per square inch" of market power—the key to success.

**3.** Dell developed a set of parallel business processes to align the whole company on a monthly, weekly, and daily basis.

**4.** The seeds of success were rooted in the need to survive a severe business setback. The company faced the choice of innovating or failing. Consider the relevance to struggling companies in a difficult economic environment.

**5.** Most of the Dell managers who created and implemented this strategic initiative became very wealthy. Think about how you define your job and your prospects.

---

## What's Next

The next chapter explains how to apply the principles of profitability management to retailing, showing their broad relevance throughout business. Think about Dell when you read chapter 10, "Recession Opportunities."

*Can you apply profitability management to a retailer? Absolutely. Start by calculating the profitability and return on invested capital for every item in your store.*

# 8

---

# PRECISION RETAILING

▼

**CAN YOU APPLY** profitability management to a retailer?

That was the question posed by a senior manager during a talk I gave to a group of executives in the Midwest.

In the talk I had described how to analyze the profitability of customers and products, and how to turbocharge a company's profits by increasing the portfolio of profitable business, turning around marginal business, and shedding deadweight business.

This executive explained that industrial companies and distributors have sales forces, so they can select and manage their customers. Retailers, on the other hand, put products on their shelves and seem to have little control over who comes into the store and what they buy. What can a retailer do to manage profitability?

The answer: plenty.

A few months after my talk in the Midwest, I held a strategy session for top executives of major grocery chains. In conversations and correspondence afterward, a number of participants offered a similar view of their industry. Here's what one executive said:

"I suppose that if supermarket executives sat down, they would agree that probably 25 percent of the customers that walk in the door cost them money. All the profit comes from the 25 percent with the largest baskets—not necessarily the largest revenue. . . . Well over half of that profit comes from 10 percent or less of the base."

## Retail profitability management

A few years ago, the CEO of a major retailer decided to assemble a small high-level work team to radically improve the company's profitability. Using profit mapping, in a relatively short time they created a PC-based model that calculated the profitability and return on invested capital for every product in every store. Not surprisingly, they found islands of high profits in a sea of marginal business. There were large opportunities for profitability improvement, even in this well-run multibillion-dollar retail company.

As they probed the areas of embedded unprofitability, and uncovered the pools of potential new profits, they identified five high-impact profit levers for major profitability improvement.

**Assortment management.** When it comes to assortment management—deciding what to put on a store's shelves—more is not always better. This is true for two reasons.

First, overly broad assortments, especially for technical products, can be confusing for both sales associates and customers. In many retail situations, more than 60 percent of the customers enter the store with a generic need, such as a radio to play at the beach, rather than a particular branded product.

Hence, there is a need in each product category for a relatively tight selection of products that fill certain roles: key price points, traffic drivers, technical icons, fashion showpieces, and so on. Within this context, a retailer might choose to carry a somewhat broader assortment in a particular dimension to emphasize its positioning and strategy.

But beyond this, overly broad assortments can diminish sales, increase inventory costs, and cause inordinate markdowns. The exception is a specialty retailer competing in a narrow segment with sophisticated buyers.

Second, tight assortments are particularly critical to the success of smaller (lower sales volume) stores. A smaller store should not be simply a scaled-down version of a larger store. It must be assorted in a much smarter way.

Overly broad assortments can diminish sales, increase

inventory costs, and cause inordinate markdowns.

▼

A large store is like a fast-flowing river: if you make the mistake of stocking a product that doesn't sell, or if you have too much of a product at the end of its lifecycle, the error flushes through the system relatively quickly. But a smaller store is like a slow stream: if you make a product mistake, it's like throwing a big rock into the water. The shelves get clogged, and it takes a long time to free them up for a new, fast-moving product. The profit map showed clearly that this was the source of a disproportionate number of this major retail chain's profitability problems.

**Customer service management.** Again, more is not always better. Here, substitution groups are critical to successful profitability improvement.

A substitution group is a set of products that fulfills the same role in a store's product assortment. An example would be a low-priced printer. Here, a store might have two or three products that fully meet a customer's needs. This is a substitution group. Nearly all retailers monitor in-stock positions on each individual product, but it makes much more sense to monitor the substitution group—because customers are indifferent to one product or another within the group. This can save a retailer a huge amount of money on inventory, especially late in the product lifecycle. Most important, it aligns store assortments with what customers really want and experience.

Substitution groups are also important because they give a retailer an opportunity to execute a Dell-like strategy of managing demand, or "selling what they have," especially with short-product-lifecycle, high-end products.

Within a substitution group, a sales associate can steer customer purchases, when needed, toward products with excess stock and away from products with thin stock. This requires a strong link between the merchant group and the stores. But it needs to take place perhaps only 5 to 10 percent of the time, and it will have an especially big, positive impact in lower-volume stores late in the lifecycle.

Retailers can also use merchandise presentation to steer customer purchases, especially toward high-profit products and those with excess stock levels. Products can be emphasized or deemphasized by repositioning the product on the aisle, or on shelf-end displays (endcaps).

For example, one prominent retailer analyzed which products would likely spike in sales at the start of the war in Iraq. On the first night of the war, it repositioned key products—guns, Bibles, and flags—in every one of its stores. Sales soared the next day.

**Customer management.** In retail, as in most businesses, a relatively small proportion of customers provides most of the profits. What can a retailer do? Identify them, hunt them down, drive them in, and get more of them.

First, use profit mapping to identify your most profitable customers. Then you can use direct mail and other highly targeted means to drive them into your stores more often, and to increase the scope and frequency of their purchases. Loyalty programs are critical in this process. Once you secure your best customers, proactively find more like them.

Consider the implications for assortment management. Try this: take a few representative stores and analyze the breadth of products your high-profit buyers purchase. Are they buying your entry-level products? Your on-sale products? Your traffic drivers? Or are they buying high-profit, higher-end products at predictable times, often early in the product life-cycle? If the latter, you can focus your assortment to maximize your sales to your power buyers, and stop losing money on marginal products sold to unprofitable customers.

**Product flow management.** This area is a source of major potential profit gains in retail today, made famous by Wal-Mart's well-known cross-docking process (a distribution center procedure for moving products directly from inbound trucks to store delivery lanes without putting away and picking). Retail product flow management is based on two important principles: supply chain differentiation and flow-through logistics. Both are explained below.

In a well-differentiated supply chain, products are grouped into clusters corresponding to their demand characteristics, merchandising characteristics, and physical characteristics. Think about the differences in an apparel retailer among staple high turnover products like white underwear, seasonal products like bathing suits, and promotional products like sports team championship T-shirts. Each of these clusters requires a different set of operating policies and a different supply chain. Each requires a different game plan for effective management. (Chapter 20, "You Only Have One Supply Chain?" explains how to do this.)

Flow-through logistics is a process for minimizing inventory and handling. For example, relatively fast moving products should flow from vendors through distribution center cross-docks to stores in regular pulses with minimum inventory and handling. This process gives you major cost savings while maintaining service levels, but it requires a high degree of organizational coordination, both internally and with vendors.

Assortment management is crucial to streamlining product flow in two key ways. First, by compressing assortments, you build in the remaining products the volume and demand stability necessary for flow-through logistics. Second, substitution groups offer considerable opportunities to focus and stabilize demand. For example, in a substitution group with three vendors, you might offer all of the group's demand upside (i.e., spikes in demand, or demand above predicted levels) to one vendor in return for guaranteed capacity and flow-through logistics; the other two vendors would see extremely stable demand, which would facilitate flow-through logistics on their part.

**Best-practice management.** By developing profit maps that show profitability and return on invested capital for every product in each store, you can construct detailed profit profiles that compare similar stores. In many retail chains today, stores are clustered, compared, and managed geographically, a practice that dates back to the days before computers, when regional managers had to visit stores frequently to judge performance. Geographic clustering is ineffective because it combines many dissimilar stores. Profit mapping enables you to cluster, across regions, stores that are similar in size, demographics, competitive situation, and other key factors, and analyze their relative performance. This provides an invaluable complement to geographic-based store-operations management.

Within a peer group, you can observe best practices and spread them quickly. The store managers and store operations group can systematically move the peer group of stores to its best-practice standards. Internal best-practice benchmarking is one of the fastest and most productive ways to improve performance. However, it is important to be sure that store manager compensation is based on absolute performance, not performance relative to the peer group, so the store managers do not have an incentive to hide their best practices.

## Culture of profitability

The most effective way to create sustained high levels of profitability is to build a culture of profitability within your company. This is true for retailers as well as for all other companies.

▶ The merchants must understand the end-to-end net profitability, from vendor to shelf, as well as the return on invested capital for every one of their products in every store. It is not enough to focus only on a product's revenues and gross margins.

▶ The supply chain and logistics managers must know their supply chain productivity, not just efficiency. Supply chain productivity is comprised of two factors: (1) the net margin of a product in a store as the numerator; and (2) the invested capital, chiefly inventory, supporting that product in that store as the denominator.

▶ The store operations managers must see the net profitability and return on invested capital performance of all the products in all of their stores, as well as the comparison of their respective stores' performance to the best practice of their peer group of stores.

▶ The key managers in these functional groups must get together periodically to systematically review the performance of their stores and products. Together, they control all the elements essential to profitability, and together they must coordinate to develop joint initiatives to manage and improve profitability.

▶ All three groups must share the same performance and compensation metrics: net profitability and return on invested capital. Ultimately, putting in place this critical behavioral driver is the most important ingredient for bottom-line success.

When you get all five of these elements right, you will create a culture of profitability in which your managers will drive your retail company to its fullest profit potential.

---

## THINGS TO THINK ABOUT

**1.** Retailers have the same profitability pattern—islands of profit in a sea of red ink—as companies in all other industries.

**2.** Like most companies, retailers have many more profit levers than one might think at first glance. Profit mapping is the key to uncovering them and creating an effective action plan.

**3.** A key part of the profitability management process in a retailer is creating a set of overarching measures of profitability to align the functional departments whose actions combine to determine profitability. The same is true of companies in all other industries.

**4.** Many retailer profitability problems stem from the management of late-lifecycle products in low-volume stores. A few relatively simple management measures can turn these lemons into lemonade.

# What's Next

This section so far has described the problem of embedded unprofitability, the opportunity for improvement, the historical context, and how leading companies have successfully developed profitability management programs to create major improvements. The next question is: what is the role of the CFO, and how can he or she be effective in the process?

*Companies suffer from embedded unprofitability. The answer: build grassroots profitability management processes into your company's core management activities.*

# 9

# NEW CFO ROLE: CHIEF PROFITABILITY OFFICER

▼

**EMBEDDED UNPROFITABILITY IS** a huge issue in every company.

It causes three enormous problems: (1) reported profits are much lower, often half of what they could be; (2) the best customers generally receive only average service, which raises a critical risk of competitors picking off the profitable piece of the business by offering better service; and (3) the company loses the opportunity to shift resources to the highest-payoff activities.

With the insights that profitability management provides, a company can secure its best business, focus on finding more of the best business, devise targeted measures to turn around the marginal business, and steadily shed the residual unprofitable business that can't be fixed. Not only is it very realistic to eliminate embedded unprofitability but it generally costs almost nothing and quickly generates large amounts of new profits and cash.

Why isn't this an essential business process in all companies? Why isn't the CFO—and the other top finance managers—involved in driving this?

■ ■ ■

# Barriers to profitability management

Here's a paradox. An enormous number of companies have large blocks of business that are unprofitable by any measure, and their managers agree that this is true. Yet, very few companies move aggressively to turn this around. Why is this so?

I probed this question in numerous conversations with CEOs, general managers, vice presidents, and CFOs over the past few years. Four structural barriers to effective profitability management emerged.

**First.** Financial and management control information is not structured to surface the problem and opportunity areas. All departments have budgets. Sales has a revenue budget, and operations has a cost budget. Yet, even if all departments make budget, the company can still be 30 to 40 percent unprofitable. Why? Because virtually all budgets start with a company's existing pattern of profitability (and embedded unprofitability), and challenge managers to make improvements from this baseline. If a company starts with a large amount of embedded unprofitability, and a manager makes a noticeable cost reduction or revenue improvement, the budget looks good, but the company still will be performing well under its potential.

> Even if all departments make budget, the company can
>
> still be 30 to 40 percent unprofitable. Why?

▼

**Second.** Everyone is doing something. Managers' projects range from product selection to cost reduction to market segment development. These initiatives are useful to some degree, but they almost always miss the huge opportunity that comes from getting the day-to-day activities of the business right all the time.

**Third.** Paradoxically, public companies have strong investor pressures that constrain top managers from turning around embedded unprofitability. Many managers are concerned that eliminating unprofitable blocks of business would require reducing revenues substantially, and this would hurt the company's stock price. These managers make the incorrect assumption that reducing embedded unprofitability means firing customers. In fact, by carefully choosing a set of profit levers and deploying them in well-selected situations, managers can turn most problematic accounts and products into profitable business.

**Fourth.** In most companies, *no one* is responsible for systematically analyzing and improving profitability. This is an astonishing assertion. Yet, I have found that while all executives are involved in activities to improve profitability, no one is responsible for the microlevel profitability of accounts, products, orders, and services, and for eliminating embedded unprofitability.

Certainly, a CEO or general manager is responsible for profitability. But most of these individuals are focused on major strategic initiatives, important customer relationships, and making sure their key managers make budget. The problem of analyzing the profitability of orders, accounts, products, and services, and improving them through precisely targeted measures, falls between the cracks.

What about CFOs? Virtually all CFOs, and other top finance managers, are very focused on profitability in terms of meeting revenue and earnings targets. They are also involved in asset productivity initiatives, asking questions like, Why do we spend so much money on payroll? Should we outsource? And, of course, they are highly focused on managing cash, even to the point of acquiring or shedding divisions of the company to keep the cash flow in balance.

However, it is very unusual for a CFO or other top finance manager to focus systematically on identifying and rectifying embedded unprofitability, and on building this process into the company's core set of ongoing management activities.

## New CFO role

How can a company break this apparent logjam and overcome these barriers to effective profitability management? The key is to define a powerful new role for the CFO: *Chief Profitability Officer*.

This may seem like a strange suggestion, as virtually all CFOs view profitability as a central part of their existing jobs. But to be fully effective, a CFO must go beyond broad, departmental performance measures to build grassroots profitability management processes into his or her company's core management activities. This task has three key components.

**Road map.** The effective chief profitability officer (CPO) needs to develop a systematic understanding of the company's baseline profitability through profit mapping. This will reveal the precise areas of high profitability, low profitability, and negative profitability, going far beyond gross margins, market segments, and product families. This view will form the basis for laser-targeted initiatives to systematically improve profitability.

**Process.** Building a set of ongoing organizational processes and incentives for profitability management is a critical CPO job. This starts with integrating profit-mapping information into day-to-day jobs throughout the company. Think about this familiar example. A supply chain manager works hard and achieves a 15 percent inventory reduction, but this inventory is supporting unprofitable business. At the same time, a sales rep brings in a 20 percent revenue increase that actually *reduces* profitability. In most companies, these two individuals would be rewarded like heroes—even though they actually caused the company's profitability to drop. This should be a major CPO concern.

The key to success is for the CPO to get his or her organization in front of the problem through integrated market planning. In this process, the sales and marketing groups join with the operations group to define a set of account relationships, ranging from highly integrated to arm's length, and to target accounts for specific relationships. That way, the company's operating cost structure can be aligned in advance with the business mix. If this sounds like a tall order, it really is not. However, it is a different way of doing business, and leading companies have already seen great increases in profits and market share in this way.

Profitability management opens a new realm of

opportunity for the creative CFO.

▼

**Transition management.** Transition management will make or break profitability management initiatives, especially in public companies. CPOs are right to be concerned about possible stock price repercussions from simply eliminating unprofitable revenues. However, many profit lever initiatives will increase profitability of marginal business at little cost, and with no revenue loss. Similarly, securing and growing your most profitable business by shifting sales and service resources from unprofitable business is only a matter of prioritization, training, and adjusting sales compensation. Together, these can give you major increases in revenues, profits, and cash flow.

For example, one auto accessories company that pursued this strategy actually increased its penetration of high-potential, underpenetrated accounts by more than 40 percent within a few short months. At the same time, it created an agent network to service its marginal, low-potential accounts that were far from its depot network. This reduced its costs and freed up resources. Revenues shot up, costs dropped, and the company's stock price tripled in about three years.

The remaining issue is eliminating residual unprofitable revenues that can't be turned around. Here, the key is to bring in new high-profit revenues before the unprofitable revenues are phased out through appropriate pricing.

Profitability management opens a new realm of opportunity for the creative CFO. Using it, a CFO can generate revenues, profits, and cash surprisingly quickly. But it requires that the CFO move beyond his or her traditional domain and become a central player in creating an effective profitability management process and a culture of profitability that pervades the whole company—maximizing profitability from the grassroots up, not just from the global budgets down. In this way, the effective CFO can truly become the company's Chief Profitability Officer.

---

### THINGS TO THINK ABOUT

**1.** For CFOs and all financial managers, profitability management offers the opportunity of a lifetime—a chance to drive profit improvements of 30 to 40 percent or more without the need for capital investment.

**2.** There are powerful reasons why these opportunities have been hidden for so many years. The good news is that it is not very difficult or time-consuming to identify the opportunities and to craft a program of improvement.

**3.** There are very important issues of transition management that can make or break a profitability management program.

**4.** The CFO must become very skillful at coordinated change management in order to be a successful chief profitability officer. He or she must join with the other top finance managers to create a new culture of profitability and new business processes to support it. The payoff in results and satisfaction is enormous.

## What's Next

Difficult economic times—whether a general recession or company-specific problems—provide a critical window for a results-oriented manager to drive fundamental change. The last chapter of this section explains why and how.

*It's true: a crisis is a terrible thing to waste. Difficult
economic times bring rare and valuable opportunities to
drive lasting change in your company.*

# 10

# RECESSION OPPORTUNITIES

▼

**RECESSION. IS THIS** the worst of times or the best of times?

The answer is both. Difficult times bring difficult problems to all managers, but they also create rare opportunities for renewal.

Consider cost cutting. In a recession, revenues fall, cash is depleted, and stock prices plummet. In most companies, the instinctive reaction is "all hands on deck" cutting costs. The problem with cost cutting, however, is twofold: managers often do it wrong, and cost cutting is not enough.

Managers charged with cost cutting in recessionary times all too often focus inordinately on short-term incremental gains, and miss major strategic opportunities. This means that there is a bad way and a good way to cut costs. The bad way is to cut across the board ("let's get inventory and travel expenses down").

The good way is to look very carefully at your company and identify the winners and losers in terms of profitability and growth potential. The key is to shift resources systematically from the losers to the winners. This will enable you to lock in and nurture the profitable portion of your business, and to find and land more high-potential business. In the vernacular, you should "shoot one, promote one."

## Opportunity for change

Economic difficulties present a critical opportunity to drive progressive change in a company.

In good times, managers are busy improving their companies in traditional ways. It is very hard for top managers to move a company to change its fundamental business processes when it's doing well, even when they know that it will create lasting improvements.

Recession changes all of this. Difficult economic times present one of the most important opportunities to drive renewing change in a company. In difficult times, with the company in jeopardy, managers throughout the company are very worried. It is precisely at this time that they will be most receptive to initiatives and change. The same is true for customers and suppliers.

> Difficult economic times present one of the most important opportunities to drive renewing change in a company.

▼

The essential question for a manager is how best to take advantage of this rare opportunity. In my experience working with companies in hard economic times, there are four major areas of opportunity.

## Manage profitability

A few months of profit mapping will show you where your company is making money and where it is underwater. With this view, you can double down on the best parts of your business, target and secure more business with the potential for high profitability, improve your marginal business, and phase out the unprofitable parts of the business. This will enable you to redeploy resources and rapidly increase your profitability and cash flow.

Two points are important here. First, it is critical to refocus your sales force to sell into high-potential underpenetrated accounts using your own systematized best-practice account penetration process. This will enable you to quickly generate profitable new revenues to more than replace any falloff in sales from phasing out unprofitable accounts.

Second, a few well-selected profit levers will turn around a surprising portion of your unprofitable business. In many cases, customers are unprofitable for reasons that may not be apparent to them. For example, volatile customer order patterns require you to carry high levels of inventory, disrupt warehouse operations, and incur costly delivery charges. Importantly, this is very costly for your customers as well. Both parties will gain from an improvement.

## Enhance customer and supplier profitability

In tough times, customers and suppliers are desperate for improvements in their own profitability and cash flow. They will be unusually receptive to new ways of doing things. This creates a unique and valuable opportunity for managers to lock in high-value-added relationships with the best partners.

Customer operating partnerships can have a huge impact on customer and supplier profitability and cash flow. (These are arrangements that suppliers and customers create with each other to coordinate their intercompany product flow, reducing costs and increasing responsiveness; they are described in detail in chapter 17, "Profit from Customer Operating Partnerships.") Intercompany operations like vendor-managed inventory can greatly increase your best customers' profits and asset productivity (efficient use of the customer's assets, such as inventory and equipment) on handling your products. At the same time, you can gain control of their order pattern, and through this process significantly lower your own cost of operations. The benefits of these operating partnerships are so strong that sales often increase by 30 to 40 percent, even in highly penetrated accounts.

For your suppliers, the same partnership benefits are available. You can invite key suppliers to suggest ways that they could improve your company's profitability. Most suppliers implicitly assume that their customers are not open to serious operational innovations, and the most capable will jump at the chance to work closely with a willing customer.

In addition, you can proactively analyze your own purchase pattern from your suppliers' perspective. It is relatively easy to figure out ways to reduce both your suppliers' costs and your own costs at the same time. Gain sharing is a natural next step.

You will seldom have this strong an opportunity to drive permanent innovations upstream and downstream in your supply chain. If you act now, you will reap the rewards for years, and it is likely that most of your competitors will be paralyzed by their obsession with unfocused cost cutting.

## Drive customer innovations

Recessionary times present an important opportunity to greatly improve the value proposition that you offer your customers. The previous paragraphs described how a supplier can increase a customer's profitability through an operating partnership. But the opportunity to improve a company's value proposition goes beyond this.

A supplier typically has very deep and detailed information on its products and markets. This often includes valuable information on customer best practices across a range of noncompeting customers. In good times, when demand is strong, customers can achieve strong sales using only the sort of routine product and market information that is traditionally provided by suppliers.

In difficult times, however, customers need as much help as they can get. The problem is twofold: (1) customer-supplier relationships are often implicitly adversarial, and (2) customers may not know what helpful information the supplier has within its organization (this information may in fact be "buried" within the supplier's organization and not be readily available to the sales and marketing managers who normally interface with the customer).

There is great value for a supplier to proactively approach its good customers (and high-potential underpenetrated customers) with the proposition that both supplier and customer have a lot to gain by jointly rethinking the way the customer is using the products and bringing them to market. Often, it quickly becomes apparent that the supplier has detailed information that can improve the customer's own value proposition.

For example, a supplier of industrial products faced the problem of differentiating its products like safety equipment, which were viewed by the customers as commodities and were subject to extreme price competition. In a great move, the company's marketing group worked with its best distributors to create special catalogs and customer Web sites that focused on helping the distributors' customers select the right products for particular applications and use them correctly. This had tremendous value for the ultimate consumers, and drove large sales increases through the whole channel, benefiting company, distributors, and customers alike.

In a recession, the instinct is to hunker down and focus on short-term measures to minimize the pain. This is exactly the wrong thing to do.

▼

## Create strategic innovations

When is the best time to innovate? The answer, surprisingly, is when you don't need to. Think about the situation of GE's aircraft engine business. In the months after 9/11, airline traffic dropped precipitously, and orders fell off a cliff.

At the time, the company was developing a new generation of fuel-efficient engines. At first, it appeared that the company's timing was terrible—developing a costly new product while the industry was in turmoil. But in reality, this was exactly the right thing to do. It took some time to complete the development cycle, and the engines were brought to market when the airlines were emerging from the slump, the market was strengthening, and jet-fuel costs were rising.

## Timing is everything

All this is profoundly counterintuitive. In a recession, the instinct is to hunker down and focus on short-term measures to minimize the pain. This is exactly the wrong thing to do.

Insightful managers will realize that difficult business conditions create a rare and valuable opportunity to renew and change their companies, with a lasting impact on their long-term profitability. Now is the time to be proactive and creative. Not only will you reenergize your organization but you will reap the rewards for years to come.

■ ■ ■

**1.** Financial pressure—whether from economic recession or company-specific problems—presents a very important opportunity to develop and implement a profitability management system that produces both fast and lasting results.

**2.** There is a good way and a bad way to cut costs. Unfortunately, most companies are mired in the mass-markets mentality outlined in chapter 3, "The Age of Precision Markets," so they cut across the board with disastrous long-term consequences.

**3.** Your customers and suppliers will be looking for solutions as well, and they will be especially receptive to positive change. This creates a very critical opportunity to create innovative new programs with your channel partners for your mutual benefit.

**4.** Like all things, hard times pass. Managers who have the foresight to create positive changes and initiatives in difficult times will see their companies' performance turbocharged when business picks up. This holds true for managers at all levels of a company. Competitors who were frozen in the headlights and afraid to act decisively will fall further and further behind.

## What's Next

This section of the book gives you a framework to understand how to think for profit, and tells you how several leading companies have achieved stunning success using this process. It's not difficult, but it is very different from business as usual in the era of mass markets. The next two sections build on this knowledge by explaining how to create profit levers in the sales and marketing process and in the operations management process, respectively. The final section of this book explains how to lead change, and how to organize your company for high sustained profitability.

# SELLING FOR PROFIT

# INTRODUCTION

**HOW CAN A** company bring in business that maximizes profitability when the sales reps are compensated primarily on revenues, and all sales dollars are not equally profitable? Which account should a sales rep call on? What should he or she accomplish in the call?

This section focuses on two critical profit levers: sales management and market development. The chapters explain how to structure and focus your sales process to maximize your company's profitability, develop deeply integrated relationships with the right customers—and avoid the trap of doing this with the wrong customers—and translate your business objectives into concrete sales results. It also explains how to develop a market-planning process that integrates and aligns your whole company.

## How can a manager focus and improve the sales process?

**Chapter 11, Account Management: Art or Science?** explains how account management can be systematized and focused. Without a systematic process for selecting and penetrating the right accounts, profitability can't be maximized.

**Chapter 12, Profit-Focused Selling,** narrates the step-by-step process that the general manager of a distribution company used to restructure his sales process, increasing his company's net profits by 50 percent in three years.

**Chapter 13, Use Best Practice to Fire Up Your Sales Team,** demonstrates how you can identify and codify your own company's best practice sales process, and teach it to your whole sales force.

**Chapter 14, New Management Tool: Potential-Based Sales Forecasting,** explains how to transform sales forecasting from a process that perpetuates average performance into one that drives revenue growth and change.

## When and how should a company form a deep relationship with a customer?

**Chapter 15, Is Your Organization Reptile or Mammal?** describes the fundamental choices a company faces in engaging with its market. Sales reps face the same choices. Many companies and sales reps falter because they refuse to choose.

**Chapter 16, Out-of-the-Box Customer Service,** describes how you can create powerful new innovations that increase your customers' profitability—in the process driving up your revenues, locking in your best accounts, and reducing your costs.

**Chapter 17, Profit from Customer Operating Partnerships,** gives a step-by-step process for developing an integrated supply chain with a key customer, and illustrates it with the example of a company that did this very successfully.

**Chapter 18, Product Companies: Don't Undersell Services,** explains how to deploy related services that increase revenues and build competitive advantage while reducing costs. Many companies view related services as a nuisance, and they lose enormous opportunities for profit gains.

*In many companies, the science of account management is neither well understood nor systematically applied. And that means lost profits.*

# 11

# ACCOUNT MANAGEMENT: ART OR SCIENCE?

▼

**IS ACCOUNT MANAGEMENT** an art or a science? Account management is the process of developing new customers and managing your customer relationships. This is a critical question: the answer determines whether the sales process can be systematized and subjected to constant improvement. And effective account management is one of your most important profit levers.

The answer, not surprisingly, is that both aspects are important. But in many companies, the science of account management is neither well understood nor systematically applied. In high-performing companies, on the other hand, the science of account management is the centerpiece of the sales process, and within this context, artful selling produces the most effective results.

The science of account management has four key elements: (1) profitability management, (2) account relationship selection, (3) relationship migration paths, and (4) account planning. With these four elements in place, plus aligned sales compensation, the sales process will produce great results.

Over the years, I have participated in a number of high-level sales management and business unit leadership meetings. A frequent comment is that sales would improve dramatically if only the sales reps had more contact with the CEOs of their accounts. This often leads to a suggestion to hire new reps with high-level account contacts.

My reaction is that many managers find it easier to spend money than to improve management processes. This is a big mistake. Most sales reps are quite capable of outstanding performance if they are managed well and work within a well-structured process. Conversely, high-performing sales reps from other companies would be much less effective if inserted into a company with a poorly structured, poorly managed sales process.

The prime responsibility of a company's management is to provide its sales reps with a systematic, effective process through which they can understand how to succeed. The essence of sales rep effectiveness is to have an extremely clear understanding of what task needs to be accomplished in every account call. This process is the science of account management.

## Profitability management

The first and most important element of account management is to ensure that each and every sales rep has a clear working understanding of profitability management. All sales dollars are not equal. Some business will produce high profitability, and other business will actually degrade the company's earnings.

**The sales rep's** objectives, in order of importance, are as follows:

▶ First, secure the most profitable business
▶ Second, obtain more of the most profitable business
▶ Third, help make the marginal business more profitable
▶ Fourth, downsize the inherently unprofitable business

Artful sales achievements that bring in the wrong business or fail to secure the best business will actually decrease profits. Here, the more successful the art of sales, the more the company is hurt.

## Account relationship selection

Relationship selection can make or break the profitability of an account. Relationships range from very resource-intensive ones, such as customer operating partnerships, to moderately resource-intensive configurations, such as product flow management (managing the customer's order pattern), to the arm's-length relationships that characterize many buyer-supplier interactions.

It is critical to be extremely clear in advance about what relationship fits which account. The key factors in account relationship selection are: (1) potential margin dollars, (2) operating fit, (3) relationship versus transactional buyer behavior (whether or not a customer is loyal to its suppliers), and (4) customer willingness and ability to manage internal change.

In many cases, an account that would be profitable with an arm's-length relationship would be unprofitable with a customer operating partnership or its equivalent. Here, an artful sales rep who skillfully sold the wrong relationship could hurt the company's performance, often for years on end, even if revenue dollars constantly increased.

Artful sales achievements that bring in the wrong

business or fail to secure the best business will

actually decrease profits.

▼

For example, a supplier of electronic components may have a relatively small customer located far from its distribution center who wants a very integrated relationship, including on-site personnel and vendor-managed inventory. In this situation, it may well be profitable to offer an arm's-length relationship with telesales and next-day service, because providing significant on-site services would make the relationship unprofitable. It is critical for companies to develop and offer a range of relationships, each with clear, measurable benefits. Sales reps must be adept at matching these relationships to customer situations.

The real art of selling relationships is to understand in advance where each relationship should end up, and to systematically steer each account into the most profitable buyer-supplier configuration, even if it means convincing one that wants an inappropriately intensive partnership to be happy with less.

■ ■ ■

# Relationship migration paths

In most companies, products and services can be structured in a way that provides clear migration paths to deepen the account relationship. For example, many entry-level products and services can be designed to enable the company's operating and sales personnel to make contact with a wide range of high-level managers in the account.

By leading with products and services that are designed to provide an opportunity to quickly widen and deepen the relationships with the account's buying center (everyone significantly involved in the decision to purchase), management can help the sales rep to accelerate account penetration. With thoughtful product and account planning, a company can build a bridge for its sales reps to their accounts' key decision makers, without the need to hire outsiders with preexisting contacts.

Astute marketing managers structure their products and services in a way that naturally leads from one sale to another, as the account's buying center is penetrated and the sales rep gains customer knowledge and trust. Here, the art is for the sales rep to work a well-structured process, and not simply to sell products in a reactive, unmanaged way.

# Account planning

The goal of account planning is for the sales rep to manage the account's decision-making process so that he or she is continually moving up the relationship ladder. An effective account plan focuses on building a robust relationship with all the relevant people in an account, so that strong sales with compensatory prices continue even if a particular individual in the account leaves. Short-run sales tactics are only part of a good account plan.

A well-conceived account plan provides the basis for coaching, measuring progress, and analyzing and solving problems. If resources, such as account development time (customer calls) or promotional investments, are needed, the account plan becomes a committed business case. It also provides milestones for sales compensation in situations where lengthy relationship building precedes sales, or where critical early products bring in only minimal revenues.

An effective account plan should cover at least six critical sales rep actions. Here's a checklist for sales reps and their managers:

**Develop an account profile.** This should include potential sales volume, margin potential, operating fit (customer service needs), relationship versus transactional buyer behavior, customer willingness and ability to change, and account history.

**Identify whom you are hunting.** Profile the key individuals in the buying center, including influencers. Generally, a surprisingly large number of individuals are involved.

**Identify their needs.** Determine what each individual needs to make your product or service most buyable. Is it support? Resale value? Lifetime value of a customer relationship? Price? Endorsements? Quick visits or lengthy talks? Often this will vary by individual.

**Determine how to open each door.** For each individual in the account's buying center, what is the key reason why he or she will listen to you? What questions will be most compelling and show that you are in tune with his or her key needs or worries? This is a critical step, and the answers are not obvious. If this is not done well, the sales process turns into simply going in and asking for business; this is especially fatal when dealing with an account's top managers.

**Create an action plan with steps, resources, metrics, and milestones.** This should be a program that is tough, thorough, and robust. It should follow directly from the previous analysis. In the absence of a tight link, the action plan again will amount to simply going in and asking for business. The plan should have expected outcomes that can justify the investment of time and resources. Specify clearly what support or resources are needed from other departments in your company.

For example, a multistep action plan might start with a one-month period of mapping the account (identifying the individuals in the buying center, estimating account potential, and determining the competitors' strength of relationship). The next step may be to move into a two-month account penetration phase in which the rep calls on the key individuals and gets the account to try an initial sample. Each of these early steps would have a concrete measure of success, an expected time period, and a set of resources required (e.g., rep time, promotional materials, telesales support).

**Create a coaching plan.** It is critical that the *sales rep* identify the key points at which he or she will need sales manager coaching. Sales reps must be creative and proactive in using their sales managers as one of their most valuable resources.

■ ■ ■

## Successful account management

The essential top management task in creating a successful account management program is to structure a very well thought out process to ensure that the sales reps have extreme clarity about what task needs to be accomplished in each and every customer interaction, and to ensure that this process will consistently produce the most profitable results.

Within this context, creative selling will be most effective, as the art and science of account management blend to maximize a company's bottom line.

---

### THINGS TO THINK ABOUT

**1.** The key to sales force productivity is task clarity. Each sales rep must be extremely clear about what he or she must accomplish in each sales call every day. It is management's responsibility to give the sales force a systematic, effective process through which they can achieve this task clarity.

**2.** Without this framework, sales reps are at sea. Some will figure out how to succeed, some will fail, and most will be much less effective than their personal potential suggests.

**3.** Sales compensation must be aligned with the sales system. If all revenue dollars are treated as equally desirable, your company will have high embedded unprofitability.

**4.** The four key elements of a great sales process are: profitability management, account relationship selection, relationship migration paths, and account planning. With these in place, your sales reps will achieve task clarity.

---

## What's Next

The first four chapters of this section focus on important aspects of sales force effectiveness, and give concrete examples of companies that have succeeded in this area. The final four chapters explain when and how to build customer relationships that push the frontier of customer value creation.

*This chapter relates the story of a general manager's three-year program to increase sales force productivity and dramatically enhance company profitability.*

## 12

# PROFIT-FOCUSED SELLING

▼

**HOW CAN A** manager achieve consistently high levels of sales force productivity?

Many managers simply assume that sales force productivity is all about increasing revenues, while reducing costs is an operations problem. This is a very costly assumption.

A company's sales force has a crucial role to play in both revenue and profit maximization. Here is how one general manager (GM) developed a profitability management process that met both essential goals.

## The General Manager's story

The GM of a paper and janitorial supply distributor in the southern United States wrote to me in response to one of my columns, "We have sliced our numbers as you described and found the eighty-twenty rule throughout [i.e., about 20 percent of the customers and order lines produce roughly 80 percent of the profits]. We then segmented and stratified our customers to be handled by different sales methods (outside sales, inside sales, and customer service). Our results are significant—gross profit per order has increased 82 percent in the last four years. Also, our net profit will be up over 50 percent over three years ago. I want to take our business to the next level, and I would be willing to share our experiences with you."

About seven years earlier, the GM took charge of a successful seventy-year-old distribution company. The company sells its products to a variety of customers, including universities, manufacturers, health-care providers, and food processors. The sales force averaged twenty years of experience.

Two years later, the GM started looking for ways to improve profitability. Over a three-year period, he instituted a powerful process that dramatically increased sales force productivity and company profitability. The process reflects the three key elements of profitability management: profit mapping, profit levers, and a profit management process.

## Profit map

The GM began by working with his IT manager to develop a process to analyze account profitability. To calculate account profitability, they started with order and account gross profit, and subtracted a set of sales and operating costs. This gave them a rough estimate of operating profit for each order and account, which I think of as the supply chain net (gross margin less operating and selling costs).

They then clustered the accounts by sales rep, and ranked the accounts in descending order by operating profit. When they showed the results to the reps, the typical reaction was that the data had to be wrong because "my top account is second from the bottom." If a rep contested the data for an account, they jointly looked up the details and reviewed the calculations. In all, only thirty of twenty-four hundred account calculations needed adjusting.

When they showed the results to the reps, the typical reaction was that the data had to be wrong because "my top account is second from the bottom."

▼

■ ■ ■

# Profit levers

The GM quickly saw that one of the key profitability drivers was the operating profit of an order. At the time, each order was taken by a sales rep during a visit to the customer. Because the visit was costly, each order had to generate a minimum amount of gross profit in order to cover the cost of the visit and related costs. (I think of this as the gross-margin-to-driving-time ratio.) In light of this, the GM developed several initiatives to increase profitability.

In the first initiative, the GM reduced the account load for each sales rep from 240 to 56 customers. The objective was to force the reps to get deeper penetration in the highest-potential accounts. The GM saw that the reps had to learn to get past the purchasing managers, and form better relationships with the key decision makers in the accounts. To accomplish this, he created an account profile template that the reps could use to develop a more systematic understanding of their accounts.

In the account profiling process, the rep identified the decision makers, competitors, and customer strategy, and devised an account penetration strategy. Developing the profiles required that the reps interview their customers. They were surprised to find that the customers liked talking about themselves and about the competitors, and even volunteered their views of competitor weaknesses and ways that the company could generate more business.

Several reps commented to the GM that the customers thought the company was even better than the reps thought. This went a long way in developing the reps' confidence in the wisdom of focusing on deep penetration of high-potential key accounts. The GM also instituted team sales calls, in which several key company operating managers (distribution manager, IT manager, finance manager) would walk through the customer facility and suggest ways for the customer to reduce cost.

In his second initiative, the GM developed appropriate sales channels for the smaller B and C accounts. Initially, he designated all the accounts below a certain operating profit threshold as house accounts. An inside customer service group (telesales) serviced these accounts. Next, the GM started a middle-market hybrid inside-sales group, focused on the 600 to 750 midsized accounts. This group combined inside sales with occasional face-to-face meetings.

The GM's third initiative focused on customer education. The reps told the smaller customers that they had to provide a minimum number of orders of a certain size in order for the company to continue to service them. Most customers changed their purchasing process and order patterns in order to continue the relationship with the company.

## Profitability Management Process

The GM changed the sales compensation system to ensure that the sales reps followed the new profitability management process. Under the new system, the direct sales reps' compensation had three components: (1) 45 percent of the compensation was salary, (2) 35 percent was based on commissions, and (3) 20 percent was composed of a bonus based on growth in gross profit per order over the previous year. Moreover, the GM instituted a minimum order size to qualify for a commission.

The profitability management program was a great success. The GM observed, "The key is to show the numbers to the employees, and explain the logic to the customers."

The GM's pervasive focus on raising operating profit per order had stunning results. The company's operating profit per order increased by more than 80 percent, and net profits soared by more than 50 percent.

Most customers changed their purchasing process

and order patterns in order to continue the relationship

with the company.

▼

## You are what you sell

Your sales force is like the front-wheel drive of a car: it pulls you through the marketplace. Regardless of your plans and intentions, your company is what it sells.

What, then, do you sell? To answer this question, just look at your sales compensation system. In most companies, the sales force is rewarded for bringing in revenues, occasionally for gross margins or units of product, but rarely for profitability. Yet all revenue dollars are not equally profitable. This is the essence of the problem—and the opportunity.

The GM increased his company's profitability by more than 50 percent, without capital investment, by shifting from revenue-focused selling to profit-focused selling. He did this in three ways:

**First.** The GM identified the highest-potential accounts, and tightly focused his direct sales resources on these accounts. Contrast this with the president of another company, who said to me in frustration, "My sales reps are like bumblebees, bouncing from flower to flower." By reducing the account span of the direct sales reps, the GM forced them to focus all their energy on penetrating and broadening their relationships with the best customers. This secured the company's key sources of profitability.

**Second.** The GM created a multitiered selling system. The best accounts received intensive direct-sales attention, the middle-market accounts received a blend of inside sales plus occasional visits, and the small accounts were served by inside sales customer service reps. By doing this, the GM focused his direct sales force on the highest-potential accounts, and matched the cost of his selling resource to the margins generated by their accounts.

In essence, if the gross margin of an order, or transaction line, is less than the cost of selling and servicing the order, it will be unprofitable. By developing a multitiered selling system, the GM reduced the sales expense relative to gross margin for the smaller B and C accounts. Not only does this system increase account profitability but it can also better meet customer needs. If your company supplies a relatively small proportion of a customer's overall purchases, the customer often will prefer a crisp, effective inside sales relationship to prolonged direct sales visits.

> The GM instituted a powerful profit-focused selling system that drove up penetration in the highest-potential accounts and turned bad accounts into good accounts.

**Third.** The GM took several measures to increase the operating profit of orders by inducing the customers to consolidate their orders. He drove the sales force to accomplish this by developing the new sales compensation system and complementing it with an extensive customer-education program.

Through these three measures, the GM instituted a powerful profit-focused selling system that drove up penetration in the highest-potential accounts, turned his "bad" accounts into "good" accounts, and converted his company's embedded unprofitability into a 50 percent profit increase.

---

**1.** Think about the power of a simple, well-coordinated profitability management process. The GM of this company achieved a stunning profit improvement in a relatively short period of time using a few carefully selected actions executed with great consistency and effectiveness.

**2.** Profit mapping was the key to developing this action plan. It enabled the GM to identify the right set of initiatives, and gave him the facts to convince his sales reps that he was doing the right thing.

**3.** Note how the GM reduced each rep's deck of accounts in order to focus them on increasing their share of wallet in their high-potential accounts. The results proved that the reps really could accomplish this. Here's something to think about: Why didn't the reps do this on their own before the GM forced the issue? If you were one of the reps, would you\have done this before the GM made the change?

**4.** The GM skillfully aligned his company's business model with account potential by creating a multitiered selling system and enforcing a policy of minimum order sizes for all accounts. These profit levers ensured that even low-volume accounts were profitable. The GM didn't just throw the low-volume accounts overboard, he made them profitable.

## What's Next

The first chapter of this section explains how to develop an effective sales process, and this chapter gives a concrete example of a company that increased its profitability by more than 50 percent by doing this. The next chapter tells you how to look inside your own company to find the most effective selling practices, and how to use them to move all of your sales reps to a level that approaches that of your best performers.

*This chapter explains how best practices developed by
your A performers can be used to train and motivate
B and C performers.*

## 13

## USE BEST PRACTICE TO FIRE UP YOUR SALES TEAM

▼

**MANY MANAGERS ASK** me for references on best practices in sales force management that they can observe and replicate. In virtually every company I've seen, the answer exists within the company itself.

I'm always amazed by the variety of practices within a company. Think about this: if you took a video of everything your sales force did last year, edited it carefully, and played the best parts, I'll bet that you would have an absolutely stellar, world-class performance.

The problem, however, lies on the cutting-room floor. This is where the evidence of the unevenness of practice in your company appears. But here's the good news: it shows how much money you could make if you could bring your whole team up to your own best-practice standards.

The observed overall performance of your sales force is the weighted average of your best practice, your average practice, and your problematic practice. The fastest and easiest way to improve your bottom line is to move all your employees up to your own best practice. This is an especially powerful profit lever for your sales force.

Most managers take for granted that their company has A players, B players, and C players, particularly in their sales force, and that their company's overall performance reflects this inevitable reality. In my experience, this assumption is almost always false.

The flaw in this view is the implicit assumption that the sales process, or any business process, cannot be analyzed, codified, taught, and coached so that even an employee of average ability can perform with consistent excellence. Why not?

## Changing the changeover process

I recall visiting a major manufacturer several years ago. This was during the time when manufacturers were shifting from the long production runs that characterize mass production to the shorter production runs of quick-response systems. The difficulty in shifting production to quick response is that it requires very rapid changeovers of the production line from product to product.

For example, an appliance manufacturer with long production runs might produce perhaps three months of a particular stove model every three months, and have to change the production line only every couple of days. However, the same manufacturer utilizing quick response manufacturing would make a different combination of products every day. In the latter situation, the company's success depends on figuring out how to change the manufacturing line from one product to another very quickly.

This manufacturer developed a simple but ingenious approach to solving the changeover problem. The manufacturer's changeover team actually took videos of their product changeovers. The whole work team analyzed the videos to identify improvements, much like a football coach watches game films.

With clear information before them, the factory workers developed new procedures. They also created a way to codify and teach the new changeover methods, as well as measures to monitor implementation. Changeover times dropped dramatically.

> The flaw in this view is the implicit assumption that the sales process, or any business process, cannot be analyzed, codified, taught, and coached so that even an employee of average ability can perform with consistent excellence.

▼

## Standards of care

In medicine, there is a guiding principle called standards of care. If you meet with a doctor before surgery, he or she will describe the procedure that you are going to experience. Most likely, the doctor will say something like, "If I see A, I'll do B; if I see C, I'll do D."

In this conversation, the doctor is describing well-established best-practice standards of care. These standards are based on rigorous research and well-analyzed experience. They are accessible and followed by practitioners throughout the field. These standards represent the shared understanding of best practice. Leading researchers and practitioners are always trying to improve the standards of care, but no one should mistake this process for "winging it."

The standards-of-care process is extremely powerful. It allows the participants to systematically analyze and identify best practice, and ensures that all practitioners adhere to it as closely as possible. The best surgeons will always be the most capable practitioners, but the standards-of-care system ensures that the rest of the surgeons practice as capably as possible. It also offers a way for leading specialists to subject the best-practice standards to constant improvement and to spread the gains rapidly.

Managers can apply this process to dramatically improve their own businesses.

## Business standards of care

Some may argue that the sales process is inherently idiosyncratic: every customer is different, every sales rep is unique, and it's virtually impossible to systematize the process.

In my experience, this view is counterproductive and wrong.

For example, initial penetration of a company that should become a major account is one of the most important but difficult processes in business. Many sales reps, particularly inexperienced ones, avoid trying to penetrate high-potential underpenetrated accounts. The rep may feel that these accounts are locked in a relationship with a competitor, or may even be hostile because of a past incident. Yet, turning around a high-potential underpenetrated account is almost always the highest-payoff use of the sales rep's time.

In several companies, I've had an opportunity to investigate this problem. The results were strikingly similar.

In each company, when I interviewed the best-performing sales reps independently of one another, they typically had a very methodical and remarkably similar view of the account penetration process. They knew almost meeting by meeting, month by month, what contacts and activities they would be working on—and they knew what results to expect at each point. They understood that the process would vary somewhat from account to account, and they knew how to handle these variations. However, it quickly became clear that within each company, the top performers were all on the same page.

The B and C players, however, were on a very different page, or very different pages. They had widely varying views of the process, either very optimistic or very pessimistic. The overly optimistic reps quickly got discouraged by the seemingly slow initial phase of the penetration process, while the overly pessimistic reps simply avoided the whole process. In fact, the high-performing reps could even tell you at what point the B and C players would give up on a turnaround account and refocus on more comfortable accounts.

Contrast this with the standards-of-care system in medicine, where everyone knows what to do and what to expect.

In my experience, high-performing reps within a company, the A players, have independently discovered a set of best-practice standards that are strikingly similar from rep to rep. They have refined these standards over time to accommodate the variations in the sales process that occur naturally from account to account. Typically these standards are not systematically gleaned and codified, but they exist nonetheless in parallel practice among the top performers.

Talking to these high-performing reps is very much like talking to an accomplished doctor: "If I see A, I'll do B; if I see C, I'll do D." But this is where the parallel ends.

The B and C players in a sales force generally do not have the experience or capability to discover best practices on their own. All too often sales training is too general, focusing on developing broad capabilities like discovering customer needs rather than helping the company's reps master critical company-specific best-practice procedures.

Sales managers often succumb to the error of exhorting reps to improve their results, or coaching parts of the process piecemeal, rather than teaching and drilling critical company-specific best-practice standards of care. The absence of systematic best-practice knowledge and process-specific training creates the great variance in sales performance that so many companies experience.

> Harnessing the power of your own best practice is the
> best of all worlds.

▼

## Best-practice process

Here is a seven-part process to create standards of care in your own company's sales force:

**Identify best practice.** Try interviewing your top performers. Focus on key processes like territory management, account selection, the account-penetration lifecycle, and day-to-day fundamentals like sales visits and follow-up.

**Codify best practice.** Here, the key is to concentrate on a small number of high-payoff activities that can be translated into replicable processes, your standards of care. To take an analogy from football, try dividing the world into fundamentals and game plans. Fundamentals include things like crisp sales calls and the ability to talk comfortably with customer managers and engineers; game plans include an account prioritization process, and a small number of well specified alternative account-penetration-lifecycle profiles.

**Train the process.** The most effective training must go far beyond teaching general sales capabilities. It must focus on systematically teaching your reps your company-specific best-practice standards of care. For example, in the account penetration process, there likely will be a small number of well-proven game plans, and each of these will have several identifiable stages with particular critical activities at each stage. Every rep should know your best-practice process, and master the essential skills necessary for success at each stage.

**Coach the process.** Consider the words of Tom Brady, the New England Patriots' star quarterback: "The goal of winning three consecutive Super Bowls should take a backseat to putting together three straight quality practices." In the account penetration process there will be certain identifiable critical points at each stage. For example, if a rep is moving into an account penetration stage in which the critical element is talking to engineers, the manager should coach and drill the rep in the process of talking to engineers until his or her performance is consistently excellent.

**Measure the process.** All too often, sales measures are too vague and broad. In account penetration, measuring progress in moving an account from stage to stage is critical. Sometimes, important progress does not yield immediate revenues.

**Compensate the process.** The compensation system must be aligned with the best-practice process. If turnaround account management is critical, a significant component of compensation should be tied to account penetration milestones.

**Constantly improve the process.** Like any standard of care, your best performers will always find ways to make the process better. The key is to identify and capture these improvements and systematically move your whole sales force to this new and better level.

## One Company's Experience

Here's how one company instituted this process in a very effective way:

▶ First, the company's executive vice president of sales appointed a team consisting of two high-performing regional sales managers and gave them responsibility to develop a new sales process. The team systematically interviewed the top sales reps throughout the company. They saw that the largest sales gains came from turning around high-potential underpenetrated accounts. While most reps shied away from these accounts, the top sales reps treated these situations as prime opportunities.

The team also saw that these high-potential accounts fell into four generic categories, reflecting differences in their purchasing behavior and the strength of the current suppliers. When the team went over the interviews, they discovered that the top reps all had very similar processes, or game plans, for penetrating the accounts in each category, and that they had figured out how to quickly diagnose which category best fit each prospective account. These game plans involved key elements, like specifying the number and nature of sales calls and who was called on, the points at which certain promotional and telesales support was needed, and the likely results at each stage.

▶ Second, the team assembled their findings, and showed it to the top sales reps. The reps were surprised that others had figured out similar approaches. But they agreed that the game plans were correct, and that it was possible to quickly tell which game plan fit a new turnaround account.

▶ Third, in order to develop a training plan, the team started by teaching the new process to the sales *managers*. They met with them, explained the game plans, and gave each manager five high-potential turnaround accounts to penetrate. At first, the managers were puzzled that they had to go out in the field to personally sell accounts, but soon they saw that the process really worked. This hands-on experience was essential in teaching the managers how to teach their sales reps.

▶ Fourth, after a couple of months, the team reconvened the group of sales managers to develop the training materials and process. The group decided that the best way to coach the process was to give each sales rep only five high-potential turnaround accounts. This would allow the managers to keep the reps focused, and to closely monitor and coach the reps' progress. Throughout this process, the managers were able to identify the points at which reps typically encountered problems, and to be proactive in coaching them in advance.

▶ Fifth, the team worked with the sales managers to break each best-practice game plan into a series of steps, each with a specific milestone delineating the completion of the step. In addition, they very quickly developed an understanding of the amount of time a rep required for each step of each game plan, if he or she were doing well. This allowed the sales managers to be very specific in their progress reviews with reps, and to identify problem situations early enough to intervene with focused coaching.

▶ Sixth, the team changed the sales compensation system. They assigned a large bonus to account penetration milestones to really motivate the reps, and to compensate them for the time spent away from their "bread and butter" accounts. At first, most reps complained about having to spend time on the five high-potential turnaround accounts. But after the first month, they discovered that sales went up by an average of 40 percent in these accounts. Immediately, many reps who had complained about having to work five turnaround accounts now wanted ten or more. The managers responded that they could have only five, and that when an account reached a critical mass of sales (an explicit milestone), the rep would get another to replace it—but each rep would have only five turnaround accounts at a time.

▶ Seventh, as the sales management group became experienced with the new sales process, they saw that the reps naturally experimented with variations in the game plans. For example, one rep found that she could profitably deploy a telesales rep to do research on prospective accounts. Another rep discovered that an important set of prospective accounts did not really fit any of the existing categories or game plans, so he developed a new one. Once the company's account development process was codified and made explicit, the whole sales force systematically and relentlessly improved the process and spread their new best practices. Everyone was on the same page, and the process just got better and better.

## Cultural consistency

The most powerful aspect of harnessing your own best practice is that your sales force will be very receptive to the improvements. Your own best practice is literally your own. It was developed by your own top performers, whom everyone in your company respects and admires. The accounts in which the best practices worked are your own accounts, often legendary turnaround successes. Your reps will be hungry for an understanding of how they could do the same.

Harnessing the power of your own best practice is the best of all worlds. Your standards of care are available within your own four walls. You can identify, codify, teach, coach, and spread them rapidly and effectively. And your own sales force will readily accept and embrace them, with a big, lasting impact on your bottom line.

**1.** The secret to rapidly increasing your sales force productivity lies within your own company. Look to your own best practice. Then ask yourself whether all of your sales reps are systematically following your own best practice, and if not, why not.

**2.** In my experience in company after company, turning around high-potential underpenetrated accounts is the fastest and surest way to rapidly increase sales. Most reps shy away from this, mostly because they do not have a well-understood process to accomplish the task. Yet when one asks the highest-performing reps in a company how they would accomplish this (what they would do month by month, and what would result), they almost always give the same answer. This is your best practice.

**3.** You can identify, codify, and teach your best practice to all of your reps, and you can systematically subject it to constant improvement.

**4.** Your sales reps will be eager to learn it—after all, it is your own company's best practice, and not an abstract training regime. You will be amazed at how readily it will be accepted, and how fast your results will improve. And it won't cost you a penny.

**5.** If you're a sales rep, why wait for your company to act first? Why not develop this understanding on your own? In my experience, most successful reps are very happy to adopt the role of teacher. But remember, you have to develop a systematic understanding of the process (game plan plus tactics), and not just trawl for anecdotal tips.

## What's Next

This part of section 2 focuses on sales force productivity. The next chapter explains the crucial role of sales forecasting. In many companies, forecasting actually retards sales improvement by breeding complacency. But it doesn't have to be this way.

*Is your sales forecasting perpetuating weak practices?*
*Potential-based sales forecasting is a powerful new way to*
*drive revenue growth and change.*

## 14

## NEW MANAGEMENT TOOL: POTENTIAL-BASED SALES FORECASTING

▼

**SALES FORECASTING SHOULD** be the centerpiece of revenue improvement in every company. Yet, all too often, managers treat forecasting merely as a necessary distraction from productive work.

The reason why sales forecasting so often fails to live up to its potential is that in most companies, it is implicitly treated as a descriptive rather than a prescriptive process. This means that managers use the process to try to predict future sales based on average current performance, rather than using it to analyze, manage, and improve the revenue stream. This embeds current practices, both good and bad, in the forecast, and managers lose the all-important opportunity to improve their sales force productivity and company results.

### What's wrong with this picture?

Typically, sales forecasting occurs in one of two ways. First, in companies like distributors and manufacturers, with identifiable accounts, forecasters try to distill and predict the sales pipeline. Second, in companies like retailers, with masses of customers, forecasters look at the demographic and competitive landscape, and try to relate these factors to sales.

Consider Company A, a distributor of maintenance products. The company has a typical sales force: each sales rep has about 120 accounts, with 5 to 10 large accounts, 10 to 15 medium accounts, and about 100 small accounts (some of which are really small businesses, but many of which are very underpenetrated large companies). Each rep calls on the large accounts weekly, the medium accounts biweekly, and the small accounts monthly, if that often.

The sales force uses a popular sales management software package in which each rep tracks his or her progress. The software produces reports that calculate the expected value of upcoming sales based on amount, likelihood, and timing. This becomes the core of the sales forecast.

Company B is a retail chain with about 500 stores. The marketing group has developed a forecast model in which each store's sales is related to the demographic and competitive characteristics of its trade area. Based on this model, the company develops sales forecasts both for existing stores and for new locations.

What's wrong with this picture?

## The missing element

Both companies A and B have forecast processes that are designed for financial projections, not for improving the business. They implicitly assume that the companies will continue their current activities, and therefore they can be projected into the future.

The point of management, however, is fundamentally different: It is to identify the key leverage points to improve the business, and to rapidly change the company for the better.

The objective of great forecasting should be to discover the company's own best practices, and to build these improved practices into the forecast, instead of perpetuating weak practices. A well-designed sales forecasting process should accelerate positive change, while a typical backward-looking process actually retards it.

> The objective of great forecasting should be to discover
>
> the company's own best practices, and to build these
>
> improved practices into the forecast, instead
>
> of perpetuating weak practices.

▼

# Distributor forecast management

Let's start with Company A, the distributor. For this company's top management, the key to success is to deploy a two-step potential-based forecasting process.

**First.** Forecast *account potential,* not actual sales, for all significant accounts in a territory. This may seem daunting at first, mostly because few companies do it today. However, in practice a manager can do this effectively by focusing on the company's own best practice—its most highly penetrated accounts—and understanding what characteristics these accounts share (e.g., revenues, number of machines). As with profit mapping, aim for a 70 percent accurate picture of account and sales territory potential.

Based on this analysis, it is not difficult to identify the salient characteristics of the company's other accounts, and to estimate the *potential sales* to each. In addition, several good commercial databases show rough account potential. The combined picture is generally quite accurate, and a few telesales calls usually can confirm account potential. Because account potential generally does not change much from year to year, the information is relatively easy to maintain once it is developed.

Several important surprises emerge at this stage. Some of the small accounts that received little attention in the past because they had low actual sales are really high-potential underpenetrated accounts. A critical mass of rep attention, combined with systematic rep training in the company's own best-practice account-turnaround process, can produce significant sales increases in these accounts.

**Second.** For each account with significant potential sales, simply estimate the difference between account potential and actual sales. This straightforward calculation gives a measure of *unrealized potential* for both individual accounts and overall territories. It also gives reps and their managers a key measure of the reps' effectiveness in converting potential sales into actual revenue dollars. It shows, for example, whether a rep is a great performer with an inherently meager territory, or a moderate performer with an inherently great territory. This perspective is critical for effective sales management and compensation.

With this picture, sales managers can direct reps to devote a portion of their time to turning around individually targeted high-potential accounts, rather than simply deploying rep time against historical account sales. This key profit lever will rapidly increase your sales force productivity.

Potential-based forecasting can be very accurate, even in the context of changing and improving revenues. The analysis of account and territory potential enables managers and reps to target the highest-payoff accounts in each territory. Because they can project the sales amounts and timing that the company's top reps' best-practice methods would have produced in each account, they can get an upper bound on this revenue growth. Because managers can gauge the relative effectiveness of individual reps at growing sales in turnaround accounts, they can accurately forecast the proportion of best-practice sales growth a particular rep can achieve.

## Retailer forecast management

In retail, the two-step potential-based sales forecasting process is again critical to revenue improvement. However, here the process works a little differently.

Let's return to the case of Company B. This retailer sells a variety of products in several related categories. In the past, the company had developed a forecast model that related store sales to a set of broad measures such as trade area aggregate population, average income, and competitive intensity. It used this model both for forecasting existing store sales and for locating new stores.

For this retail chain, the key to improvement was to deploy a two-step potential-based sales forecasting process, analogous to Company A's process.

First. Forecast each store's sales potential. This retailer, like many, collected customer zip code information at its registers, giving it a picture of customer purchases by zip code. The company found that within a store trade area, and throughout the chain, sales varied widely from zip code to zip code, even when the zips were very similar in demographics, distance from the store, and competitive intensity.

When the management team saw this zip-to-zip variance, they decided that simply forecasting average store sales was not giving them a good enough answer.

Instead, they decided to estimate the potential sales in each zip code. They profiled the best-practice zips by relating their sales to relevant factors, such as zip demographics, distance from the store, and competitive intensity. With this information, they were able to estimate the *potential* for each store's non-best-practice zips, projecting what the company's best-practice zips with similar characteristics would have produced.

This was analogous to the distributor's process of estimating account potential by focusing on its most highly penetrated accounts.

**Second.** In a second step, the managers simply subtracted each zip's actual sales from its estimated potential sales, yielding a picture of the *unrealized potential* of each store's trade area, zip by zip. This gave the management team a precise road map of where to deploy marketing resources in order to turn around the high-potential underpenetrated zips.

By comparing actual and potential sales from store to store, the top managers could gauge each store's relative effectiveness in mining its trade area. When the managers ranked each store's effectiveness, they could not only see the unrealized potential of each store relative to that store's own best practice but also estimate the additional potential sales that a top-selling store could have achieved in each lower-performing store's trade area.

With these measures of trade area potential and relative store effectiveness, plus an understanding of the speed of best-practice market development, the management team could accurately forecast sales improvement with the expectation of improved sales practices built in. They could also use this information as a standard to gauge their managers' progress in bringing their stores' sales up to best-practice potential.

In retail, zip-code-based analysis is not the only useful approach. Some store chains find customer market segmentation to be a powerful forecast variable. However, it is often very difficult to get a good measure of market segment actual and potential sales, and, in any event, sales potential almost always declines very rapidly as customer distance from a store increases. This suggests that for most retailers, zip-code-based analysis is a good place to start.

Potential-based sales forecasting can be a prime driver of

rapid revenue increases.

▼

## Sharp performance improvements

Potential-based sales forecasting can be a prime driver of rapid revenue increases. The key to success is to recognize that forecasting should not be built on the past and embed weak approaches to selling. Instead, forecasting should be based on best-practice potential, and it should drive sharp improvements in your company's overall performance through the two-step process. With this process, a manager can create a very profitable future, rather than simply projecting the mistakes of the past.

## What's Next

The first four chapters of this section give you a framework for sales force productivity, a concrete example of a company that greatly improved its results, and an understanding of how to improve your company's performance by identifying your best practice and developing potential-based sales forecasting. The next four chapters tell you how to create value-laden customer relationships.

*When it comes to customer and supplier relations, some companies are like reptiles, some are like mammals, and some haven't quite made up their minds. This chapter explains why you need to know the difference.*

## 15

---

# IS YOUR ORGANIZATION REPTILE OR MAMMAL?

▼

**WHEN IT COMES** to customer and supplier relations, some companies are like reptiles, some like mammals, while others haven't quite made up their minds. Let me explain.

Reptiles and mammals are fundamentally different in two crucial respects: reproduction and metabolism. First, reproduction. Reptiles, like snakes, lay dozens of eggs in the hope that a few will survive. Mammals, like bears, generally give birth to a few young and nurture them over a period of time. Second, metabolism. Reptiles are cold-blooded, which means that they are at the mercy of their environment, while warm-blooded mammals have the ability to control their destiny, but at a steep cost.

### Reptile strategy

Most companies have customer and supplier relationships that at their core resemble reptile or mammal reproductive strategies. For example, most catalog companies send direct-mail marketing pieces to thousands of potential customers. They often work from purchased mailing lists of relevant magazine subscribers and other sources. If a company achieves a success rate of 2 or 3 percent, the investment usually pays off. This approach to the customer market is analogous to the reptile reproductive strategy: the catalog company touches thousands of prospects in the hope that a few will convert to customers.

On the supplier side, consider a company that sources most of its products from a network of alternative suppliers on the basis of bids. It might send RFPs (requests for proposal) to dozens of companies, or might simply source its products from online auctions and marketplaces. This transactional buyer behavior also resembles key elements of the reptile reproductive approach.

## Mammal strategy

Look at the sales process in companies that have well-designed integrated account management systems. The best of these companies have carefully defined a hierarchy of customer relationships, ranging from arm's length to integrated operations, that they can develop. Their account managers, marketing managers, and supply chain managers work together to map the market. They have sorted current and potential customers using qualifying measures like potential margin, operating fit, transactional versus relationship buyer behavior, and willingness and capability for internal change management.

These companies have established account relationship migration paths in which they might engage a new customer with a core set of value-added services, and then progressively layer on other services to deepen the relationship if the account potential warrants. They develop and nurture deep relationships with the highest-potential accounts, gaining economies of scope in their account-development efforts while building barriers to entry through account knowledge, account trust, and the ability to manage change within their key customers.

This complex form of relationship selling over an extended period of time is analogous to the mammals' reproductive focus on essentially doing fewer things better.

## Vendor codestiny

Vendor codestiny (Unmei Kyodo Tai, literally "destiny-sharing organization") is a Japanese concept that represents the ultimate in mammal-like buyer-supplier relationships. This concept describes a relationship in which the supplier is treated as an extension of the buyer's company, and vice versa. These relationships are characterized by extensive information sharing, longer-term partnering, and a greater scope of products purchased from one supplier.

> Vendor codestiny is a Japanese concept that represents
>
> the ultimate in mammal-like buyer-supplier relationships.

▼

In these arrangements, both customer companies and suppliers gain great operating efficiencies and quality improvements. Because each partner has a deeper knowledge of the other and a lasting commitment to the relationship, each can adjust its business practices and even make long-term investments to accommodate the other's needs. In this way, they change the fundamental operating paradigm and cost structure of doing business together. Vendor codestiny produces the ultimate win-win.

The potential hazard of vendor codestiny, of course, is that a company gets deeply committed to a key business partner. This means that great care must be taken in both partner selection and structuring the relationship. For example, contracts must be written to contain migration-out clauses that specify how to unwind the relationship in a way that leaves both parties whole again if either elects to withdraw. This ensures that the relationship remains in the best interests of both parties. Benefit sharing also requires careful thought. These are all solvable issues, and best practice exists to guide companies interested in these relationships.

Vendor codestiny offers a number of sweeping benefits, and manageable risks. In fact, McDonald's employed codestiny relationships with its key vendors from the start, and these suppliers became enormously successful as McDonald's grew and prospered.

## The platypus choice

Think about Dell: reptile or mammal strategy? Dell might be described as the platypus of the customer relations world. A platypus is a mammal that lays eggs like a reptile, but in a very special mammalian way. The platypus usually lays two small eggs that stick to the fur on the mother's belly. When the babies emerge, they attach themselves to the mother's hairs, and the mother cares for them. The upshot: don't be fooled by the eggs.

Dell conducts what appears to be a broad market outreach through e-mailings, advertisements, and Web site activities; in this respect, the company appears to have a reptilelike approach to market development. But when you look carefully, Dell is systematically and relentlessly mammal-like in its go-to-market philosophy. It does this in three ways.

First, Dell conducts a major portion of its business with large corporate accounts. In these business activities, Dell employs a classic mammal-like account management process. For example, with its largest customers Dell establishes comprehensive intranet sites within the customers' businesses; these sites feature custom-designed configurations and other special features agreed upon with the account.

Second, through its pricing, Dell seeks relatively sophisticated repeat buyers who do not need extensive technical assistance either in the buying process or after purchase. Dell specifically prices its products above most competitors' products, and uses this pricing strategy to select the customers it wants. This pricing policy enables Dell to keep its customer service costs under tight control.

Third, Dell carefully analyzes its customer lists, looking for (1) buyers that fit the company's target profile, and (?) purchase patterns among the target customers. This information enables Dell to focus its outreach activities on the customers it wants to keep, and to target offers to individual customers based on when they are most likely to buy.

There is an important lesson here. Most companies necessarily have some elements of broad outreach, or prospecting, coupled with more intensive key-account sales. What separates the successful companies from the unsuccessful ones in this area, however, is whether, like Dell, a company has made an explicit choice of which strategy will dominate its market development efforts. In the absence of this explicit choice, a company generally winds up in the untenable position of pursuing two fundamentally different go-to-market strategies, often with the go-to-market team similarly split and the two factions competing with each other for resources and attention.

## Metabolism: Who's in control?

Reptiles and mammals differ fundamentally in a second important area. Reptiles are cold-blooded. This means that they cannot regulate their internal temperature and must find environmental situations that enable them to survive. Picture the lizard sunning itself on a rock to gather energy to sustain its hunt for food.

Mammals, on the other hand, are warm-blooded. This means that they can keep their bodies at a constant temperature almost regardless of the environment. Being warm-blooded gives mammals more flexibility to do what they want when they want, but it requires a big investment in obtaining the additional food-based energy to fuel their constant internal temperature. Think of it this way: cold-blooded reptiles are controlled by their environment, while warm-blooded mammals control their environment.

Here, the analogy to business shifts from company to individual, and offers insight into two classic forms of sales rep behavior. If you look carefully, you can see that some sales reps have more reptilelike selling strategies, while others are more like warm-blooded mammals in this respect. Some reps are relatively passive in market development. They send out general prospecting pieces, and find some accounts willing to buy. They may go for long periods of time in this transactional mode, probing the environment and happening on satisfactory situations almost by chance. Much like a lizard in search of a warm rock.

When these salespeople find repeat buyers, they return to them time after time, using the meetings to chat in generalities with the purchasers to keep the relationship warm, sort of like the lizard on a rock. This strategy has the inherent danger of leaving the environment in control of the sales rep's situation: if the purchaser leaves the company, or a competitor befriends the purchaser's boss, the relationship dissolves.

By contrast, other sales reps are much more mammal-like in their sales approach. They invest in developing ways to control their selling environment. They prospect vigorously for new accounts, and qualify them carefully to ensure that the reps' time is as productive as possible. When these reps land an account, they sell by carefully managing the customer's decision-making process in a way that inexorably increases their account penetration.

Mammal-like strategies require more upfront
investment, which takes energy, discipline, and
organizational coordination.

▼

These proactive reps do indeed chat with customers in sales calls, but here the parallel ends. The reps with a mammal-like strategy are always listening for an opening in the conversation to improve their selling position by (1) looking for an opportunity to suggest a new product, service, or further contact; or (2) seeking to understand how the customer's business is changing so they can position favorably into the change. When one travels with one of these reps, one can ask in advance about the objective of the sales call, and the rep's answer will be very specific and action-oriented, not just "to keep the customer happy."

The mammalian sales approach takes a lot of upfront energy and investment of time, in terms of understanding the accounts, qualifying them carefully, discovering the unfolding situations in them, and thinking through how to penetrate and manage the customer's extended buying center. These reps often talk about the importance of studying a customer's purchases for clues about how the account's buying activities are changing. They always strive to deeply understand the customer's business, and to devise new ways to create value for the customer.

Like warm-blooded mammals, these reps are always investing in their ability to control their environment, rather than being controlled by it. Not surprisingly, they are always the most successful producers, with great results that endure even as their selling environment changes and evolves.

## Lessons for managers

Here are three lessons for managers charged with overseeing or executing customer-supplier relations:

1. Both companies and individuals with reptile-like approaches to business can survive, but they are at the mercy of their environment. Remember what happened to the dinosaurs.
2. Mammal-like strategies require more upfront investment, which takes energy, discipline, and organizational coordination, but both companies and individuals pursuing this approach gain control over their environment and earn the ability to create their own success.
3. Beware of not choosing. This dooms a company or individual to the worst of both worlds, not the best. While most companies necessarily have elements of both strategies, the key to success is to have clarity on your basic operating mode, and to drive all buyer-supplier activities toward consistency with this core operating vision.

Beware of not choosing. This dooms a company or an
individual to the worst of both worlds, not the best.

▼

| THINGS TO THINK ABOUT |
| --- |

**1.** A company has to make a clear decision on its fundamental go-to-market strategy—either laying out a lot of lines in the hope of catching a few fish, or doing fewer things better. The former is a reptile strategy, the latter is a mammal strategy.

**2.** Both strategies can succeed, but the mammal strategy gives you an opportunity to shape your future. Think about how this relates to this section's first four chapters, which explain how to be both purposeful and effective.

**3.** Companies and individuals that fail to decide which strategy to pursue are doomed to the worst of each.

**4.** Mammal strategies—doing fewer things better—require more forethought and planning, but they give you more predictable results, and the ability to systematically analyze and improve your performance.

**5.** Think about what actually happened in your company last year. Which strategy best describes your activities? Did you visit your customers regularly, mostly keeping your relationships warm, or did you spend a lot of time trying to systematically find ways to do things differently? Did you actively look for best practice in penetrating the high-potential underpenetrated accounts in your territory?

## What's Next

The next two chapters explain how to create new high-value customer relationships. These are critical for success in developing a strategy with high sustained profitability and competitive barriers to entry.

*In today's ultra-cutthroat environment, leading companies create a competitive advantage by redefining customer service through building relationships, anticipating needs, and helping customers become more profitable.*

# 16

# OUT-OF-THE-BOX CUSTOMER SERVICE

▼

**TAKE A MOMENT** to think about the following question: what is your worst customer service nightmare?

At a recent MIT executive workshop, I asked a group of high-level managers about their customer service nightmares. At first, they offered chilling scenarios involving missed delivery dates, unanswered phone calls, and impatient customers waiting endlessly for technical support.

Next, I asked the question in a different way: what customer service move might your *competitors* make that would be your worst nightmare? The answers included the following:

- ▶ identify a critical service I missed and offer it to my customers
- ▶ create a culture of cooperation and collaboration that brings them closer to my customers
- ▶ become organizationally aligned around my customer, and build close working relationships among all of their company's departments and their customer counterparts
- ▶ enter the market between my company and my customers

- generate better customer information and use it to offer new services to my customers
- integrate multiple divisions and present one contact point for the customer

This set of answers differed from the first set of scenarios in a crucial way.

## The new customer service

The shift in the executives' answers reflects the fundamental change taking place in customer service today. In the past, customer service essentially meant companies keeping their promises to customers. Phrases like "meeting customer expectations" and "giving customers what they want when they want it" reflect this objective.

Today, however, leading companies are redefining customer service. Phrases like "building a relationship with the customer," "being proactive, anticipating customer needs," and "understanding the customer better than the customer understands himself" exemplify this new objective.

These executives all agreed that their customers are reducing their numbers of suppliers by 40 to 60 percent, and that to grow market share a vendor must create new forms of customer service that dramatically increase customer value.

This new view of customer service requires commitment, and entails understanding the customer well enough to dramatically increase the customer's profitability. Importantly, well-designed customer service innovations often reduce your own operating costs at the same time. Creating a deep relationship with the customer implies a new definition of customer service—mutual change management—in which the goal is to create innovations that radically increase the customer's profitability.

These are the hallmarks of business success in the Age of Precision Markets.

> This new view of customer service requires commitment and entails understanding the customer well enough to dramatically increase the customer's profitability.

▼

# The case of Nalco Chemical

In today's aggressive business world, simply meeting customer expectations by delivering the right products on time is the price of admission. It is what every company must do to stay in business. The way to differentiate your company is through customer service innovation. This enables a company to expand the boundaries of its business and increase its domain of value creation. I call this *building a bigger box around your business*.

Consider Nalco Chemical, a specialty chemical maker whose water-treatment chemicals were becoming a commodity. Nalco installed sensors on the customers' chemical tanks so that it could monitor them as customers drew down the chemicals. This gave Nalco big cost savings in routing the replenishment trucks, and even greater cost reductions in manufacturing due to better production scheduling.

Nalco then realized that these sensors could be used for a new purpose. Because Nalco knew the water-treatment systems that were using the chemicals, it could predict the rate of chemical use if the systems were functioning properly. Nalco started to compare actual versus predicted chemical use as an indicator of possible problems in the overall water-treatment system. When there was a problem, Nalco called to alert the customer.

Since the cost of a major municipal system malfunction might amount to many times the annual cost of the Nalco chemicals, the benefits were huge. At contract renewal time, Nalco issued report cards on itself to the customers, showing the large benefits relative to the much smaller chemical costs.

Nalco redrew the boundaries of its product offering, providing an innovative customer service that brought benefits to both parties. The customers benefited from systems savings that more than paid for the chemicals, while Nalco received price increases and lowered its operating cost.

Nalco redrew the boundaries of its product offering,

providing an innovative customer service that brought

benefits to both parties.

▼

# Out of the box

Nalco provided out-of-the-box customer service. It went far beyond merely meeting customer expectations for on-time deliveries with accurate amounts, which might be described as in-the-box customer service.

By expanding business beyond its traditional boundaries, Nalco opened new opportunities to create customer value, block competitors, and lower its own costs. In doing so, Nalco redefined its products and expanded the boundaries that traditionally defined its business; it drew a bigger box around its business. In the process, Nalco secured its best accounts and significantly raised its profitability.

# Differentiated ball bearings

The case of SKF Bearings provides another example of innovative customer service.* Traditionally, ball bearings were relatively undifferentiated. However, SKF carefully analyzed its customers' needs and extended its product to meet them more fully, drawing a bigger box around its business. For example, SKF operated in two important, and very different, aftermarket segments.

In the *vehicle aftermarket* (repair parts for cars and trucks), mechanics have three problems with ball bearing repairs: (1) where to find the replacement bearing, (2) how to install the new bearing, and (3) where to obtain accessories needed for the installation.

SKF's response? Create ready-made repair kits. These kits included all components required for the repair, including competitors' products where necessary, as well as installation materials and instructions.

By contrast, in the *industrial equipment aftermarket* (repair parts for industrial machines and equipment), the cost of machine downtime is much greater than the cost of repair. Ball bearing longevity is critical. Longevity depends on four factors: (1) the quality of the product, (2) how the product is installed, (3) how well protected the ball bearings are from environmental contamination, and (4) maintenance quality.

---

* For more on this, see SKF Bearings, IMD/ECCH #591-018-1, authored by Professor Sandra Vandermerwe and Dr. Marika Taishoff.

In order to meet the needs of this market, SKF created planned-maintenance programs aimed at reducing machine downtime due to bearing failure. The programs included elements such as specifying lubricants, automatic lubricating devices for difficult-to-reach bearings, cleanliness programs, sealing products, and monitoring and maintenance management services.

SKF extended the ways in which it could create value for its customers—changing from simply selling products to helping the customers reduce their total cost of product purchase and use. By doing this, SKF provided out-of-the-box customer service, and drew a bigger box around its business.

## Walk in your customer's shoes

The process of developing out-of-the-box customer service innovations requires two elements: (1) an understanding of the customer's business, and (2) an understanding of channel costs (joint operating costs spanning your company and your customer). It is fundamentally different from the process of providing flawless in-the-box customer service, which typically involves performance feedback loops and process adjustments.

**Customer understanding.** First and foremost, in order to create an innovation that increases your customer's profitability, you must be able to walk in your customer's shoes. This involves developing a thorough understanding of your customer's business, generally through on-site observation and interviews.

Often, a company's sales reps are the prime link to the customers. But sales reps are generally focused on selling more products through in-the-box service excellence. In contrast, out-of-the-box innovations require that your operations and marketing managers gain detailed customer knowledge through direct customer contact and on-site visits.

The key to identifying these potential gains is to spend enough time on enough customers to figure out what they really need. Ask yourself this question: what would you do to change your customers' operations if you really wanted to improve things—and you were managing them yourself? If you don't have enough information to answer this question in a precise way, it would be extremely productive to spend time developing a more systematic understanding of your customers.

Most important, out-of-the-box customer service innovations require seeing customer operations in a new way, with a focus on discovering opportunities to improve the customer's business. The Nalco and SKF innovations required, more than anything, a fresh view of a traditional customer relationship. Developing these insights did not involve detailed analysis or specialized technical knowledge, just clear vision and an open mind.

**Channel map.** Understanding the cost of providing the service is the second critical element. This requires a quick, effective cost model spanning your company and a few typical accounts. A channel map provides this picture. It is a representation of the physical product flow across an extended supply chain, spanning your operations and your customers' operations, with associated time, activities, costs, and order variance at each step. It gives you a clear picture of the current situation, and enables you to quickly spot the largest pools of cost and potential gain—the most important profit levers—both in your customers and in your own company. As with so much of strategic analysis, 70 percent accuracy is the key to success.

Here is an example of how one company developed a channel map using a small work team:

> The team started by examining the movement and accumulation of a small sample of products in one operating region over a three-month period. They traced the product flow through their own company and through a small sample of their customers, from point of supply to point of consumption. This overview allowed them to develop an understanding of the underlying patterns of consumption, product movement, and inventory. In addition, the team charted the activities (e.g., transportation, unloading the trucks, stocking warehouse shelves, picking customer orders) at each stage, and approximated the cost of each stage (using the techniques described in chapter 6, "The Hunt for Profits").
>
> The team not only looked at its own company's replenishment, shipment, and inventory patterns, but also visited several customers and suppliers to understand their operations and identify the internal factors that were creating these patterns. In one customer, the team did a brief on-site cost study, in which it confirmed its rough estimates. With the relatively small number of products, and manageable sample of customers and suppliers, the team could gather specific information on the actual product movement and cost structure. The team used this information to develop a set of PC-based cost models depicting the company and its key customers at each point in the progression of product

flow. Once the complete picture of activities and costs became clear, the team identified the large pockets of cost that could be eliminated, both internally and in its customers.

At this point, the team decided to focus on coordinating with its biggest customers to improve forecasting and eliminate the volatility in the customers' order patterns. The team then expanded the analysis to cover a number of other products, regions, customers, and suppliers in order to confirm its hypothesis that this was the best way to reduce costs quickly.

The team made rough approximations of the new costs that could be achieved, discussed these with the customers and suppliers it had visited, and reran its cost models using revised information in order to generate order-of-magnitude estimates of the overall benefits both for the company and for the customers. Finally, the team identified the key changes needed for the new system.

## Strategic customer service

A company that offers well-constructed packages of out-of-the-box services can change its strategic position from a commodity-like supplier to a highly differentiated provider.

For this shift to occur, the vendor must offer a well-packaged set of customer services that improves its *accounts'* profitability. Not only will this provide superior value, but importantly, it will move the locus of the customer's purchase process from cost-oriented lower-level employees to value-oriented general managers.

The package of customer service offerings must be developed in the context of competitor activities. Some out-of-the-box customer services, such as vendor-managed inventory, will effectively block competitor incursion into key accounts. Here, first-mover advantages are decisive.

Out-of-the-box customer service innovation is highly interactive with account and product selection. Different accounts have different service needs, different perceptions of value, and different readiness to change. The process has to be carefully managed. Simply offering a menu of innovative customer services misses this crucial point and risks failure.

■ ■ ■

*Out-of-the-box customer service innovation is highly interactive with account and product selection.*

▼

There is usually a logical sequence to moving accounts from arm's-length to service-differentiated relationships. Some out-of-the-box customer services offer an opening to deepen your ties with your customers, other services create a natural migration path to an even more value-laden relationship, and still others lock in the relationship. This sequence has to be well understood and integrated into your account planning process. Account coordination must involve your operations managers as well as your sales reps.

In most companies, few new skills are needed to develop and offer out-of-the-box customer service. Instead, the necessary new ingredient is a commitment to gaining a new understanding of your customers' businesses. This involves a resolve to break down traditional organizational barriers, especially within your own company, in order to bring all of your resources to bear on building powerful new customer relationships.

Importantly, most out-of-the-box customer service innovations actually generate cash from the onset, as unneeded inventory is liquidated and redundant functions are eliminated.

## First-mover advantages

Out-of-the-box customer service is fundamentally different in all respects from in-the-box customer service. It involves new value creation in the customer, and often lowers vendor costs significantly at the same time. It is an essential component of profitability management because it locks in your best accounts, and increases sales and profitability for both your best customers and your own company.

There are critical first-mover advantages. The risk of not moving fast is the real possibility of losing your best customers if they consolidate their suppliers and your competitors beat you to the punch with their own out-of-the-box innovations.

Unlike price competition, if a competitor wins one of your customers through out-of-the-box customer service innovation, your company probably will not get the customer back. Conversely, if you move creatively and rapidly, you can secure the best customers, with their essential flow of profits, for years to come.

**1.** In the Age of Precision Markets, the nature of customer service is changing dramatically. Traditional customer service (on-time deliveries, returned phone calls) is the ante. Developing powerful new ways to increase your customers' profitability is the way to win.

**2.** Your customers are reducing their supplier bases by 40 to 60 percent. Your ability to create out-of-the-box innovations will determine whether you stay or go. The benefits in profitability and market share are huge.

**3.** A channel map will enable you to identify the best out-of-the-box innovations for your customers. Look for the biggest improvements with the least disruption, and search your customer base for savvy early adopters.

**4.** Attention, operations managers: you have a central role in this process. It is crucial that you develop relationships with your operations counterparts in your customer companies, so that you can work directly with them to develop new ways to jointly make things better.

**5.** If you sell an innovative product to a customer, a competitor with a better product can easily dislodge you. But if you engage a key customer in an innovative relationship with interlinked business processes, it is nearly impossible for a competitor to elbow you aside. These relationships enable you to build strong barriers to entry through customer knowledge and trust, and through your ability to manage constructive change within your customers.

## What's Next

The next chapter explains when and how to create customer operating partnerships with your best customers. These are especially powerful relationships that enable you to reduce mutual costs, increase profits in both companies, and build high barriers to entry. As a result, they can give you a sales increase of 35 percent or more, even in your highest-penetrated accounts.

*Need to increase profits? Consider creating "customer operating partnerships" that involve tightly linked extended supply chains. The payoff? Share increases in even your most profitable accounts.*

# 17

## PROFIT FROM CUSTOMER OPERATING PARTNERSHIPS

▼

**HOW CAN YOU** secure and grow the 20 to 30 percent of your business that contributes the lion's share of your profits? Customer operating partnerships are a particularly powerful profit lever that will enable you to accomplish this.

Customer operating partnerships are customer-vendor arrangements that involve tightly linked extended supply chains. They offer tremendous gains, including (1) 20 to 35 percent share increases even in your highest-penetrated, most-profitable accounts; (2) a shift to a strategic positioning as a highly service-differentiated supplier, even for companies that are stuck as commodity providers subject to constant price wars; (3) a direct-sales relationship with value-oriented top customer executives, rather than price-oriented purchasing managers; and (4) a highly defensible competitive position with switching costs.

Most leading companies are now reducing their number of suppliers by 40 to 60 percent. The most desirable customers are seeking more intensive operating partnerships with fewer, more capable suppliers. Price is no longer the primary deciding factor. This is creating a historic opportunity for managers who develop and offer these out-of-the-box arrangements.

Conversely, managers who fail to initiate customer operating partnerships with their best customers run the risk of losing them, and the lion's share of their company's profitability, to competitors who move first.

While customer operating partnerships are very different from ordinary customer relations, most company managers have the capability to develop these arrangements with their most important customers. It is crucial, however, to understand the management measures that you must put in place.

Managers who fail to initiate customer operating

partnerships with their best customers run the

risk of losing them.

▼

## The case of the hospital supply company

Let's look at the case example of how a major national hospital supply company developed one of the first vendor-managed inventory systems. This customer operating partnership gave it sales increases of more than 35 percent in its highest-penetrated, most-profitable accounts.

At the onset, the company was facing an increasingly untenable situation. It manufactured and sold a variety of hospital supplies, but its anchor categories were relatively undifferentiated and subject to constant price wars. For example, if the price of a liter of a typical intravenous (IV) solution was about $1.00, a five-year contract would hinge on whether the quoted price was $0.97 or $1.03.

The company's sales reps called on hospital pharmacists and purchasing staff, who focused on minimizing price. They interacted with high-level hospital executives only rarely.

The hospitals' order patterns fluctuated severely, causing inventory, service, and production problems. This fluctuation had three causes. First, the nurses in the patient care areas ordered from the hospitals' stockrooms infrequently and in large amounts. Second, although the hospitals had agreed to semiweekly order and delivery schedules, they placed orders almost every day and expected next-day delivery. Finally, quarter-end sales drives by the company's sales force were common.

The company's operations managers had been careful to control operating costs and to keep staff levels lean. But the company was stuck trying to respond efficiently to an inherently inefficient situation.

## Mowing the lawn around Stonehenge

I remember the company's president telling me, "We're getting very good at mowing the lawn around Stonehenge, without ever asking why the stones are there."

At one point, a major hospital asked this executive to consider becoming a prime vendor, a master supplier who would funnel supplies from a variety of sources through one warehouse to the hospital dock with consolidated invoicing. The president assembled a small team and asked them to analyze this request. The team decided to follow the supplies downstream from the distribution center, across the hospital receiving dock, to the actual points of patient consumption in several large hospitals.

When the team developed a systematic channel map, they saw a very disjointed, redundant supply channel. In the first segment, within the distribution center walls, the company received hospital orders, picked the supplies, packed them, shipped them to the hospital, and invoiced for them. In the second segment, the team saw the mirror image once the supplies reached the hospital: the hospital issued the orders, received the supplies, unpacked the boxes, put the supplies away in the stockroom, and paid the invoices. In a third segment, the hospital patient care areas ordered from the stockroom and put away the supplies.

The team conducted in-depth studies of several large hospitals, mapping product flow and measuring hospital operations. They found that the hospital materials management organizations were costly, as expected, but they also found surprisingly large amounts of hidden costs in areas such as nursing. When the team checked these findings, the hospital personnel were amazed at the true costs.

When the team assembled the true picture, they found that the total cost by the time the product reached the patient's bedside was about five dollars, contrasted with the one dollar sales price at the hospital dock. Of the four-dollar increment, the internal hospital supply chain costs comprised about half, while the other half represented other factors.

A startling new perspective emerged: *more than 80 percent of the business was outside the company's traditional business definition.*

For years, the company had simply assumed that its job was complete when the customer received its products at its receiving dock, and this assumption seemed so obvious that no one had ever thought of examining it. New communications and computer technologies, however, had given it the capability to extend that boundary far into the customers' operations for their mutual benefit. But no one had seen this possibility before.

## The Stockless System

The team saw a great potential for joint hospital-company economies by (1) eliminating redundant steps and stock; and (2) altering the picking, materials management, and information processing systems. After doing a careful cost analysis in several hospitals, the team determined that between one-third and one-half of the two dollars in internal hospital materials costs could be eliminated, even while providing the hospital with a substantial increase in service levels.

After discussions with target hospitals, the team developed the initial operating partnership model, which they called the Stockless System. This was one of the first, and most widely followed, vendor-managed inventory systems.

As a first step, the team analyzed each patient care area's product usage patterns and specified the stock requirements. Next, they implemented this process: an on-site company employee counts the stock in each patient care area each day or every few days; the employee transmits this information to the company's distribution center, where a replenishment order is derived and packed into patient care area-specific containers; then it is delivered directly to the patient care area, where the company employee puts the stock away; finally, the company invoices the hospital.

The Stockless System had a huge impact on the company: it moved the domain of its value creation to the whole extended supply chain, and enabled the company to shift its selling focus from the $0.97 to $1.03 negotiation, to mutual value-creation on a much larger scale. It enabled the company to build a new competitive position as a highly service-differentiated supplier. The company had drawn a bigger box around its business.

■ ■ ■

# Great benefits

The Stockless System gave the company great strategic benefits in four areas:

**Cost reductions.** The Stockless System created large cost reductions for its customers and itself. The hospitals eliminated several steps in the supply chain, and greatly reduced their inventories. Valuable space was released, and hospital personnel were redeployed into patient care. The company gained large, unexpected operating benefits because the Stockless System smoothed the erratic hospital order pattern. Moreover, the Stockless System business unit was now being paid to process the orders that were previously processed by the company's customer service department.

> The hospitals' order pattern fluctuated severely,
>
> causing the company great inventory, service, and
>
> production problems.
>
> ▼

**Sales increases.** The company's sales increased dramatically, even in highly penetrated accounts. This increase was directly driven by (1) the operations-to-operations relationship that formed between the head nurses in the patient care areas and the company's patient care area coordinators, who were personable lead hands from the warehouse, not sales reps; and (2) the near-perfect service levels that allowed the sales reps to focus on selling new products, rather than on solving supply problems.

**CEO relationships.** The president was able to establish close working relations with the CEOs of the major hospitals because the Stockless System involved large savings and major changes. Several important new joint business initiatives resulted.

**Competitive advantage.** The company developed immediate strategic advantage over its competitors, enabling it to secure and grow its largest, most profitable accounts. The Stockless System operating partnership rested upon four essential elements: (1) confidence of the customers, (2) demonstrated ability to perform, (3) company commitment and resources, and (4) joint end-to-end business understanding and operations-to-operations relationships. Once the company established this new way of doing business, its competitors could not easily follow.

# Quantum change

Both the company and the hospitals had to make significant changes in
five areas:

**Account selection.** The company's management realized early on that
account selection was crucial to success. They had to be very careful in
their choice of partners because these relationships were very intensive.
The top managers carefully screened and prioritized their customers
according to their potential gain, operating fit, relationship versus transactional buyer behavior, and willingness and ability to change.

**Account coordination.** In the old paradigm, the sales rep was the primary link
to the account, sales plans were confidential, and operations personnel
were largely excluded. In the new relationship, the president formed a set
of multifunctional account teams to plan and develop partnerships with
important target accounts. Once this account planning process was stabilized, he invited the customers to send managers to participate. Rather
than having an adversarial tenor, account planning became a process for
jointly moving the partnership forward, much like the trucking company
described in the first section of this book.

**Selling the Stockless System.** The process of selling the operating partnership to a hospital CEO was very different from the normal product
sales process. Because the partnership entailed a new customer-supplier
relationship, a close CEO-to-CEO link was needed. The company made
its first sale to a smaller hospital that was run by a particularly innovative
CEO, and then brought others in to view the showcase. At one point, the
president assembled a focus group of hospital CEOs, and asked them for
suggestions on how to sell the Stockless System.

**Operations.** Operations changes were needed in several areas. First,
operations managers were integrally involved in developing the new
operating process and estimating the gains; they had to understand
internal hospital operations even better than the hospital's personnel did. Second, the operations staff had to learn to manage sensitive,
scatter-site operations within customer premises. Third, they had to
restructure the supply chain to deliver near-perfect service without
incurring additional cost, and this required that the Stockless System
inventory be protected from the rest of the company, even large strategic
accounts. Fourth, the operation had to become more flexible to adapt
to the changing customer-partnership mix, and the operations managers had to master the complexity of a dual-distribution system. Finally,

the operations team had to learn to participate in the multifunctional account planning process.

**Management.** Because the Stockless System represented a new way of doing business, the company's management had to take the lead in developing new, more open relationships with key customers. The operating partnerships increased the risk and stakes for management because the relationships were more complex, the standards more stringent, and a failure could mean the loss of a major account. Important management control and sales incentive changes were needed because the Stockless System eliminated quarter-end sales drives, which led to significant short-term sales reductions as inventory was drawn down, and required new incentives to encourage operations involvement in the sales relationship.

## A historic opportunity

The case of the major hospital supply company shows how customer operating partnerships can dramatically improve a company's market share in its most desirable customers, its strategic positioning, and even its asset productivity. However, care must be taken in matching these arrangements to specific accounts.

As the best customers move aggressively to reduce their number of suppliers, many leading companies are finding that customer operating partnerships are crucial to maintain and grow the profitability of their best accounts. And there are important first mover advantages: once a company secures its key accounts with operating partnerships, it is very difficult for competitors to encroach or for profitability to erode.

Important changes are required. Companies that have failed in customer operating partnerships have done so primarily because they have neglected the underlying management process changes.

To be successful, a manager must carefully segment the account base, understand that these intensive, high-profit relationships can be developed only with fewer partners, systematically qualify the target accounts, and explicitly accept a multitiered account relationship system. And the company's top managers must understand and create the parallel changes that must occur in the company's sales, operations, and management processes.

**1.** Customer operating partnerships offer a way to turn a commodity supplier-customer relationship into a highly differentiated one. They also provide a pathway to reduce costs and increase profitability, both for your own company and for your best customers.

**2.** These partnerships require a different way to relate to customers, and a different way to manage your customer relationships. Your operations managers are essential to the process—for account penetration, for account development, and for integrated account management.

**3.** Consider this question: If you were a key manager within your best customer, how would you increase that customer's profitability by 30 to 40 percent? What would you ask your key suppliers to do? If you know the answer, step on the gas with your operating partnerships. If not, try inviting your key customer-counterpart managers to lunch—often.

**4.** Think about your company's activities last year. What did your company actually do to dramatically increase your best customers' profitability? What barriers to competitive encroachment did you build with the 20 to 30 percent of your customers who create most of your profitability? Is your relationship secure at the highest level of these customers because you are providing so much unique value that the customer wouldn't even think of changing suppliers?

**5.** How would your strongest competitors answer these questions? How would your most innovative competitors answer?

## What's Next

This chapter and the preceding one explain how to create high-value relationships with your best customers. These relationships offer revenue growth, high profitability, and sustained barriers to competitive entry. The next chapter describes how to develop and manage related services as a critical component in a full package of compelling customer value.

*The strategic use of services offers major opportunities
for product companies to build real value and customer
trust in three areas.*

# 18

## PRODUCT COMPANIES:
## DON'T UNDERSELL SERVICES

▼

**MANY MANAGERS OF** companies that make or distribute products lose important profit opportunities because they don't capitalize on the strategic benefits of related services.

This is natural. They are focused on managing their products. Consequently, they regard designing and managing related services, such as express delivery, information support, and vendor-managed inventory, almost as an afterthought, a nuisance cost to be recouped if possible.

I recall discussing this topic in a meeting with a group of visiting managers at MIT. In preparation, I was given some materials that suggested how best to deal with these services. There were two key points: (1) understand the costs of the services; and (2) offer a menu of services at prices that hopefully recoup the cost, and ideally turn a profit. This approach missed the big opportunities.

The argument reminded me of the situation in transportation about a decade ago. At that time, most suppliers quoted prices on a "delivered basis," which meant that the price of the product included the cost of the freight to move it to the customer. When some astute customers looked carefully, they discovered that the vendors were often making more money by overcharging for the freight than they were making on the product's actual price.

This practice added no value, and alienated the customers. In response, customers created freight conversion programs, in which they renegotiated product prices based on pickup at the vendor's factory and paid the freight charges themselves. Customers viewed these programs as righting previous vendor wrongs. For years, they soured vendor-customer relationships.

## Strategic use of services

Selling more products can give a vendor additional business with customers, but selling the right related services can give a vendor a new strategic positioning, even more product sales, and a host of other valuable benefits. This can be critically important in reversing a vendor's slide toward commoditization and price competition.

> The strategic use of services is a critical profit lever
>
> that offers major opportunities to build real value and
>
> deep customer trust in three areas: (1) new strategic
>
> advantage, (2) new account management and selling
>
> advantage, and (3) new cost reduction advantage.

▼

Consider the parallels between the major hospital supply company described in the preceding chapter and a national trucking company that developed an innovative set of third-party logistics services for its key customers. (Here, a company's main line of business is treated as its product, even if it is technically a service, like the transportation services of a trucking company or the audit services of an accounting firm.)

The hospital supply company developed a new set of related services that involved managing the ordering, inventory, and distribution of its products within its hospital customers. The trucking company created a comprehensive service to manage the warehouse and transportation network of its major accounts. These innovative new services enabled both companies to dramatically improve their competitive positioning and reverse their fortunes.

In the past, the hospital supply company had sold commodity products on a price basis to low-level purchasing managers. It had formed only limited relationships with hospitals' top managers. The new service, however, had a major impact on hospital costs and operations. Consequently, the company's top managers needed to have extensive dialogues with hospital top executives throughout the service development and sales process.

The same dynamic occurred for the trucking company. Initially, the company had sold commodity trucking services to transportation purchasing managers. These individuals bought services based on lowest price, and often put their traffic out for bid. In essence, these services were commoditized, like the hospital supplies in the parallel example.

In the new situation, however, the overall package of customer logistics services was so important and complex that few trucking companies could credibly offer the service. The deciding factor in awarding service contracts was whether the customers' top managers became convinced that they could trust the trucking company's performance and its ability to reduce costs. Consequently, for both the hospital supply company and the trucking company, tight, trusting management-to-management relationships naturally evolved.

Once the new hospital service was in place, the company's competitors were effectively blocked from developing similar relationships with hospital officials. Simply selling more products at arm's length never could have achieved this advantage. The trucking company experienced the same dynamic.

Selling more products can give a vendor additional business with customers, but selling the right related services can give a vendor a new strategic positioning even more product sales, and a host of valuable benefits.

▼

During the process of developing the new hospital service, an important question arose about whether the company should distribute competing vendors' products through its new system. Predictably, the competing vendors objected, but the hospital CEOs required them to comply or they would lose the business. Importantly, the company's own product managers objected strongly to using the new system to distribute competitors' products. They felt that the new service should be used to promote their own product sales instead.

The company's CEO had the wisdom to overrule his product managers. He understood that the company's new strategic relationship with the hospitals as a trusted partner would create new value for the hospitals, and with it, deep customer understanding and trust. He saw that this would win out in the long run. In fact, this happened surprisingly quickly, and sales rose almost immediately.

This issue also arose widely in third-party logistics. Some providers decided to favor their own assets, or to offer them exclusively. Customers quickly gravitated to the service providers who were neutral in their offerings, and who they perceived were motivated to do what was best for the customer.

The hospital supply company's in-hospital operating personnel formed close, day-to-day working relationships with the hospitals' operating personnel, especially the head nurses, and these head nurses had a key role in product selection. The customer knowledge and trust that developed created natural barriers to competitive entry. As a result, sales of the company's products increased by more than 35 percent, even in the most highly penetrated accounts. The trucking company experienced a parallel dynamic in its third-party logistics service, particularly when its operations personnel were resident in the customers' facilities.

In a final parallel, both new services led to important cost reductions for both the providers and the customers, as both the hospital supply company and the trucking company were able to create savings by coordinating their customers' operations with their own.

## Managing related services

Product company managers have a clear opportunity to move past dealing with related services from a tactical perspective, begrudgingly offering them and upcharging at every opportunity. The key is to focus on both the crucial underlying strategic opportunities and the broader cost savings. Here are the essential elements in developing and getting the most out of related services:

▶ Related services can change the fundamental strategic positioning of a company. We saw this in chapter 17, "Profit from Customer Operating Partnerships." This is especially important for companies whose products are becoming commoditized. By carefully designing these services, product managers can build pathways to deepen their customer relationships. This gives them the ability to strongly influence product selection, and to effectively lock competitors out of its best accounts.

▶ Paradoxically, the larger the change created by the new services, the easier it is to sell the new relationship—because it captures the attention of the customer's top managers, who typically are relationship-oriented value-buyers. Think about the difference between a company selling electronic components to a major manufacturer and another company developing a relationship in which it has partnered with the manufacturer to create joint teams chartered with reducing the manufacturer's costs and codesigning the next generation of the manufacturer's products.

▶ Product managers can use related services to help customers change their businesses, opening huge new avenues for value creation. For example, after the hospital supply company developed the vendor-managed inventory service, it approached the hospitals with the possibility of a new distribution service that would support the hospitals' development of a network of scatter-site clinics. The hospitals alone could not have managed the logistics of this service. In a parallel situation, many companies turn to their third-party logistics relationships for the knowledge and capability to develop their international business operations, or to move quickly into new areas.

▶ It is important to integrate related services into account planning and account management. Some services, like helping a customer with developing new lines of business, by their nature allow account managers and operations personnel to build relations and trust with managers throughout the customer's buying center. Once this trust is developed, they can influence customer product selection in a comfortable and natural way.

▶ Beware of developing and offering services as simple profit centers in the absence of the broader strategic, competitive, and account management context. The grave error of the vendors who alienated their key customers by charging phony freight rates illustrates this.

▶ Vendor managers must be prepared to say no to good accounts that don't fit the service package, (e.g., due to geographic location). They have to develop one or more fallback packages that also offer value.

▶ Very often, related service costs are not incremental. Well-designed related services can actually reduce your costs. Consider the example of the hospital supply company. While there was a measurable incremental cost to offering the vendor-managed inventory (VMI) service, this cost was more than offset by unexpected vendor cost savings in the areas of delivery, product flow, factory scheduling, and inventory. Beyond this, the VMI system led to major sales gains. The same occurred for the trucking company.

> Well-designed related services can actually
>
> reduce your costs.

▼

Related services must be a critical profit lever in every product manager's portfolio. Handled well, they offer rapid and lasting strategic account management, and cost reduction advantages. Not only that, they also create unexpectedly large increases in product sales as well.

---

### THINGS TO THINK ABOUT

**1.** Related services offer important opportunities to build your value package with your key customers. They can strongly improve your basic strategic positioning and create barriers to competitive entry.

**2.** Beware of the temptation to treat related services as an auxiliary profit center. It is crucial that you integrate related services with your mainstream product offerings to create maximum value for your customers. Otherwise, you risk having your best customers lose their trust in you.

**3.** Related services are critical in building relationship-migration paths with key accounts.

**4.** Well-developed related services can actually reduce your costs and increase your profitability, even while they produce new value and new profits for your key customers. Channel mapping will show you the best opportunities to do this.

**5.** The acid test for whether related services will really contribute to your company's profitability is whether they are managed and measured on overall account health and profitability, and not on narrow profit-center contribution.

## What's Next

The chapters of this section explain how to sell for profit—how to generate new revenue streams that increase your profitability, and how to build high-value relationships with your best customers. The next section of this book explains how to operate for profit—how to create powerful profit levers in your operations and extended supply chain. The final section tells you how to manage and lead your company to create high sustained profitability.

# OPERATING FOR PROFIT

# INTRODUCTION

**SUPPLY CHAINS ARE** the operational links that govern product movement and service provision within a company, and join suppliers with customers. These can range from the streamlined product flow that is at the heart of Wal-Mart's business to the customer service and support system that a software company provides to its accounts. All companies, no matter what their business, have supply chains that make a big difference in maximizing profits. When supply chains work well, they create tight, productive customer relationships, major sales gains, and huge profit increases. They also build strong barriers that keep profits high and competitors out.

The chapters in this section explain why most companies need multiple parallel supply chains, how to structure and manage them, how to match your supply chain with your customer relationships, and how to manage your supply chain organization to maximize your supply chain productivity. This section also describes how a proactive manager can use supply chain innovations to create enduring profitability and strategic advantage.

## What is the value of multiple parallel supply chains?

**Chapter 19, Supply Chain Management in a Wal-Mart World,** explains how integrating your supply chain with a major customer can drive enormous sales and profit increases, but developing a highly integrated customer relationship with the wrong accounts can be very costly.

**Chapter 20, You Only Have One Supply Chain?** tells you how to develop and manage multiple parallel supply chains that fit your company's product and account needs.

## How can supply chain and operations management lower costs and raise revenues?

**Chapter 21, The Dilemma of Customer Service,** explains how to get out of the trap of high-cost/poor-service that plagues so many companies.

**Chapter 22, Profit from Managing Your Product Flow,** shows how volatile order patterns from a few major customers and products can have a big effect on your operations costs, and what practical steps you can take to fix this problem.

**Chapter 23, Nail Customer Service,** explains how to structure customer service in a way that increases customer satisfaction while lowering your cost.

**Chapter 24, Winning with Make-to-Order Manufacturing,** describes how one effective company cut its production cycle time from several months to a few days, dramatically reducing its inventories and other operating costs.

## How can supply chain managers have the most impact?

**Chapter 25, Achieving Supply Chain Productivity,** explains how supply chain managers can dramatically increase their impact on their companies' profitability by broadening their focus from narrow cost-control to broad supply-chain productivity.

*The Wal-Mart supply chain management structure is not one-size-fits-all. How do you keep everyone else happy? Apply service differentiation to your strategic accounts.*

## 19

## SUPPLY CHAIN MANAGEMENT IN A WAL-MART WORLD

▼

**HERE'S A SUPPLY** chain dilemma: now that you've learned how to do business with Wal-Mart, what do you do with everyone else?

Over the past decade, Wal-Mart has famously invited its major suppliers to jointly develop powerful supply chain partnerships. These are designed to increase product flow efficiency and, consequently, Wal-Mart's profitability.

Many companies have stepped up to the challenge, starting with the well known Wal Mart/Procter & Gamble (P&G) alliance, which incorporated vendor-managed inventory, category management, and other inter-company innovations.

P&G even fielded a dedicated account team in Bentonville, Arkansas. In a very creative approach, the team members represented key P&G functions: (1) sales/marketing, (2) supply chain management, (3) IT, and (4) finance. In the eyes of one P&G vice president who was centrally involved at the time, Wal-Mart's CFO became the key internal customer, because P&G's objective became maximizing Wal-Mart's internal profitability.

Increasingly, top managers have learned how to create powerful customer operating partnerships that integrate their supply chains with major customers like Wal-Mart. Much has been written about the need to develop customer partnerships, and most companies have at least one project in this area. What most companies have not sorted out, however, is what to do with all of their other customers.

## Now what?

A common answer to the question of how to structure relationships with other customers is to try to apply the Wal-Mart relationship to all customers. This approach is implicit in commonly shown PowerPoint slides that offer a view of a company's evolving supply chain. In one version, the company starts as a stable supplier, evolves into a reactive supplier, then an efficient reactive supplier, then an efficient proactive supplier, and finally becomes a revenue and margin driver.

This may seem logical, with the company's supply chain capabilities inexorably increasing in sophistication over time, enabling the company to develop ever-more-effective operational integration with its customers.

The problem, however, is that developing Wal-Mart–like supply chain partnerships requires a lot of resources and management attention. It also requires willing, innovative partners with a great operating fit. Pursuing this approach too widely would be both costly and frustrating.

> Developing Wal-Mart–like supply chain partnerships
>
> requires a lot of resources and management attention.

▼

## Beyond one-size-fits-all

In the past, suppliers to the retail trade typically had rather monolithic supply chains suited for their mass markets. The order fulfillment process was designed with a one-size-fits-all approach. Customers received the same list price regardless of ordering efficiency. There was very little effective forecasting. Suppliers gave some inventory priority to major customers in the event of allocations, but this was the exception. Products were delivered in the manner that customers requested, regardless of inefficiency. This pattern characterized suppliers in most industries for years.

Today, the retailers themselves are changing dramatically. There is very visible consolidation, with the top ten retailers expected to comprise about half of the industry's revenues in a few years. Retailers have very different degrees of willingness and ability to innovate, and the innovators are growing fast. Most retailers have long had significant buyer power, and many are still focused on exerting price pressure on their suppliers rather than seeking increased profitability through process innovations. At the same time, the leading retailers are consolidating their supplier bases. They are looking more and more to major suppliers for supply chain innovations and prioritization, and in return they are giving them increasing shelf space.

As a result of this history, major retail suppliers find themselves stretched. They are forced to meet the increasing needs of their largest customers, while they are devoting disproportionate resources to their smaller customers. This untenable situation is forcing major suppliers across a range of industries to rethink their account relationships and extended supply chains.

## The importance of service differentiation

Service differentiation is the key to providing excellent, consistent service at a reasonable cost. This important profit lever is a process in which a company sets different service policies—ranging from order cycles to degree of operations integration—for different groups of accounts. The company always keeps its promises, but the promises are different to different groups of customers.

This concept can guide the development of an appropriate set of supply chain policies. It is essential to successful profitability management, because it enables a supplier to match its cost structure and innovation initiatives to account potential. An astute supplier can use service differentiation to avoid the common pitfall of overinvesting in service to demanding low-potential accounts, and underinvesting in more costly but worthwhile service initiatives that would prompt sales increases in underpenetrated, high-potential accounts.

Service differentiation is also good for the customers. It enables them to plan their operations around a very clear set of service standards, and a very consistent level of service. However, it does require that customers establish well-disciplined operations, as each of these relationships features a specific set of agreed-upon processes.

The sea changes that retailers and their suppliers
are now experiencing are starting to play out in
industry after industry.

▼

## Service differentiation matrix

The Service Differentiation Matrix depicted in Figure 6 provides a way to organize and structure account relationships. In this two-by-two matrix, account size is represented on the vertical axis, and willingness and ability to innovate is represented on the horizontal axis.

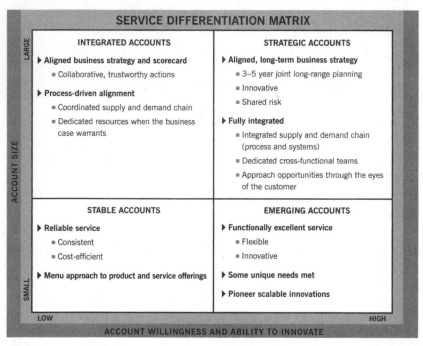

Figure 6

The matrix has four cells: (1) strategic accounts—major accounts with the willingness and ability to form integrated supply chain partnerships; (2) integrated accounts—large accounts, important but often somewhat smaller than strategic accounts, and with less willingness and ability to join in supply chain innovations; (3) emerging accounts—smaller accounts that are very innovative and usually fast-growing; and (4) stable accounts—smaller accounts that are generally reluctant to innovate significantly. Each account cluster requires a very different set of account relationships and supply chain structures.

**Strategic accounts.** These major accounts both warrant and require a high degree of operations integration, customization, and innovation. This is manifest in two main areas.

First, the supplier and the strategic account should develop an aligned, long-term business strategy. This typically involves a three- to five-year shared strategic plan for the relationship, and joint long-range planning. The relationship should be innovative and involve shared risk. For example, a very large, innovative retailer asked a prominent consumer products company to experiment with some promising new services. The retailer observed that the supplier shipped products from its factories to its distribution centers, then on to the retailer, entailing costly double handling. The retailer proposed that instead the supplier ship directly from its factories to the retailer, bypassing the distribution centers and saving money. Although this was a new way to do business, which made sense for only a few very large retailers, the supplier was willing to develop a unique process to make this work.

Second, the companies' supply chains should be fully integrated. This should involve both supply chain processes and systems. Replenishment should be continuous, often involving vendor-managed inventory rather than discrete orders. For strategic accounts, the supplier should dedicate cross-functional account teams and expend significant resources to understand and improve the customer's structure and business.

For example, some suppliers are pioneering efforts to develop new vendor management processes and systems that extend all the way to the retailer's shelf rather than to the distribution center. Today, when most suppliers ship to their retail customers' distribution centers, their involvement ends. However, some innovative suppliers are experimenting with RFID (radio-frequency identification, little electronic "tags" that identify a product when they are scanned by an electromagnetic field). This technology enables a supplier to track its products even within a customer's stores. This would allow the supplier to develop new ways to observe, analyze, and manage the retailer's entire product flow—right to the shelves.

**Integrated accounts.** These important accounts warrant significant care and resources, but not extensive customization. This can be seen in two areas.

First, a major supplier and integrated account should develop an aligned business plan and scorecard. The joint business plan will not be as customized as in the case of a strategic account. The plan should have a shorter time horizon, perhaps one year, but the relationship should be collaborative and trustworthy.

Second, the companies' supply chains should be coordinated, but not necessarily fully integrated. The supplier should use existing internal processes to respond to orders from integrated accounts. Vendor-managed inventory systems may be appropriate for these accounts, as they are a cost-saving measure. However, new systems that would bring vendor management to the store shelf may not be warranted.

**Emerging accounts.** These smaller accounts are very innovative and fast-growing. They warrant significant supplier attention both because of their growth and because they provide a low-risk opportunity for the supplier to develop and showcase new systems and processes that can be quickly deployed into strategic accounts. Yet, because these customers are relatively small, suppliers need to limit their investment.

The supplier should provide service that is both functionally excellent and flexible. The service should be efficient and largely standardized, or costs will quickly go out of control. However, the supplier often can justify meeting some unique needs, especially if the innovation can be scaled to the larger account base. These accounts are important because they force the supplier to be very innovative.

**Stable accounts.** These accounts typically cause a disproportionate amount of cost because many are unsophisticated and have idiosyncratic processes. For example, a stable account may order by fax rather than electronically, and may have unusual shipping specifications.

The key to supplying this group profitably is to offer a menu of service offerings, along with clear rules of engagement, such as minimum order sizes for various lead times, weekly ordering, and shipments to distribution centers only. In this way, the supplier can provide reliable, consistent, cost-efficient service. This will ensure transactional efficiency for both the supplier and the customer.

It is likely that the supplier will need a transition strategy for this segment of accounts. Some major suppliers already have withdrawn from a direct relationship with some of these customers, and instead have chosen to serve them through master distributors.

■ ■ ■

# How it plays out

The sea changes that retailers and their suppliers are now experiencing are starting to play out in industry after industry. The evolving retail supply chain provides a model for top managers in these other industries as they face the seemingly impossible dilemma of providing excellent service while increasing profitability in the presence of escalating customer demands.

## THINGS TO THINK ABOUT

**1.** Service differentiation—offering the right relationship to the right set of customers—is the key to providing consistent, excellent service at a reasonable cost.

**2.** Different sets of customers should get different relationships, ranging from highly integrated supply chains to arm's-length transactions. The Service Differentiation Matrix, which classifies customers by size, and willingness and ability to innovate, provides a great starting point for this process.

**3.** Underlying the process of service differentiation is the clear strategic dictate that you can't be everything to everyone, and one size does not fit all. The strong temptation in so many companies to have a uniform set of customer policies is one of the most problematic legacies of the Age of Mass Markets.

**4.** Note the composition of the integrated account management team that P&G fielded in Wal-Mart—representatives from sales/marketing, supply chain management, IT, and finance—all critical to creating and managing powerful out-of-the-box customer service innovations. How does this compare to your company's account teams in your key customers?

## What's Next

The theme of service differentiation is developed in the first three chapters of this section. The next chapter explains how to create multiple parallel supply chains, essential to custom-tailoring your supply chain to a variety of customer and product situations while, at the same time, lowering your costs.

*When it comes to supply chains, having three or more may be just what you need to meet the needs of your best customers.*

## 20

# YOU ONLY HAVE ONE SUPPLY CHAIN?

▼

**WHEN IT COMES** to supply chains, having two is better than one, and three or more may be best of all. Let me explain.

A few years ago, I met with the top supply chain executives of one of the largest manufacturers of telecommunications equipment. The company produced products ranging from expensive digital central office switches to the cables that run from pole to pole to replacement parts for past and present generations of equipment in the field.

We spent the day in a conference room reviewing their supply chain, discussing ways to make it more productive. The executives explained how their supply chain worked. First, the company manufactured products in its factories; then it shipped them, generally in full truckloads, to its field distribution centers scattered around the country; finally, the products were stored in the field distribution centers until customer orders arrived.

As we talked about the process, it became clear that the company was running a one-size-fits-all supply chain. For example, the company produced small circuit boards, valued at more than thirty thousand dollars, to upgrade electronic switch capabilities. Yet they traveled side by side with all of the company's low-value products from the factory to the distribution centers, often waiting for a full truckload before shipment took place.

## Having two supply chains is better

This suggested a thought: why not have somebody stand at the end of the production line putting the circuit boards into Federal Express envelopes and shipping them directly to customers? That way, the company would save a lot of money in inventory costs, even with the higher transport cost. There really was no good reason why these compact, expensive circuit boards should move through several echelons of warehouses, wait for trucks to be fully loaded, and sit in inventory all over the country.

This may seem like an obvious solution, but think about this question: why did nobody see it years before?

The answer is that the company's supply chain was designed in an earlier era, when the company produced far different products. It was set up to efficiently transport heavy, low-value products like telephone cable. These products were produced in high volume, and because transportation cost was much more important than inventory carrying cost, they had to be transported efficiently in full truckloads and stored in field locations near the customers.

> The company's supply chain was designed in an earlier
>
> era, when the company produced far different products.
>
> ▼

When the company started making expensive, compact electronic switch components, the managers simply assumed that these products would move through the existing supply chain. This was a very costly assumption.

Here, two supply chains were indeed better than one. The company needed one supply chain for its bulky, inexpensive traditional products, and a second completely different one for its small, valuable electronic components.

Supply chains typically involve long-lived facilities and equipment, like distribution centers and bar-code scanners. In many companies they were designed to reflect the company's operating needs ten to twenty years earlier. This was the root cause for the telecommunications equipment company's problems, and it is a core source of poor supply chain performance for many businesses today.

In many companies, not only does one size *not* fit all products, but surprisingly often it is the *wrong size* for most.

## Three supply chains is even better

Consider the supply chain needs of a major clothing retailer. This company has three types of products: (1) staple products, like white underwear; (2) seasonal products, like wool slacks; and (3) fashion products, like stylish blouses. Each needs a different supply chain.

**Staple products** are sold steadily throughout the year, often at relatively low margins. These products are easy to forecast, and should flow through the supply chain like water through a pipe. Inventories should be kept primarily in stores, with small safety stocks in field distribution centers. These products should be transported in efficient truckload quantities.

**Seasonal products** experience strong peak demands that are hard to predict. For these products, the retailer must build inventory in advance of the season and carefully manage the pace at which it pushes product out to the stores. However, the supply chain for these products is even more complex than that.

In retail, high-volume stores can support much higher inventory levels, relative to sales, of seasonal or short-lifecycle products than can lower-volume stores. In fact, in many retailers, a very large proportion of marked-down inventory is late-product-lifecycle stock in lower-volume stores. High-volume stores need a different supply chain than do lower-volume stores, and this need increases as the product moves through its season or lifecycle.

**Fashion products** are characterized by very unpredictable demand. A product may take off, or it may be a dud. It may take off immediately, or later in the season. These products require very special supply chains.

For example, Zara, a Spanish fashion-oriented retailer, utilizes dual sourcing. Picture the demand for a product over time as waves in the ocean. All products have a stable, predictable portion of demand (the water below the waves), and a more volatile, unpredictable portion (the waves). However, some products have much more volatility (bigger waves) than others. Fashion products, by their nature, have a lot of large, unpredictable waves—the retailer does not know when a product will get hot, and when it will fall out of fashion. Zara sources the "waves" (volatile portion of demand) from local vendors with higher cost and fast response time, and the "ocean depths" (stable portion of demand) from Eastern European vendors with lower cost but poor response time. That way, Zara gets the best of both worlds.

The economics are compelling. Think about this: one major retailer has structured a supply chain with a forty-eight-hour response time on fashion products sourced in the Far East. If you buy a fashion garment from one of its stores in your local mall, the data is transmitted to a factory in the Far East. The factory keeps semifinished products in stock, and that day it cuts and tailors a replacement for the one you bought. The garment is flown to the United States on a chartered air freighter, cleared through dedicated customs, and driven through the night to the store in your local mall to replace the one you bought.

Does this sound expensive? It is. This expedited supply chain adds a few dollars to the cost of the garment. But the garment's margin is many times that incremental cost, and the sale otherwise would have been lost. So it makes perfect sense.

## More than three may be best of all

So far, we have looked at several dimensions of supply chain differentiation:

- ▶ Product characteristics—value, bulk (to this we could add criticality and availability of substitutes)
- ▶ Product demand—staple, seasonal, fashion (to this we could add other categories from other industries)
- ▶ Time—stage of season or lifecycle (early, middle, or late)
- ▶ Store type—high volume, low volume (to this we could add other categories such as specialty or mass-merchant stores)

Here's another important supply chain differentiator:

- ▶ Customer relationship

The preceding chapter introduced the concept of customer service differentiation, tailoring your supply chain to the customer relationship. Order cycle time—the time from customer order placement to customer receipt of product—is a very important profit lever. (The next chapter will explain more systematically how to manage this.)

In a nutshell, high-volume steady accounts should get fast order turn-around time in return for the bulk of their business and cooperation with forecasting. Occasional accounts should get longer turnaround time to allow you to bring product from centralized inventories if needed. If the occasional accounts want faster service, they can upgrade their relationship with you.

The key is to always keep your order cycle promise to every customer, but to promise different order cycle times to different accounts based on your relationship. The same goes for your degree of operations integration with your key accounts (as the previous chapter explains). It makes both economic and marketing sense to have different supply chains for different account relationships.

## Supply chains of the future

There is a fundamental change occurring in supply chain management. In the Age of Mass Markets, most companies had relatively static supply chains with a one-size-fits-all, mass-market orientation. A few had dual supply chains coexisting side by side (regular and rush orders), but once the configuration was in place, things didn't change much.

The static supply chains of the past reflected two factors: (1) until recently, supply chain IT was not capable of dynamic management; and (2) everyone was in the same boat, so there was little competitive disadvantage.

As we enter the Age of Precision Markets, things are changing fast. Modern supply chain IT is becoming more capable of dynamic management, assigning the right product to the right supply chain at the right time. Already, some competitors in nearly every industry are using these supply chain innovations to sprint ahead of the pack.

Think about this image of the supply chains of the future. Products are flowing from suppliers to customers through supply chains that look like networks of pipes, valves, and reservoirs. The flow of products is determined by thoughtful supply chain managers using an intelligent supply chain IT system that takes into account the factors discussed above.

The IT system would identify the essential characteristics of each product/customer situation—where the product is in its lifecycle, the size and volatility of the customer's order pattern. Based on this, the IT system would channel the product flow through a predetermined supply chain that best fits the situation. As the situation changes, the product flow would shift to a different, more appropriate supply chain. Supply chains thus will become much more dynamic, responsive, and cost-effective, with products channeled into and out of predetermined flow plans as circumstances warrant.

It makes sense to have different supply chains

for different account relationships.

▼

In this way, companies will deploy multiple parallel supply chains in a very flexible, cost-effective manner. These innovative new supply chains will drive up their profits by giving them the ability to provide customers with highly tailored packages of service at far less cost.

Soon competitive pressures will force most companies to employ dynamic, differentiated supply chains, and there are compelling first-mover advantages. The supply chain managers who create these innovative systems will create strong new streams of profits, and competitive advantage.

---

### THINGS TO THINK ABOUT

**1.** Most supply chain assets, like facilities and equipment, are long-lived. Consequently, in many companies, they are mismatched with evolving business needs. This causes a lot of inefficiency, especially in companies that have a one-size-fits-all distribution system.

**2.** With careful thought, and today's software, supply chain managers can create multiple parallel supply chains that are well tailored for their companies' product and customer needs.

**3.** These multiple parallel supply chains do not require new capital investment in bricks and mortar. Instead, in a well-managed supply chain, predetermined game plans and decision rules allow you to channel your products through your existing facilities in different ways to meet your changing product and customer needs. This substantially lowers your cost and raises your profit margins.

**4.** It is important to carefully monitor your products and customers so your supply chain is dynamic, quickly changing sets of products from one game plan to another in response to your ever-changing business needs.

## What's Next

The previous chapter explains how to match your degree of supply chain integration to your customer relationships. This chapter describes how to create multiple parallel supply chains that move your company from a one-size-fits-all customer approach to one in which you are doing the right things for your products and customers at all times. The next chapter continues the theme of service differentiation by explaining how to develop a set of customer service policies that are tailored to meet real customer needs while reducing your costs.

*Service differentiation is the solution to the high-cost/
poor-service spiral. The dilemma of customer service can
be resolved by thinking carefully about your customers' real
product requirements, your customer relationships, and
your supply chain economics.*

## 21

# THE DILEMMA OF CUSTOMER SERVICE

▼

**CUSTOMER SERVICE IS** one of the most important levers of profitability, but one of the least understood. Most managers can improve customer service and lower costs at the same time, but this requires that they reexamine some important assumptions about how customer service is defined and managed.

### Two frustrated managers

Consider the case of a vice president of distribution at a major industrial company. He was responsible for a wide product line and numerous field warehouses, but his customer service was problematic and declining steadily. The lower the customer order fill rate (percent of complete orders delivered on time), the more inventory he sent to the field warehouses. The warehouses were stuffed, costs were rising out of control, and customer service continued to plunge. It seemed that there was no way out of the spiral of escalating costs and worsening service.

When the vice president of distribution met with the company's executive committee to discuss the problem, the executive vice president of sales and marketing exclaimed, "Our customer service policy is like a pendulum. One quarter, we ring the fire bell on costs and cut our inventories, so service falls and the customers scream. The next quarter, we load up our warehouses, and costs go out of control. The customers don't trust our service, so they keep tightening the delivery time, making it impossible to meet their service demands. How do we get out of this cycle?"

## Service differentiation

Many companies face the dilemma of escalating costs and problematic service. Their managers react by trying to find the right balance of cost and service. What could be more logical?

The problem with this approach, however, is that the management actions with the highest profit impact are not those that rebalance one-size-fits-all service standards and out-of-control costs. The most effective actions are those that create *service differentiation*—setting appropriate order cycles (the time between your receipt of a customer order and the customer's receipt of your product) for different sets of customers and products. Given an appropriate set of order cycles (promises made), a manager can provide all customers with near-perfect service (promises kept) at a reasonable cost.

This is a very common problem across all businesses. Some companies have to carry a lot of costly inventory in local field warehouses just in case it is needed, while others have to staff expensive service personnel such as installers, repair techs, or software consultants. This chapter illustrates service differentiation with the example of a company with physical inventory, but the principles apply directly to service businesses as well.

The key question is how to set appropriate, differentiated order cycles. A manager can develop a highly profitable service-differentiation strategy by utilizing a three-step process.

### Step 1: Understand real customer needs

This sounds simple enough—just ask the customer, right? There are two problems with simply asking the customer what order cycle he or she requires. First, the customer may not know his or her real needs, especially in companies where the purchasing group is separate from the operations group. In the absence of this understanding, it is safest for the customer's purchasing staff to simply demand faster and faster service. Second, most customers will ask for shorter and shorter order cycles if they don't trust the vendor to keep its delivery promises.

In fact, all products require flawless *service levels*, but different products need different *order cycles*.

Consider the following examples from the hospital supply industry. Products such as IV solutions that are high-volume, critical, and costly for the customer to store require tight order cycles. However, other products can easily tolerate longer lead times, as long as the supplier is extremely reliable. These products include many slower-moving products with adequate on-site customer safety stock, such as odd-sized bandages, as well as products with a prescheduled use, such as a special scalpel that a particular surgeon may want to try.

> All products require flawless service levels, but different
>
> products need different order cycles.

The only way to understand real customer needs is for your operations managers to spend time on the customer's premises observing the product inventory and usage patterns and developing a joint understanding with the customer's operations managers on appropriate order cycles. While this requires an investment of time, the payoff in improved service and reduced cost is very high.

### Step 2: Align order cycles with customer relationships

Not all customers have equal importance, although you'd never know it from most companies' distribution policies. In most warehouses, the standing rule is first-come first-served, unless severe rationing of a crucial product is necessary.

The problem with first-come first-served is that it hurts your best customers—important accounts with established loyalty and steady, high volumes. This is especially problematic when an occasional customer places a large, unexpected order, often because the customer's primary supplier is out of stock.

Most companies' order fulfillment and service measurement systems do not differentiate between important customers and intermittent customers. The supplier gives both the same order cycle commitment, and the service-level measurement will appear to be the same regardless of which customer receives an incomplete delivery. But the impact on your business will be very different.

The only way to understand real customer needs is to

spend time on the customer's premises.

▼

The answer is for the managers in both your sales and supply chain groups to come together and set appropriate order cycles for different groups of customers.

### Step 3: Align your supply chain with the order cycle

Once a manager has defined appropriate order cycles for sets of products and customers, the next step is to align the supply chain to produce near-perfect service at low costs. A *Customer Service Matrix* is the critical starting point in figuring this out. It segments customers and products into four quadrants: core vs. non-core customers, and core vs. non-core products. Managers can assign appropriate service intervals to each quadrant. This matrix provides a focal point for sales managers and operations managers to get aligned.

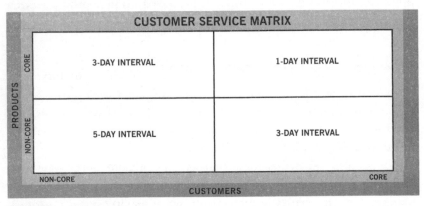

Figure 7

Figure 7 shows a Customer Service Matrix with examples of service intervals. Let's illustrate how this works by returning to the example of the hospital supply company.

**Core customers/core products.** The core/core quadrant corresponds to important products ordered by important customers (such as IV solutions for important hospital customers). Here, order cycles must be short because the customers keep only minimal inventory on site and stockout costs are very high. Generally, a supplier should keep these products in field warehouses near these customers.

**Non-core customers/core products.** These might be critical IV solutions ordered by an occasional customer. This quadrant causes the most customer service problems.

Often, the sales rep acts as an advocate for the occasional customer, arguing that it is an opportunity to get a foot in the door. The problem is that it is prohibitively costly to carry enough local inventory to quickly satisfy both loyal customers with steady orders and occasional customers who place large unexpected orders. If you don't differentiate between these two categories of customers and give priority service to your loyal accounts, you will wind up chronically shorting your best customers. In most companies, this is the most common reason why important customers receive problematic service, and in response insist on faster and faster deliveries.

The solution to this difficulty is to offer the occasional, non-core customers longer, but reasonable, service intervals. In the example Customer Service Matrix, core customers receive one-day service while non-core customers receive three-day service on core products. This gives the supplier an extra margin of time to bring in products from a regional warehouse, if needed, to fill an unexpected order from an occasional customer. Most of the time, non-core customer orders can be fulfilled more rapidly, but the extra interval time lets the supplier always keep its service promises without incurring the large cost burden of just-in-case inventory.

**Core customers/non-core products.** In our example, this segment might include a major hospital customer ordering a new type of bandage to try. In most companies, excessively high distribution costs are caused by inappropriate service intervals in this quadrant.

Here, even your best customers will accept longer order cycles, such as three days, because they keep ample safety stock on-site and the product is not critical. This extra order-cycle time allows you to keep only a small amount of inventory in local field warehouses, and to support this by bringing in stock from a regional warehouse, if needed.

**Non-core customers/non-core products.** Here, think odd bandages for occasional customers.

In this quadrant, order cycles should be set to enable the company to bring products from a regional warehouse to the local warehouse, or to ship directly from a centralized facility. In the example Customer Service Matrix, this interval is set at five days. The longer interval enables a manager to give priority to the loyal core customers by shipping from local or regional inventory, while serving occasional customers economically from a regional or national facility. This allows the supplier to meet the promised delivery dates without having to keep an enormous amount of inventory in every local warehouse. Great service and kept promises, all with rock-bottom low costs.

## Profitability lever

Service differentiation, setting appropriate service intervals for different customers and products, creates enhanced profitability, and crucial competitive advantage, in three ways:

**First.** Your service levels (promises kept) will improve to near-perfect levels, tightly binding your best customers to your company.

**Second.** Virtually all customers, even occasional ones, will strongly prefer your flawlessly reliable service at longer, agreed-upon order cycles to a competitor who offers faster service but with lower reliability.

**Third.** Your sales reps will be happy to have an opportunity to sell an upgraded relationship by offering high-potential, occasional customers the incentive of moving to faster order cycles in return for a commitment of product volumes and loyalty.

> Service differentiation can create crucial competitive
>
> advantage in three ways.

▼

You can resolve the dilemma of customer service by thinking carefully about your customers' real product and service requirements, your customer relationships, and your supply chain cost structure. Service differentiation is the solution to the high-cost/poor-service spiral experienced by managers in so many companies. It is a critical profit lever that can turn many problematic accounts and products into very profitable ones.

**1.** The essence of great customer service is always keeping your promises to your customers.

**2.** But the key to smart, profitable customer service is to make different promises to different sets of customers for different sets of products. Remember: always keep these promises.

**3.** In creating service-differentiated order cycles, you need to balance real customer needs, your actual customer relationships, and your supply chain cost structure. Getting these in alignment creates a very powerful profit lever that will turn a lot of your unprofitable business into good business, and a lot of your marginal business into great business.

**4.** All customers, even occasional ones, will strongly prefer your predictable flawless service, even with longer order cycles, to a competitor who promises faster service but often fails to keep the promise.

## What's Next

The first three chapters of this section explain how to develop a supply chain that delivers great service at low cost. The next chapter tells you how to work with your key customers to smooth their order pattern and make it more predictable. It explains how to use this profit lever to drive down costs both for your company and for your best customers.

*Here's how artful product flow management can lead to improved earnings and happier customers.*

## 22

# PROFIT FROM MANAGING YOUR PRODUCT FLOW

▼

**PRODUCT FLOW MANAGEMENT** is an important profit lever that managers can use to raise earnings and benefit key customers. The objective is to influence your customers' order patterns, which is one of *your* biggest operational cost drivers.

Erratic, unpredictable customer orders require you to keep a lot of just-in-case inventory or maintain excess service personnel time, especially for a key customer's core products and service needs. Most managers simply assume that customer orders are a given, and that their operations managers' job is to respond as efficiently as possible. This is a very costly assumption.

Some leading operations managers have figured out how to work with their customers to change their order pattern, making it less volatile or changing the order quantities for more efficient handling. In this way, they profit handsomely from managing their product flow. The same principles apply directly to service companies managing their customers' service orders. (Chapter 12, "Profit-Focused Selling," gives a good example of this process.)

The case of a leading industrial supply company illustrates the power of product flow management.

# The case of the industrial supply company

Faced with the apparent need to build several facilities and with customer pressure for significant improvements in performance, the industrial supply company's executive committee authorized its senior vice president of operations (SVP) to conduct a challenge-everything study of its business operations. In order to look at the company's business in a new way, the SVP shifted his focus from the company's internal operations to the product flow through the whole channel, including his customers and suppliers.

As a first step, he decided to visit some of his key customers to see what happened to his products after his company delivered them to the customers' receiving docks.

What he saw was surprising. The end users within the customers' operations consumed virtually all of his high-volume products very steadily—with very little fluctuation from day to day, or week to week. Yet, when he looked at these customers' orders, they exhibited a surprisingly erratic order pattern.

Because these were key customers, and the products were critical to their production processes, there was no question of fulfilling the orders immediately. This forced the company to carry very high local inventories. Moreover, because these products and customers were so important, his manufacturing group often had to interrupt their production schedules to meet the unexpected peaks in demand. When this happened, the factory placed costly emergency orders on the company's suppliers.

To his amazement, everyone in the supply chain was hugely affected by this unnecessary fire drill, which generated a surprisingly large portion of the company's costs.

When the SVP saw this, he wondered if the problem was caused by all customers or just some accounts. He decided to look at a few key products, and analyze the order patterns of all the customers in a representative region.

When the SVP looked at each customer's orders over a three-month period, he found that a few large customers caused most of the problem. He was happy to see that most of the big customers ordered relatively steadily, and that the small accounts averaged one another out. The few key customers with large, unpredictable orders created the big spikes in product demand that caused so much trouble. This concerned him because they were large, loyal customers with long-term contracts, and not occasional accounts.

> The few key customers with large, unpredictable orders created the big spikes in product demand that caused so much trouble.

▼

As he traced the impact of the orders, he saw that these peaks in demand were amplified as each company in the channel ordered from the next, and that these erratic orders were very costly for the customers as well.

When this became clear, the SVP realized that everyone had focused on responding as efficiently as possible to a fundamentally illogical order pattern. In each company, managers were even being rewarded for improving their responses. The SVP was astonished to realize that no one had seen that the underlying problem was that the order pattern itself was all wrong.

Why not? The problem had remained hidden because it lay *between* the companies rather than within a company. Everyone simply assumed that customer orders are a given, and that his or her job was to respond as efficiently as possible.

## The Solution

The solution seemed startlingly simple: do something to fix the few large customers that accounted for most of the fluctuations. If the company could do this, the logjam would be broken, and product would flow smoothly and steadily from the beginning to the end of the channel.

The SVP thought about different ways to fix the problem. He decided to develop a relatively simple standing-order arrangement with the few key accounts that were causing the problem. His company provided semi-weekly deliveries of the steadily consumed high-volume products in pre-determined amounts. Importantly, his operations managers met monthly with their counterparts in the customer companies to review and reset the delivery quantities, and they developed contingency plans to expedite emergency orders if unexpected needs arose.

This steadied the product flow for these important customers. The

SVP could greatly reduce his inventories, discipline his manufacturing process, and eliminate the emergency orders his factory placed on his suppliers.

The results were startling. The company's operating costs fell by more than 35 percent. Inventories were cut in half, the company was spared a multimillion-dollar capital program, and stockouts were virtually eliminated. Labor costs decreased greatly because the warehouses now had a much more stable workload. With steady customer orders, many high-volume products could simply flow through the distribution center in cross-dock mode, moving directly from replenishment trucks into customer delivery lanes without being put away and picked.

The company's operations managers discovered that when they had standing orders with key accounts, they could pack the products onto pallets in a standard configuration, so the customers could easily find each product, rather than simply getting a jumble of boxes. This made it very easy for the customers to receive the products and put them away. This seemingly small improvement was a really important benefit to the customers' operations personnel. The whole process significantly reduced the customers' handling costs and inventories.

Inventories were cut in half, the company was spared

a multimillion-dollar capital program, and stockouts

dropped substantially.

▼

Because its order patterns were now predictable, the company stabilized its manufacturing schedules. This allowed the company to issue firm, long-range forecasts to suppliers, with firm commitments to purchase the materials; in return, the suppliers significantly lowered their prices and guaranteed supply availability. Everyone in the channel experienced great benefits.

The company's sales process improved in unexpected ways. The new system freed the sales reps from the need to spend the lion's share of their time on customer service complaints, and allowed them to focus on end-user selling. New relationships and trust developed in newly created, periodic operational review meetings that included the company's regional operations managers and the customers' purchasing and operations managers. The increased focus on more productive selling, coupled with the efficiency of the product flow, led several large customers to broaden their purchases of the company's product line. Key account sales rose through the ceiling.

## Why did it take so long?

Even though the company was well recognized for its sophisticated management, and its customers and suppliers were well managed, it took years for the company to discover this deceptively simple, and seemingly obvious, solution. And, in the past, a major competitor had tried and failed to implement a similar standing order system.

This raises two important questions: (1) why did it take so long for operations management to recognize the problem? and (2) why did the company succeed while competitors failed? The SVP faced three problems that are common to the process of managing product flow.

**First.** There was no previous awareness of the opportunity for improvement or the root causes of the problem. The company's operations and manufacturing managers simply had taken the order and replenishment pattern as a given, not within their control, and had focused on optimizing the company's response. All previous operations' improvement efforts were conducted within this traditional introspective framework.

The possibility of *altering* the customers' order patterns, and the impact of dramatically improving so many aspects of the company's performance through product flow management, simply did not surface in the company, its customers, or its suppliers—more than five hundred companies in all—until this SVP had the vision to challenge everything.

**Second.** Despite the company's sophisticated computer capabilities, it lacked the data needed to understand many of the costs of intercompany product flows. The SVP had to gather new data to analyze the order patterns and their costs. The company's customers and suppliers had similar blind spots in their operations analysis, and in their cost accounting systems.

**Third.** Implementing the standing order system required important organizational changes. Several managers were affected: regional operations managers met periodically with key customers to review service and adjust standing order levels; facility managers reconfigured and downsized their warehouses; materials managers tracked products beyond the company's boundaries; purchasing managers developed long-range purchase commitments with suppliers, in return for price reductions and guarantees of priority service and contingency backups; and manufacturing managers changed their schedules and procedures to draw new efficiencies from the new demand pattern.

## Why a competitor failed

It is not surprising that a major competitor failed. This company made the mistake of approaching the standing order arrangement simply as a new marketing program. Its program had three fatal flaws: (1) the competitor had failed to isolate the key customers and products that had relatively steady consumption but erratic ordering patterns, and instead it developed an unfocused system that tried to do too much; (2) it neglected to establish frequent meetings with customer operations managers, and had no contingency mechanisms to monitor and adjust delivery levels, or to quickly react to unforeseen problems; and (3) the competitor failed to reconfigure its distribution facilities, and reorganize its manufacturing and supply processes in order to gain new cost efficiencies.

## Powerful profit lever

Product flow management is a powerful profit lever that can increase your company's earnings while raising your customer service levels—all while increasing your key customers' efficiency and profitability.

The preceding chapter explains how to match order cycles with real product needs and customer relationships. The biggest opportunities for product-flow-management gains come, not surprisingly, in the core-customer/core-product quadrant of the Customer Service Matrix, where high-volume products flow to big customers. In this key quadrant, order pattern variance is one of the primary drivers of high inventories and costly operations—for both you and your customers—and it is here that you should focus your efforts for the largest gains.

> Product flow management is a powerful profit lever
> that can increase earnings while raising customer
> service levels.

▼

By developing a strong operations-to-operations relationship with your core customers, you can influence your customers' order patterns to a surprising extent. Product flow management is a critical profit lever that creates an important win-win for both your company and your best customers.

---

**THINGS TO THINK ABOUT**

**1.** Product flow management—smoothing the fluctuations in your customers' order patterns and making them more predictable—can have a very large impact on your costs and profitability. It offers your best customers the same benefits.

**2.** The highest impact comes from working with a relatively small number of key customers on their high-volume products.

**3.** In most companies, operations managers simply assume that the customer order pattern is a given, and spend large amounts of time and resources trying to optimize their response. When operations managers work with their customer counterparts to shape and manage their order pattern, they achieve surprisingly strong results.

**4.** In all too many companies, managers do not look systematically at information on customer order patterns. This critical profit lever is not in anyone's job description. This is another problematic legacy of the Age of Mass Markets.

---

## What's Next

Customer service is much more complex than most managers realize. This is why it is such a great profit lever. With a smart set of customer service policies, you can do a lot to raise your customers' satisfaction, even while lowering your costs. The next chapter tells you how.

*When you do a good job of fixing a customer service problem, you often earn more customer loyalty than if there hadn't been a problem in the first place. Here's how to show your worth and earn your customers' trust.*

# 23

# NAIL CUSTOMER SERVICE

▼

**WHAT DO YOU** do when you're waiting for a slow elevator?

A number of years ago, a company that had just built a major building realized their elevators were intolerably slow. It was too expensive to reengineer the elevators. What could they do?

After thinking about the problem for a while, the company's architects had a great idea: they installed mirrors in the lobby and elevators. It turns out that people will tolerate a surprisingly long wait if they can watch themselves in a mirror.

Today, most tall buildings have mirrors or reflective metal surfaces in their lobbies and elevators.

Disney World had a similar problem. The waiting lines for attractions were often very long, and children were impatient. So were adults. What could Disney do?

The customer service group at Disney studied this problem at great length, and they made the field into a science. They figured out exactly how long people will wait before they need to be distracted. Consequently, when you queue up for Pirates of the Caribbean or other top attractions, you are likely to be engaged at carefully predetermined intervals by wandering characters, videos, and mirrors. Disney customer service engineers even laid out the waiting lines in a serpentine manner, providing a feeling of constant progress, and ensuring that you never see how long the line really is.

Here's how one top hotel chain, which differentiates itself through its reputation for great service, handles customer service. Every employee is empowered to spend up to a few hundred dollars without supervisor approval to rectify customer service errors. If your laundry is late, it arrives with a bottle of wine.

In this way, the hotel turns lemons into lemonade.

When you do a good job of fixing a customer service problem, you often earn more customer loyalty than if there had been no problem.

▼

Southwest Airlines has a similar policy. The front-line employees are empowered to bend the rules to meet customer needs. It is no coincidence that Southwest is widely perceived as one of the leading airlines in customer service, even though it is a low-fare carrier.

When you do a good job of fixing a customer service problem, you often earn more customer loyalty than if there had been no problem. This is when you can show your worth, and earn your customer's trust.

## What is customer service?

This raises a critical question: exactly what is customer service? Nearly every company has numerous customer service measures, but how many of these really produce the right results?

Consider the following customer service measure: a copier company has a policy that when a customer calls for repairs, 95 percent of the time a repair tech will arrive on the scene within two hours. Sound good?

Think about the following issues.

This policy treats all service problems the same. Some service calls are prompted by machine failure, while others may be caused by cosmetic issues, like a loose nameplate. The policy also treats all customers and customer situations the same. One call might be for a nonfunctioning machine that happens to be the only copier on the executive floor of a major account, while another call might be for one of the dozen copiers in the company's administrative department.

Customers' negative perception of service is largely formed by their worst experiences, not by the average. For example, even if the copier company fully met the policy above, the disappointed 5 percent would have far different reactions if the wait time were four days rather than just over two hours. By the way, did you notice that the policy focuses on when a service tech arrives, not on when the problem is fixed?

This policy reflects the cardinal error of customer service: it measures what the copier company sees, not what the customer sees. It's an operational measure, not a customer measure.

Is customer service what the customer experiences? Not exactly. *Customer service is what the customer remembers.*

The acid test of customer service is the customer's future behavior. If Disney World had managed to shorten its *actual* wait time by 20 percent, but had failed to devise clever ways to change its customers' *perception* of their wait time by distracting the waiting customers, customer service complaints would have gone through the roof. Here, the customers' perception, not the reality, is what really counts.

## Product reliability

Think about this one. The copier company develops a great quality process, and its copiers become very reliable. What's the impact on customer service?

The answer is counterintuitive. As the products become more reliable, the easy-to-fix problems go away. The ones that remain are the most intractable, those that take the most time and are most difficult to fix. When customers focus on their bad experiences, they often perceive that customer service has degraded, even if overall service actually has improved considerably.

What can you do about this? Several things.

**First.** Shape your customer's perception. Some insightful companies issue report cards to each of their customers showing their actual service to that customer. In this context, the occasional problems are seen to be just that, occasional problems.

**Second.** Get in front of the problem. Some companies carefully analyze the key points at which preventative maintenance makes a big difference. Others design machines with the capability for self-diagnosis. Some of these machines can even call for service, without human intervention, if they detect an impending problem.

**Third.** Make the products easier to fix. Most often, the root problem behind lengthy repairs is lack of quick access to needed parts.

A vice president of one major copier company created what he called the "wall of washers." He saw that the company's product design engineers were specifying unique washers for each of their products. This caused huge problems in keeping local spare parts inventories, and resulted in big delays in repairs. To emphasize the point, he had his staff collect every unique washer and paste them on a wall. By the time they finished, there were more than a thousand washers on the wall.

The vice president brought the product design engineers to see the wall of washers. They were startled. As a result, the engineers quickly began to redesign products to have a maximum number of common parts. The improvement in service intervals (the time between when a customer calls and when the machine is fixed) was striking. And inventory costs dropped through the floor.

## Product availability

Measuring customer service is a common problem in retail. Many stores have thousands of products, and it is costly and difficult to keep them all in stock. In addition, products may be inaccessible because they are present in the store but not in their proper place on the shelf. What's the right customer service measure?

The answer is more complicated than simply whether the shelf is empty. A lot depends on the customer's actual need. Many managers across a range of industries incur large, unnecessary costs because they fail to deeply probe their customers' needs.

In many retail situations customers come into the store with a generic need such as a tape measure, a plastic container, or an inexpensive television. For these situations, most stores carry two to four products that would fit the customer's need, and the customer is largely indifferent. In this context, if one of the products is missing from the shelf, the customer is still perfectly satisfied. Many industrial supply companies have the same situation.

In these cases, the proper measure is a substitution group (described in chapter 8). For many retailers, more than 60 percent of their sales engagements fit this customer behavior profile, as does a high proportion of industrial supply situations. Yet most of these companies focus on product-specific availability measures of customer service. Not only is this very costly, but they also fail to develop effective programs to help the customers identify and accept reasonable substitutes. This deficiency causes major customer service problems, and huge inventory costs in company after company.

Many service operations and factories experience another sort of customer service misunderstanding. For example, in a typical hospital, the definition of an out-of-stock situation is one in which the stockroom and at least one patient care area run out of a particular product. Yet the hospital may have a large amount of the product scattered in other patient care areas. The real problem is lack of a mechanism to locate the product scattered around the hospital.

This creates a very important opportunity. If a supplier installs a vendor-managed inventory system that includes both the stockroom and patient care areas, it will gain the ability to cross-source from one patient care area to another. Stockouts will disappear, and on-site inventories will plummet. This opportunity is one of the major hidden benefits of vendor-managed inventory.

## Effective customer service

Managers at different levels of your customer companies will have fundamentally different definitions of effective customer service.

Your company may be in grave danger if it focuses solely on providing outstanding traditional customer service (e.g., order-fill rates and responsiveness). A competitor can trump your position by engaging your best customers' top managers with a package of out-of-the-box innovations that dramatically increases the customers' profitability. Even if you make your customers' front-line managers happy, you may still lose the executive suite.

> Managers at different levels of your customer companies
> will have fundamentally different definitions of effective
> customer service.

▼

Customer service is the starting point and ending point for any effective account relationship. It is a critical profit lever that is very often misunderstood. The key to success is thinking clearly about what your customers actually perceive, and being very creative about how to shape and manage that perception. With careful analysis, you can nail customer service. But you better act fast and nail it before your competitors do.

---

### THINGS TO THINK ABOUT

**1.** Customer service is the starting point and ending point for any effective customer relationship, yet it is one of the most misunderstood areas of business.

**2.** Customers' negative service perceptions are formed by their worst experiences, not by the average, even if the glitches are few and far between. You can shape your customers' perceptions in a variety of powerful ways.

**3.** The acid test of your customer service is your customers' future behavior. The best customer service metrics focus on actual customer experience, customer perceptions, and continued customer behavior, not on your company's internal performance. What are your customer service measures designed to tell you?

**4.** Often the key to improving customer service while lowering costs lies in seemingly unrelated areas like product design. Think about the mirrors in the elevator lobby, and the wall of washers.

---

## What's Next

The chapters of this section so far have explained how to develop an effective service-differentiation program, how to match your supply chain structure to real customer needs and relationships, how to lower your costs by managing customer order patterns, and how to create and manage customer perceptions of your customer service. These are very important profit levers that lower your costs and increase your profitability. The next chapter tells you how to create a make-to-order manufacturing system that reduces your production costs while increasing your flexibility and market responsiveness. The final chapter covers the management issues involved in operating for profit.

*How make-to-order manufacturing paid off for one leading company by reducing finished-goods inventory, warehouse costs, and minimum production lot size.*

## 24

# WINNING WITH MAKE-TO-ORDER MANUFACTURING

▼

**SEVERAL YEARS AGO,** a leading appliance manufacturer revolutionized its manufacturing process, cutting its cycle time for producing stoves, refrigerators, and other white goods from four months to three days.

And this revolutionary new process didn't cost a cent. In fact, it generated cash from the start.

What did this company do? How did it do it?

The critical first step occurred years earlier. The company's top management team decided to create a culture of innovation by continually driving its managers to find new ways to do things, by giving them a lot of leeway to try new things, and by accepting the occasional failure as part of a successful innovation process. This is the company's ultimate competitive edge.

As part of this innovation process, the company's vice president of manufacturing decided to scour the world looking for new manufacturing practices. In New Zealand, he discovered a company that had developed a very effective new way of manufacturing, and he brought the process back to North America. This make-to-order process became the basis for the company's great success. It was widely followed by managers in a number of industries. Yet many followers missed key elements that underlay the company's success.

## The traditional way

Before this innovation, the company manufactured its products in the traditional make-to-inventory way developed in the Age of Mass Markets. It produced a large number of products, and each product was scheduled to be manufactured once every four months. The company used sales forecasts to set the production quantities, and each time a product was manufactured, it produced four months of inventory to last until the next scheduled production run.

Forecasting was a byzantine process. Four months before a product's production, the sales reps, key account executives, and area sales managers made projections. These projections were reviewed and adjusted by zone administrators and zone managers, then by pricing managers and sales administrators. At sixty days before production, the projections were combined into a sales forecast that then was reviewed and adjusted by the vice president of sales, the product managers, and the vice president of marketing. Thirty days before production, the manufacturing team set the production schedule and quantities.

The problem was that at this point, thirty days before production, everyone already knew that the market conditions had changed, making the schedule obsolete and the quantities wrong. But the forecasting process was so convoluted that there was no feasible way to change the plans. Consequently, the company chronically experienced both a huge inventory buildup and terrible service—all this despite the fact that each month's forecast involved nearly three man-years of effort by eighty-seven employees from twelve different departments.

## Make-to-order process

The key insight at the core of the new make-to-order process was the realization that while the company could accurately predict how much of a *product family* it would sell, it couldn't predict the right mix of products within the family. For example, one of the product families in the range business had four products (e.g., different colors and features). Each product's sales could change by up to 25 percent from one month to another, which made it very hard to forecast sales. However, the whole product family had only a month-to-month sales variance of less than 3 percent—a huge difference.

When this became clear, the vice president decided to reorganize the company's manufacturing process. Rather than producing four months of inventory for each product every four months, he dedicated a constant amount of manufacturing capacity to each product family. He then charged his managers with developing a process to alter the product mix within each product family every day. With this change, the company could move from four-month production runs set a month in advance to a manufacturing system that changed the product mix every day based on real-time demands.

## Addressing Sales' concerns

At this point, the sales group became concerned. They were worried about the company's ability to respond to unexpected peaks in demand under the new system. They saw that manufacturing capacity would be available, but what about the necessary components and parts?

In order to allay these legitimate concerns, the manufacturing group agreed to keep enough components and parts in inventory so that they could increase the production of any product, on any day, by up to 50 percent. This satisfied the sales group.

How did the company do this without an explosion of component inventory?

The vice president looked carefully at the parts that went into building the products. He saw that some parts were common to all products in the product family, but that most were unique to one or two specific products. (Does this remind you of the wall of washers in the preceding chapter?)

He had the company's design engineers move aggressively to redesign its products so that they used a maximum number of common parts. This enabled the company to dramatically reduce its component parts inventories. (Think about the positive impact it had on customer service performance and cost as well.)

This product redesign program had a huge impact. For example, in the range business, which comprised nine product families, the extra cost of carrying enough unique parts to accommodate a possible 50 percent increase in sales was about $750,000. With this extra inventory, the company was able to institute the make-to-order system and remove about $14 million in finished-goods inventory. This cut the range business inventory in half.

As the company's engineers redesigned more and more products, the $750,000 extra parts inventory declined to $300,000, and the $14 million remaining finished-goods inventory dropped to $8 million. The company's other business units (refrigerators, other white goods) achieved similar results.

The impact of this critical profit lever on the company's bottom line was startling. Orders filled on time rose from less than 60 percent to more than 95 percent. Finished-goods inventory across the company dropped from $100 million to $35 million, generating an enormous amount of cash. Warehouse costs declined by 30 percent. Minimum production-run size fell from two hundred units to one appliance. The frozen production schedule period dropped from thirty days to three days.

The company's managers implemented the new process in a very conservative, well-controlled manner. Each time the company made a major change (like changing the production process), it built its work-in-process inventory to make sure that its service would stay strong, even if it took a little while to stabilize and fine-tune the new production process. Once production steadied, however, the company removed the extra buffer, and more.

Each time the company made a major change, it built

work-in-process inventory to ensure good performance.

▼

## Parallel changes

The company instituted a set of parallel changes in several related areas of its business to enhance the effect of the make-to-order process.

▶ First and foremost, the company put all of its key managers on the same compensation performance metric. Everyone was measured and rewarded on: (1) return on sales (profitability), and (2) order fill rate.

▶ The company worked closely with its key suppliers. Initially, it picked five major vendors and helped them institute the make-to-order process in their own companies. This enabled the suppliers to reduce their inventories of parts by 60 percent over a nine-month period. In a very important move, the company reduced the number of its suppliers from thirteen hundred to four hundred in order to have more clout, enabling it to work more intensively with those that remained. The company even invited a number of these key vendors to send engineers to work as part of its product-redesign teams.

▶ The company slashed the number of distribution centers from twenty-six to three. In the past, each distribution center served a specific geographic area, and carried a full line of products with several months of inventory. In the new system, each of the three distribution centers served one of the company's three plants. Because each plant was dedicated to one business (e.g., ranges), each distribution center stocked only a single type of product, and each had visibility into national demand. This new distribution configuration combined with the efficient new make-to-order process to eliminate nearly all the company's finished-goods inventory.

▶ When the company eliminated its regional distribution centers, it established a set of regional cross-docks. In this arrangement, the three national warehouses sent products to small regional facilities, where they were transshipped directly onto delivery trucks. This allowed the company to achieve freight efficiencies and very fast response times. The company's new manufacturing and distribution systems were so effective that its order cycle time (the interval from customer order placement to customer product receipt *including manufacturing and shipping*) was six days.

▶ The company also worked closely with its key customers to increase *their* efficiency. Traditionally, these accounts had held about sixteen weeks of inventory. The company helped them reduce their inventory levels to two weeks of product, dramatically reducing the customers' costs. The company also worked with its larger accounts to get them to order at regular weekly intervals, further increasing the predictability and steadiness of their orders.

Learning by doing is a very important element of any

change process.

▼

## Key success factors

The company's top managers reflected on their experience, and offered the following tips:

1. Work with the sales reps to be sure that they are comfortable with the new process.
2. Compensation alignment is absolutely critical.
3. The process is self-financing, so "just do it."
4. Implement the new process in increments; the company started with a 120-day cycle, then reduced it to 3 weeks, then 1 week, then 3 days.
5. Supplier commitment is crucial: "If the vendor doesn't want to do it, look for another vendor."
6. Rely on your suppliers: "The vendors had far more flexibility than we ever believed; we never used our supplier base as a resource."

## Final advice

One top manager summed up the company's best practices: "Continuous improvement beats postponed perfection. Beware of analysis paralysis." The manager observed that some other companies had stumbled because they overanalyzed the process. Learning by doing is a very important element of any change process. For this company, the commitment to ongoing innovation, the willingness to try sensible new things, and the ability to understand all facets of the new process were the keys to accelerating profitability and continuing success.

The company also worked closely with its key customers

to increase *their* efficiency.

▼

**1.** The old manufacturing system described in this chapter was developed in the Age of Mass Markets, an era characterized by a relatively small number of standardized products and stable demand. This system is completely inadequate to meet the demands of today's Age of Precision Markets.

**2.** The new make-to-order system is well designed to meet the needs of business in the new era. The keys to the new system's success are to allocate capacity to product families (product families have stable demand), and to develop innovative ways to alter the product mix within each product family every day to match the rapidly changing market.

**3.** The new manufacturing system affected a wide range of related areas, including product design, supplier relations, customer relations, and supply chain structure. It allowed the company to create a whole new business system.

**4.** Note the critical importance of aligning company-wide compensation around a few key shared measures. This theme is amplified in the next chapter. Also note that the process is self-financing, and generates cash from the onset.

**5.** Consider the company's guiding principle: "Continuous improvement beats postponed perfection. Beware of analysis paralysis." This is a great example of the power of 70 percent analysis linked to decisive action.

## What's Next

The final chapter of this section explains how to focus and motivate your company's operations and supply chain organization to maximize profitability.

*Forget traditional supply chain management. Managers must be responsible for the earning power and productivity of the assets in their trust, not just cost control.*

## 25

# ACHIEVING SUPPLY CHAIN PRODUCTIVITY

▼

**WHAT IS THE** biggest problem in supply chain management today?

The biggest problem is that in many companies the mission of the supply chain organization is defined much too narrowly. All too many supply chain managers are acting like traditional logistics managers, focusing almost exclusively on controlling operational costs. When they do this, their companies lose a huge amount of potential profits.

When I work with groups of supply chain executives at MIT, I sometimes ask how many in the group are logistics managers. Everyone raises his or her hand. Next, I ask how many are supply chain managers. Again, all raise their hands.

Then I ask: what's the difference between the two?

Most of the time, I get puzzled looks. Yet, for these managers, nothing could be more important. And for their companies, an enormous amount of profitability is at stake.

The difference between logistics and supply chain management is critical. It is the difference between a logistics manager's narrow focus on minimizing operating costs with customer orders as a given, and a supply chain manager's much broader, proactive focus on managing the profitability of all aspects of a company's product flow from the first touch within the company's supplier through the company to the final use within the customer. This is a crucial difference, and it can have a huge impact on a company's profits.

The underlying problem is that many of the most important elements of supply chain management actually lie outside the supply chain organization. They are managed by other departments or, more often, not managed at all. Unfortunately, all too many supply chain managers simply assume that their job is to focus on the variables under their direct control.

## From Logistics to Supply Chain Management

Recently, I reviewed a survey of the top managers of major company supply chain organizations. High on the list of supply chain priorities were operational topics like improving supply chain visibility. When I saw this, I knew there was a problem.

Supply chain visibility certainly is a significant supply chain issue. Getting better information on the status of inbound movements, deliveries, and customer inventory will lead to cost savings. But these savings are incremental in nature, not paradigmatic improvements.

First and foremost, supply chain managers must be responsible for supply chain productivity—monitoring and comanaging the earning power and productivity of the assets in their trust—not just for cost control of these assets. This essential responsibility goes far beyond traditional logistics. It involves both revenues and costs—and how they come together to form the company's profitability.

> Supply chain managers must be responsible for
>
> the earning power and productivity of the assets
>
> in their trust.

Supply chain productivity is a measure of the earning power of supply chain assets like inventory. It is measured by a ratio called the return on invested capital (ROIC). For example, if the inventory of a product in a region is one hundred dollars, and it enables the company to earn a net profit of twenty dollars over the course of a year, the ROIC is a healthy

20 percent—one of your islands of profit. Another product with the same inventory of one hundred dollars might be *losing* ten dollars annually—this one lives in your sea of red ink.

These simple ratios can be calculated using standard desktop tools for all your customers and products with a few months' work, using the profit-mapping techniques explained in an earlier chapter. They show the company's pattern of profitability, but translated into a picture of the earning power of the company's supply chain assets. This view shows the true performance of the company's supply chain.

Of course, if only 20 to 30 percent of a company's business is profitable, a major block of the company's supply chain assets (and operating costs) are unproductive. This is a huge supply chain problem, and offers a major opportunity for paradigmatic improvement. Yet, surprisingly, few supply chain managers see doing something about it as the most important part of their job—or as part of their job at all!

Think about this familiar example: if you work hard and achieve a 20 percent inventory reduction, but these assets are supporting unprofitable business, should you be happy? It depends on how you define your job. If a manager is managing like a traditional logistics manager, he or she probably doesn't even see the problem and is delighted with the efficiency improvement. But a true supply chain manager would see the whole situation, and conclude that the most important work is yet to be done.

In most companies, the fastest and most effective way to improve supply chain productivity is to change the mix of business being sold so that it better fits what the company's operations are structured to supply. Not all revenues are equal. Some revenues will produce high profitability, and some revenues will actually degrade earnings. The differences are amazingly large. Yet very few supply chain managers systematically work to address this most important determinant of their supply chain productivity, this critical profit lever. (You might take a minute and review the sidebar in chapter 6, "The Hunt for Profits," which gives a concrete example of how to do this.)

Almost all sales compensation systems are driven by revenue maximization, or occasionally by gross profit maximization. Virtually none reflects true profitability, including the very significant operations costs present in nearly every company. This is the real cause of most poor supply chain productivity in business today, and doing something about it is simply assumed to lie outside the supply chain organization. This is the single most costly assumption a supply chain manager can make.

Faced with this reality, supply chain managers have a choice. Either they can turn inward and confine their efforts to traditional logistics matters like product flow visibility and cost control, or they can step up to the broader opportunity of maximizing their asset productivity. If they choose the latter, it will sometimes involve cost minimization, sometimes changing revenue streams, and sometimes actually increasing costs to obtain disproportional revenue increases.

However, it will always involve working intensively with counterparts across organizational boundaries to jointly create important new value.

In my discussions with supply chain executives, I have found that what they are really most concerned about is whether they are playing an important role in the strategy and direction of the business—whether they are really making a difference.

All too often, supply chain managers feel that they are overseeing a service function whose role simply is to fulfill the business that others shape and create. All too often, they feel that they are stuck trying to optimize their operations to respond to a fundamentally problematic set of business requirements. At a deep level, they are concerned with being effective, having a real impact on the company beyond meeting their cost and service targets.

## Five steps to supply chain productivity

In my experience working with effective supply chain managers, I have found that five steps are essential for supply chain managers to expand their role from cost control to supply chain productivity.

**Decide** to be responsible for supply chain productivity, the real essence of supply chain management, and not just for narrow logistics. Make the earning power of your assets a prime focus of your job. Look around the company and see who's involved in this process. The odds are that your company does not have an explicit profitability management process, and asset productivity is simply—and incorrectly—assumed to be maximized if everyone makes budget.

**Analyze** your supply chain productivity. If your company doesn't have a profit-mapping process, start one. All you need to do is create a model that (1) identifies the inventory supporting each product, each order, and each customer; (2) identifies the revenues and net profit generated by each of these assets; and (3) combines these measures to create a 70 percent accurate database of ROIC for each product, order, and customer. Chapter 6, "The Hunt for Profits," will guide you in this process.

The database will show you the asset productivity of the different elements of your supply chain. With this picture, you can quickly identify some particularly effective profit levers. Your colleagues in sales and marketing will be very interested in this information as well.

**Take the lead** in coordinating with your counterparts in sales and marketing to systematically improve ROIC. Here are a few key leverage points: (1) account selection, (2) relationship selection (arm's length versus customer operating partnership), (3) sales process selection (direct versus telesales), (4) service differentiation (different order cycles for different customers and products), (5) product life cycle management (knowing where and when to stop holding inventory on a late life cycle product), and (6) product flow management. Just review the chapters in sections 2 and 3 of this book.

These key elements come together in the account planning and account management process. It is critical that you get involved in this process, and not simply cede it to the sales and marketing groups. Account planning and account management, *more than any other process*, will determine your supply chain productivity—and your operating costs. If you are not centrally involved in this process, you will be stuck in reactive mode.

**Differentiate** your company from your competitors' using supply chain capabilities. This will have a big impact on both supply chain productivity and company profitability.

Today, most companies are reducing their supplier bases by 40 to 60 percent. The suppliers that remain see huge, immediate increases in market share. The key element that determines which supplier gets this increase and which supplier loses it all is the supplier's ability to create positive change within the customer. Winning suppliers know how to increase their customers' internal profitability. This is the fastest and surest way to increase market share today, and it is *first and foremost a supply chain management issue*.

Today, most companies are reducing their supplier bases

by 40 to 60 percent. The suppliers that remain see

huge, immediate increases in market share.

▼

Leading supply chain managers have detailed knowledge of their customers' internal processes and economics. They have the capability to work with their best customers to develop customer operating partnerships that increase the customers' inventory turns, move products directly to needed locations, and provide information that makes the customers much more profitable. These are all supply chain capabilities, and they create surprisingly large revenue increases, cost reductions, and lasting strategic advantage.

These customer relationships are crucial generators of revenues, profits, and asset productivity, yet how many supply chain managers view systematically creating them as a true centerpiece of their jobs?

**Manage change** both internally and externally. Maximizing supply chain productivity requires not only good information but, most important, great change management. Within your company, this means developing a detailed, holistic picture of ROIC, and engaging your counterparts to join you in a coordinated program of profitability management and ROIC improvement.

Within your key customers, it means much the same thing: developing an understanding of the *customer's* internal profitability and the *customer's* internal ROIC on your products, and engaging key customer managers throughout the customer organization in an effective program of change and improvement. In essence, you are creating a program of profitability management *within your key customers*.

## Managing supply chain productivity

Ultimately, shifting from logistics to supply chain management involves changing your perspective:

▶ Broaden your view from narrow cost control to supply chain productivity.
▶ Broaden your management focus from supply chain operations to overall company activities.
▶ Broaden your playing field from your own company's operations to address your customers' and suppliers' operations as well.

In short, *draw a bigger box around your job.*

More than anything else, supply chain productivity requires that supply chain managers become experts at profitability management and change management. Armed with these capabilities, supply chain managers can step up to the vital task of shaping their companies' future.

**1.** Think about the world of difference between logistics and supply chain management. The former focuses on narrow cost control, while the latter encompasses the asset productivity of the whole supply chain.

**2.** The surest way to increase supply chain productivity is for your sales reps to bring in business that fits your operations capabilities. The best way to rapidly increase sales is for your supply chain group to create customer operating partnerships with your best customers. Yet in most companies, sales and operations are separated by high partitions, and linked only through global budgets. This is one of the most problematic legacies of the Age of Mass Markets.

**3.** The best way to integrate your company is to create an overarching measure—profitability, or ROIC—that enables all relevant managers to coordinate with one another to maximize your company's profitability. This is essential for successful management in the Age of Precision Markets.

**4.** Do you have ROIC information that allows you to collaborate with your counterparts to manage your company's profitability? If not, why not take the lead in developing it? It doesn't take very long to develop this information at 70 percent accuracy—which is enough to really improve your results.

## What's Next

The first two sections of this book respectively explain how to think for profit and sell for profit. This section tells you how to operate for profit. The final section of the book describes how to lead for profit by building a high-performance, profit-maximizing organization.

# SECTION 4

# LEADING FOR PROFIT

# INTRODUCTION

**FIRST AND FOREMOST**, companies are about people. Management effectiveness is the ultimate key to maximizing your profitability and company performance. Without top management leadership and an effective management team, all profit initiatives will fall short.

The key building blocks of an effective profitability management process are change management, middle management excellence, and personal leadership. The chapters in this section explain how to manage paradigmatic change (both within your own company and in your customers and suppliers), how to build a strong capable middle management team, and how to manage culture change in your company. The section concludes by explaining how an individual can become an effective manager and leader.

## How can a manager lead paradigmatic change?

**Chapter 26, The Challenges of Paradigmatic Change,** describes the nature of quantum change, and explains how you can effectively transform your organization in advance of crisis.

**Chapter 27, Managing Change: Garden, Sand Castle, Mountain, Spaghetti,** describes the major types of change management, and outlines the measures needed to successfully accomplish each one.

**Chapter 28, The Effective Change Manager,** explains how you can develop the capability to be effective at managing sweeping, positive change.

## How can a manager create major change in a customer or supplier?

**Chapter 29, Create Paradigmatic Change in Your Customers,** describes the process of rolling out a major process innovation that involves significant customer change, and gives an example of a company that had difficulties doing this.

**Chapter 30, Manage Your Suppliers as a Resource,** tells you how to tap into your suppliers' deep expertise in order to change and improve your own company's profitability and positioning.

## What is the most effective way to develop a great middle management team?

**Chapter 31, Managing at the Right Level,** describes a situation that is all too common in business, in which managers are performing the work that should be done by those below them. This paralyzes a company, and prevents it from maximizing its profitability.

**Chapter 32, Middle Management Excellence,** outlines the key steps in developing a strong, effective, proactive middle management team.

**Chapter 33, Action-Training for Culture Change,** describes how one company developed a very effective action-training program to respond to changing industry conditions, and in the process created paradigmatic culture change throughout the company.

## How can an individual become a great manager and leader?

**Chapter 34, New CIO Role: Change Warrior,** tells how CIOs have to develop a fundamentally new role in their companies as their job shifts from using technology to improve existing processes to deploying technology that enables their companies to operate in fundamentally new ways.

**Chapter 35, Masterful Management,** describes the core capabilities of an effective manager, and tells you how to develop them.

**Chapter 36, The Essence of Leadership,** outlines the essential characteristics of leadership, and explains how to become an effective leader.

*Paradigmatic change has the potential to create major profitability gains in a business, but it requires careful management to pull off effectively.*

# 26

---

# THE CHALLENGES OF PARADIGMATIC CHANGE

▼

**I RECENTLY RECEIVED** an e-mail from a former student who is working on changing the supply chain of a major company. She noted that, to her surprise, the "hard" issues are relatively easy to solve, but the "soft" issues are the hardest to overcome. What did she mean?

My correspondent was involved in trying to reframe her company's basic business practices to improve its profitability. She was finding that defining a new system for linking the company with its vendors was intellectually challenging, but solvable. The real difficulty lay in getting the managers involved to change their longstanding way of doing business, and accept the new system.

The process of managing large-scale change that my student faced is one of the most important, and potentially rewarding, challenges of a manager's career. Several years ago, GE completed an important internal study in which it analyzed a number of projects, and related return on investment to project size. It found that really large investments had much higher returns than smaller investments. The reason was that the larger projects created fundamental improvements in ways of doing business, producing paradigmatic change. On the other hand, the smaller projects yielded respectable but lower returns, as managers invested in tuning up their existing business processes, resulting in only incremental change.

This led GE's top management to initiate a culture shift that challenged managers who asked for capital for particular projects to return in a few weeks with a proposal to spend a much greater amount to really change and improve their businesses.

## Paradigmatic change

Paradigmatic change is very important in business. It has the potential to create major profitability gains and to renew a company, but it is very difficult to accomplish in the absence of a business crisis. Managing paradigmatic change is fundamentally different from managing incremental improvements to the existing business.

When I am asked for material to read on managing paradigmatic change, I respond with a very unlikely source: *The Structure of Scientific Revolutions,* by the late Thomas Kuhn. This book is a staple at the doctoral level in business schools, but it rarely appears on popular-reading bookshelves, and it is not about business at all.

This book grew out of Kuhn's research on the history of science. Before Kuhn's work, the prevailing view of knowledge building in science was that it was a linear process centered on the scientific method. According to the traditional view of this process, scientists develop hypotheses, test them, and in this way build knowledge. However, when Kuhn looked closely at what actually happened, he found that nothing could be further from the truth.

Instead, Kuhn found that knowledge building in science was a process that was marked by occasional great lurches forward. In fact, most science took place within the context of a broad, tacit, explanatory framework that he called a paradigm. The Aristotelian system that theorized that the sun revolved around the earth is an example of a paradigm.

Within a paradigm, science is determined in a way that is consistent with the paradigm. The experiments that count as useful are the ones that support the paradigm, and this typically involves refining and extending it. Kuhn calls this normal science. The community of scientists forms a culture around the paradigm. They reject experiments and ostracize experimenters who are at odds with it. A prime example is Galileo, who bucked the existing paradigm and narrowly escaped with his life.

After a period of time, experimental evidence begins to show that the prevailing paradigm is insufficient. Kuhn calls these anomalies. What happens? The evidence is ignored, and the community of scientists goes along as if nothing had happened. Over time, more and more evidence accumulates, and still it is ignored.

Finally, a scientist will propose a comprehensive new paradigm. This new theoretical framework will be accepted *only* if it fully explains everything that the old paradigm explained *as well as* the anomalies. Moreover, the new paradigm must specify enough detail to be useful as a guide to normal science. Even then, the process of change is profoundly political, not logical, with more open-minded scientists gravitating toward the new paradigm, while others continue to cling to the old.

This is what happened when Copernicus's paradigm supplanted Aristotle's, and when Einstein's supplanted Newton's. This is paradigmatic change. Kuhn relates the change process blow-by-blow.

## Lessons from scientific revolutions

What Kuhn found in science plays out in business every day. A manager seeking to create paradigmatic change, whether in market focus or vendor integration or manufacturing process, will hit a wall of "the way we do business" that is analogous to Kuhn's paradigm.

> What Kuhn found in science plays out
>
> in business every day.

▼

As in Kuhn's process, simply showing evidence that a fundamentally different way of doing business would provide higher returns will not be sufficient to motivate paradigmatic change unless a dire crisis is clearly imminent. It will be ignored much as Kuhn's anomalies were ignored.

Consider the origin of Dell's famous make-to-order system, described in an earlier chapter. Dell's spectacularly successful new business system did not grow out of a whiteboard session showing such high prospective returns that the company was convinced to change its business.

In fact, Dell had produced a very unsuccessful PC model, and had lost so much money it was on the verge of running out of cash. The only way to raise money to keep the company alive was to liquidate all of its inventory as soon as possible. The operating officers were ordered to find a way to run the company without inventory. In the process of complying with this seemingly impossible task, they developed the now-famous make-to-order system. The key point is that in the absence of a life-threatening crisis, the management team surely would have rejected the new system out of hand.

## Change before crisis

How can a manager create paradigmatic change *before* crisis? Kuhn's observations, coupled with the experience of many businesses, suggest three key points of leverage:

**First, make a comprehensive case for upcoming disaster if paradigmatic change does not take place.** It is not sufficient to provide evidence that the old business practices are not working well (like declining sales to key customers), or that an alternative would produce better returns (like shifting resources to penetrate a new set of accounts). There must be a strong case that there is no choice but to change: there may not be a burning platform, but the clock is ticking. Otherwise, the organization will resist the needed change until there really is no choice, which most often is too late.

**Second, develop a comprehensive, concrete specification of the new paradigm.** People won't change current practices based on an abstraction. The new paradigm must be specific enough to guide the day-to-day actions that must take place within it, along with a feasible pathway of change.

Here, showcase projects are particularly valuable. A showcase is a demonstration of a new way of doing business without a previous commitment to accept the change. For example, early in the development of the very innovative customer operating partnership in the hospital supply industry (described in chapter 17, "Profit from Customer Operating Partnerships"), a showcase system was set up in a small Canadian regional hospital. This concrete working example provided enormously powerful evidence that the new system was feasible. This small hospital became the most frequently visited hospital in North America, as hospital CEOs from all over came to see the new process in action.

This small hospital became the most frequently visited

hospital in North America.

▼

Similarly, a forward-thinking auto parts distributor maintains a policy of constant experimentation. The company's management always tries new ways of doing business on one or another of its hundreds of stores. When an experiment is successful, the practice is rapidly spread; when it is not, another experiment quickly takes its place. In all, not more than one-tenth of a percent of the business is at risk at any one time, yet this process allows the company to innovate extremely rapidly and effectively.

Here's an important tip from experience: pick a relatively small customer (or supplier) who is very capable and innovative, and for whom you are an important supplier (or customer). The key is to find a situation in which all the elements are most favorable for successful innovation, and to resist the temptation to approach your biggest customer until you have perfected the new initiative. The same advice holds for selecting a product line, sales territory, or distribution center for a showcase of a new profit lever or an innovative business process.

**Third, be patient and wait until the time is right.** Paradigmatic change requires a unique set of conditions. Sometimes, the organization will reject the change several times before a critical mass of managers finally recognizes the need for change and the utility of the new paradigm. It is very important to be relentless and unwavering about the need for change, but flexible in your timing. Focus on winning the war, not every battle.

Beyond this, it makes a big difference to view the change process as analogous to climbing a tall mountain, and structure a set of "base camps" along the way. This will allow your organization to move through the change process in a systematic, effective way. (The next chapter explains in more detail how to do this.)

## Lessons for top managers

Top managers have an extremely important role to play in creating paradigmatic change. They can take measures to make their companies' cultures much more change-friendly. By encouraging showcases and experimentation, rather than rigid adherence to standard practices, they can accelerate innovation.

■ ■ ■

A company's most important asset is a management
team inclined to learn quickly by thinking and doing,
embedded in an open-minded culture.

▼

Organizational culture tends to reflect the actions and attitudes of the leaders. By being open-minded about the need to experiment with fundamentally new ways of doing business, and by viewing small setbacks as learning and not failure, a top manager can condition his or her company's culture to respond positively to paradigmatic change.

A company's most important asset is a management team inclined to learn quickly by thinking and doing, embedded in an open-minded culture. In the long run, this is the best way for insightful top managers to ensure their companies' success.

---

### THINGS TO THINK ABOUT

**1.** It is certainly possible to lead a program of paradigmatic change, but the process is completely different from managing incremental improvements to your business.

**2.** Have you hit the wall of resistance to changing the "way we do business"? If so, you're not alone. Among my clients and former students, this is the biggest problem innovative managers face.

**3.** Among the key components in the paradigmatic change process, the one that is most often overlooked is the need to specify a new paradigm (way of doing business) in enough detail to guide your company's day-to-day business activities. People won't let go of the old way of doing things until they are completely clear about how to do things differently.

**4.** One of the most important top management tasks is creating an organization that is conditioned to change, and which continually seeks and embraces positive change. This is the "holy grail" of sustained business success, and the key to enduring high levels of profitability.

# What's Next

This section is about leading for profit. The first five chapters focus on managing change—both internal change and change in your customers and suppliers. The subsequent three chapters tell you how to build the organizational capabilities that are critical to profitability management. The final three chapters explain how to be an effective manager and leader.

*In becoming an effective manager of change, it helps to think in terms of metaphors. Are you tending your change initiatives like a gardener, or are you snagged in spaghetti?*

# 27

## MANAGING CHANGE: GARDEN, SAND CASTLE, MOUNTAIN, SPAGHETTI

▼

**WHEN I THINK** of managing change, four images come to mind: a garden, a sand castle, a mountain, and a plate of spaghetti. Let me explain.

### A garden

The first image of change is a garden. My mother-in-law, who is very wise, introduced me to this image. She said that a marriage is like a garden. A garden requires constant care and work, or it gets overgrown with weeds.

As a gardener, I know this is true. Behind every beautiful garden is an amazing amount of hard work: planting, fertilizing, and endless weeding. And a really great gardener always contemplates how to improve the garden. He or she periodically changes the garden's look and composition, moving plants around, introducing new ones, and taking old ones away.

Two key points emerge here. First, a garden that isn't getting better gets worse very fast. Second, only when a garden is good can the gardener see how to make it great, and only when it is great can he or she see how to make it truly outstanding.

Does your business look like this? Are you constantly weeding, adjusting, and improving it? Or does your portfolio of accounts, products, and services simply reflect "the way we do business"?

A great business, like a great garden, requires constant work even to stay the same. An essential element, one that is very often missing, is the process of constant weeding. As the business evolves and its markets change, accounts, products, and services lose their profitability and potential. They must be weeded away. Only if this weeding process is a constant, ongoing, integral part of the business can you start and grow new high-potential initiatives to keep your company healthy.

> A great business, like a great garden, requires constant
>
> work even to stay the same.

▼

At Dell, for example, the process of "sunsetting" products (ending their lifecycle) is considered one of the company's most important strengths. It makes all the difference between success and failure. Contrast this with a company in another business whose CEO confided that the product managers were always "one day away from profitability, and one SKU away from greatness."

The failure to constantly weed leads to the situation of many companies in which 30 to 40 percent of the company is unprofitable by any measure. Once a company reaches this state, it is hard to give up revenues from the unproductive part of the business, even if profits will improve dramatically. Instead, it is far better to institute an ongoing system of profitability management and constant weeding.

## A sand castle

The second image is a sand castle. Think about the process of building a sand castle. First you pile up sand. Every time you pile the sand higher, some of it trickles down, you pile it up again, and it trickles down again. After a while, the sand castle takes shape. Sometimes, a section falls away. You go to work fixing and changing that section: you pile the sand, and it trickles down until you've replaced it. Finally, your sand castle is complete. It may look very different from the one you started building because you had to change your vision of what it would look like in response to what happened during the building process.

Contrast this with the business case process in most companies. Most business cases—requests for financial investment in a project—require a manager to identify a clear set of costs, a clear process for developing value, and a clear payoff. A business case of this sort makes sense in situations where the facts are well known, like investing in a new machine for an existing process. The problem is that the same methodology is often erroneously applied to situations in which key elements are *not knowable* at the time. These situations look more like building sand castles.

I recall advising several major telecommunications and other high-tech companies about investment in new technologies in the early 1990s. It always amazed me how our most important innovations could not have passed the business case test at the time they were developed.

Think about cell phones and PCs. Could you seriously see a major company deciding to develop a cell phone network so your teenager could call friends across the high school campus? Imagine presenting a business case to develop PCs based on the assertion that even retired people would use them once or twice a day for e-mail instead of using the phone. What is the implicit value of the customer's time? What market numbers would you use? Who would believe them?

It always amazed me how our most important

innovations could not have passed the business

case test at the time they were developed.

▼

Instead, the process of getting these enormous businesses off the ground was like that of building sand castles—piling up sand, watching it trickle down, piling up more sand, experiencing major setbacks—until the market took shape and the investments were finally clearly justified. Here, it was necessary to "prime the pump" on market development for an extended period of time, even without a clear, well-grounded value-creation process and calculation of returns. And it was crucial to accept constant minor and occasional major setbacks, and to view them as an integral, natural part of the market development process.

In an ambiguous, uncertain situation, there is necessarily a huge amount of probing the potential market and learning by doing. In fact, the really critical issue is how fast and effectively you can figure out how the market will evolve.

If a market is in your company's strategic sweet spot, it's best to start piling up the sand and to remember that setbacks are a natural part of the process. If you let business cases decide these critical matters, the market will move right past your company.

## A mountain

The third image of change is a mountain. Think about climbing a very high mountain. The most essential part of the process is establishing a set of viable base camps along the ascent route. This involves identifying proper locations, organizing and coordinating logistics, provisioning enough supplies not just for the ascent but for the descent as well, allowing for time to acclimate to the altitude, and identifying alternative routes between base camps so that the climbers can react to the conditions they experience.

By contrast, many large-scale change management processes in companies focus primarily on the objectives and payoffs, and not enough on the process of getting there. Three common errors occur.

First, some teams try to reach the ultimate objective of the change in one step rather than establishing base camps along the way. This is neither desirable nor feasible. It is generally necessary to try out new ways of doing business before settling on a final formulation. At the same time, different business functions are capable of changing at different rates. They need base camps in the change process in order to work out new ways of operating and to get realigned with one another, or performance may suffer.

Second, the teams may mistake the first base camp for the final objective. Change, like ascending a mountain, is daunting and grueling. There is a strong tendency to perceive progress toward a goal as achieving the goal. All too many change programs lack a clear definition of how much change is enough.

Third, teams sometimes reach an early base camp, and get discouraged by how much change they have left. This can occur if they fail to see, or fail to believe, that the change process is well conceived and well organized. In a well-structured change process, they will have an opportunity at each base camp to get acclimated and adjust to their new situation before moving on to the next.

The underlying problem in many large-scale organizational change programs is that managers view the change process as all or nothing.

They focus on selecting the peaks and envisioning the view from the top. In fact, the process of organizing and managing change, establishing sound base camps along the route, makes all the difference between success and failure.

## A plate of spaghetti

The final image of change is a plate of spaghetti. This is what you get if you neglect the other three.

All too many managers have a plate full of change initiatives, each of which has intrinsic merit, but together look like a plate of spaghetti. It doesn't have to be this way.

Most change initiatives fall into one of three categories: constant weeding, strategic market development, and large-scale organizational change. Each has a different nature, a different management and control process, and a different sort of outcome. All three types of initiatives are necessary, and together they enable the effective manager to deploy a program of renewing change that positions the company for today, tomorrow, and the evolving future.

> All too many managers have a plate full of change
> initiatives, each of which has intrinsic merit, but
> together look like a plate of spaghetti.

> The most essential part of the process is establishing a
> set of viable base camps along the ascent route.

▼

**1.** In managing change, it is very helpful to think carefully about the three major types of change—constant weeding, strategic market development, and large-scale organizational change. Each is very different from the others, and each requires a unique management process.

**2.** Constant weeding is often overlooked. This is where your sea of red ink comes from. Profitability management is the way to align your company so the weeds don't grow in the first place.

**3.** Business cases are completely inappropriate for strategic market development. This is the core reason why so many great companies have so much trouble when their markets change, and why smaller competitors are so much more agile.

**4.** Most managers want to lead large-scale change. This is where you make your mark and show that you are worthy of moving to the next level. Yet many managers fail because they do not analyze the *process of change* carefully enough. The key to success is defining a well-planned series of base camps along the pathway of change.

## What's Next

The first chapter of this section describes the process of paradigmatic change. This chapter explains how to manage the different types of change. The next chapter tells you how to be an effective change manager.

*Managers who rise to run a company choose to maximize the long-run profitability of the company by adroitly managing fundamental, paradigmatic change.*

## 28

## THE EFFECTIVE CHANGE MANAGER

▼

**WHAT WOULD YOU** do in this situation?

You've been given the choice assignment to set sales goals for an important market segment, but your analysis convinces you that the sales process itself is flawed. It is generating a large amount of unprofitable business, and it needs sweeping changes.

How would you convince the managers and division heads that the jobs they have been doing for years were unproductive and they never saw it? What would you do if they stonewalled you? Who would you call? Who would you write to? What would you say? How could you overcome this seemingly no-win situation?

Every week I get e-mails from readers, former students, executive program participants, and client managers asking questions like these. They see a better way to do things, but feel frustrated about getting the company to change. And a manager with great insights who can't produce successful change is ineffective.

Here's another way to frame the question: what is your responsibility as an employee?

This question may sound simple and self-evident, but, like all basic questions, it really is neither. Is the answer doing what your manager specifies? Even if there is a better way to do it, and your manager won't budge? Even if you feel that the company needs something different, but you are told that your job is to do things the way they have always been done?

The answer I give is that your responsibility is to maximize the long-run profitability of the company. Understanding what this means is critical to managing change effectively.

In most companies, you must balance long-term renewing change with the need to deliver the regular, short-term results your shareholders require. You might think of this as "changing the airplane's propeller in midflight." Ultimately, managing this balance successfully is the key to rapid career advancement, personal job satisfaction, and successful profitability management.

## Embedded business practices

First and foremost, companies are about people, in the sense that asset productivity, financial results, and all other measures are the result of what the people in a company believe, think, and do. People are able to work in organizations because they internalize well-structured ways to think about things and do things, like knowing which customers the company sells to and how it sells to them. These constructs become very firmly rooted in an organization and are very difficult to change. Often, they are so pervasive that they simply disappear from sight and operate at a tacit level as "the way we do business."

This actually is a strength, not a weakness. Without these constructs, companies would be chaotic, with everyone essentially paralyzed trying to figure out what to do next. However, times change and, over time, companies need to change in response. The problem is that these constructs are very stubborn and difficult to change. This is one of the most important sources of embedded unprofitability.

Most managers run into trouble because they are used to managing tactical change—tuning up existing business processes—and they try to apply the same techniques to more fundamental change. This is the problem the manager faced in the situation described at the beginning of this chapter. As you turn from managing tactical change to creating paradigmatic change, your change management process needs to be fundamentally different.

The first chapter of this section describes the importance and nature of paradigmatic change, transforming a company's tacit set of policies and constructs. It also offers some guiding principles for change management. This chapter focuses on the day-to-day activities you need to adopt in order to be effective at changing "the way we do things."

## Changing "the way we do things"

Managing quantum change is a complex, daunting process. That is why it is so important to bear in mind that the true north in any management process is to maximize the long-run profitability of the company. In order to reach this objective, a manager can frame an effective change process using seven principles.

> The "true north" in any management process is to maximize the long-run profitability of the company.

▼

**Identify the underlying problem.** A company's set of policies and core organizational constructs typically reflect the company's history. If you really want to understand most companies, look at their situation five to ten years ago. What they're doing today probably is an extension of the policies they developed in response to the earlier situation. This set of policies exists at a tacit level, generally unseen, rarely examined, but pervasively influential.

By analyzing this tacit set of policies and constructs, a manager can identify why a particular disconnect occurs between "the way we do things" and what is needed today. Chances are that the old policy is not "bad"; it is simply obsolete. If you can explain systematically why changing business needs caused the gap to develop, the change process becomes depoliticized and change becomes much more acceptable.

For example, a nationally known specialty retailer had been dominant in its business for a long time until a few years ago. Because this retailer had such a large market share, and so many stores in convenient locations, it was the first place most customers shopped. In this situation, the retailer's merchants (the managers who decide on products and inventory) did not have to make difficult decisions in areas like product life-cycle management and store assortment planning that a retail merchant in a hotly competitive business would have to make every day. Consequently, they became somewhat complacent. They mistakenly assumed that sales were strong because they were so good at merchandising, not because the retailer had so many well-placed stores. As time went on, hungry new competitors with really capable merchants entered the market, and the retailer lost ground quickly.

The underlying problem was the growing disconnect between the retailer's weak merchandising decision-making processes, which were adequate in its earlier period of market dominance, and the company's new business needs when the market became hotly contested. Because these processes were so fundamental and pervasive, the situation was literally invisible to most managers. In a surprisingly short period of time, the company was fighting for its life.

**Make relationships before you need them.** This is absolutely critical. The underlying problem in the situation described at the beginning of the chapter is that once the analytical process was completed, it was almost too late to start the change process.

It is very difficult for busy managers to take the time to develop relationships with their key counterparts in other departments of the company before the relationships are needed. Yet this is precisely the most effective precondition for successful management of large-scale change.

There is an old adage in ship chartering that you shouldn't talk business until the third lunch. There is a strong grain of truth in this, and it holds an important key to effective management. Effective relationships are best developed in social situations, like over lunch or at after-work get-togethers, not in structured business meetings. In an informal context, you can get to know your counterpart's hopes and concerns. With this knowledge, you can find ways to support your counterparts, and even to frame your initiatives into win-win situations where you can gain traction by incorporating their change initiatives into yours.

Effective relationships are best developed

in social situations.

▼

With a strong network of relationships, and a history of working cooperatively to help others in their own change programs, you will have the receptive ears and broad support you need throughout the company to effect major, lasting change.

**Involve others in the analysis.** In tactical change projects, managers often do the analysis themselves, or use a small team. Then they produce a business case, and use it to convince others to accept the results. This doesn't work in paradigmatic change. In large-scale change projects, it is mandatory to involve a broad range of counterpart managers in the analysis. This is true for two reasons.

First, the other managers may well have important needs and perspectives that have to be accommodated for the initiative to succeed. When you incorporate these, your project will be much more effective.

Second, they need to be immersed in the data that show the need for sweeping change. They need time and understanding in order to break down their tacit constructs and reconstruct a new way of doing things. Unless they have gone through this conversion process, most managers won't be willing to change the fundamental way they do business—even if they understand intellectually the need for change. Importantly, top management will be very sensitive to the depth and degree of buy-in of those who will have to live with the change, and this will have a big impact on whether or not you get executive agreement to move forward.

**Create a showcase.** A showcase project, described in the first chapter of this section, is a limited-scope exploration of possible new ways of doing business. In the case of the new sales process, it may well be possible to experiment with new ways of doing business in one of the company's smaller territories, or in a few smaller accounts. This allows you to develop new business processes, to learn by doing, without endangering the company's results. And you can take your colleagues to see it and "kick the tires."

**Win the war, not every battle.** Individual business decisions are almost always part of a series, rather than stand-alone, make-it-or-break-it situations.

In a paradigmatic change initiative, timing is everything. It may take a few decisions that go against the direction you are advocating to produce the evidence you need to convince people that your direction is correct. In the process of educating people, it simply takes time and persistence for a new way of thinking to sink in.

**Keep several balls in play.** Change projects have their own rhythm. Sometimes they stall simply because the organization is not ready to digest the change. If you try to force the issue, the organization will turn on you.

The key is to have several change management projects going at the same time. That way, if one stalls, you can try to move another up the field. By the time that project stalls, the first may well be ready to move forward. Having several projects going at the same time takes the pressure off you to force a decision before its time.

It is especially effective to develop in parallel several change projects focused on different aspects of the same underlying problem. That way, when you achieve success in one area, it will enhance the prospects of success in the others.

**Make change stick.** At the end of the day, the acid test for whether change will stick is whether top management is willing to adjust the company's key behavioral drivers—planning, resource allocation, and, most important, compensation—to move the company in the new direction. If you can change these, you will cement the new paradigm in place. If not, the company will revert to the old way of doing things.

Ultimately, the managers who rise to run the company are those who choose to maximize the long-run profitability of the company by becoming proficient at managing fundamental, paradigmatic change.

---

### THINGS TO THINK ABOUT

**1.** Your prime responsibility as an employee is to maximize your company's long-run profitability. My objective in writing this book is to give you a road map of how to accomplish this.

**2.** Every company has a very strong set of embedded business practices "the way we do business"—that made great sense when they were first developed. The problem is that as the world changes, these embedded business practices stubbornly stay the same. This is the underlying source of the enormous frustration that managers experience when they attempt to lead paradigmatic change.

**3.** One of the most important things you can do to become an effective change manager is to develop relationships with your counterpart managers before you need them. This may seem like the last thing you should do when you're really busy, but these relationships will be critical to your effectiveness, and they will really pay off for a long, long time.

**4.** Relationships are best built outside regular working time, and not in routine meetings working on business problems. Think about last month. How many times did you get together with your counterparts at lunch? After work? Did you discuss business issues, or just enjoy getting to know one another and brainstorming?

## What's Next

This chapter explains how to be an effective change manager inside your company. The next two chapters tell you how to manage change in your customers and suppliers, respectively.

*Selling paradigmatic change in your organization is difficult enough, so how do you sell it to customers? Here's how to overcome three large obstacles.*

## 29

# CREATE PARADIGMATIC CHANGE IN YOUR CUSTOMERS

▼

**WHAT DO YOU** do when your customer gets your vision and agrees with your vision but won't do anything about it?

### Selling products versus selling change

I've always been struck by the vast differences between the way companies sell products and the way they sell process innovations like customer operating partnerships.

For products, the process of product development, market development, and sales has been well defined for decades. Companies do market research, match product attributes to market segments, gauge price elasticity and demand characteristics, identify early adopters, map customer buying centers, cross the chasm, and so on.

The nature of selling process innovations to customers could not be more different. The reason: selling a new product generally involves only incremental change for the customer, while selling an intercompany process innovation involves paradigmatic change on the part of the customer as well as the supplier.

Because there are few widely known tools for creating paradigmatic change in a customer, many managers treat the opportunity in an ad hoc, rather than systematic, way. Yet, it is just as feasible to systematically create fundamental change in customers as it is to sell new products to them.

Three difficulties complicate the process of selling change to a customer. First, you often have to sell the change internally to other functional groups within your own company, even while you deal with customer acceptance and change. Second, the realm of vendor-customer relations in many companies is monopolized by the sales and purchasing groups. This tends to freeze out the operations managers of both supplier and customer, who typically are the agents (and beneficiaries) of change. Third, many operations managers are not experienced in the process of relationship selling.

## Changing zero-sum into non-zero-sum relationships

As daunting as intercompany innovation is, there is great value at stake. Successful creation of customer operating partnerships, which requires paradigmatic change in customers, leads to greatly increased profitability for both parties. Effective suppliers are creating major sales and profitability gains in their best customers. This is the pot of gold at the end of the successful change process.

The underlying difficulty—and opportunity—in creating major change in a customer is the task of changing a traditional zero-sum relationship into a non-zero-sum relationship. A zero-sum relationship is one in which one side's loss is the other's gain. A non-zero-sum relationship, on the other hand, is one in which both parties can wind up better off by cooperating.

A traditional customer-supplier relationship is profoundly zero-sum in nature. I charge a higher price, my customer incurs a higher cost; I make more money, my customer makes less. This underlying motivation system typically shapes the prevailing business paradigm, "the way we do business," in both companies. This is the core impediment to creating paradigmatic change in areas like customer operating partnerships and product-flow management, which are non-zero-sum in nature and leave both parties better off. It is another problematic legacy of the Age of Mass Markets.

■ ■ ■

*A traditional intercompany supply chain is profoundly zero-sum in nature.*

▼

## The manager's story

One thoughtful manager wrote a note to me describing his successes and frustrations in creating paradigmatic change: "A lot of organizations view themselves as being nimble enough for paradigmatic change . . . only to be shut down when our customers are unwilling to change their processes even when it is the right thing to do on all fronts."

When I received this e-mail, I contacted the manager to discuss his situation. He described the business problem he faced.

This manager is in the business of transporting large sheets of glass, a product that is difficult, costly, and dangerous to handle. Through innovative research and development, the company established a new system that allows for the product to be handled much faster and more safely, saving money for the manufacturer, the transporter, and the company receiving the product. Importantly, because the traditional system is difficult and dangerous, it is hard to recruit enough skilled personnel. Consequently, the transportation companies in the business cannot offer sufficient capacity to meet their customers' needs.

Although the new system will ultimately provide high returns for the manager's company and his customers, it requires some changes in the way they handle materials. In some cases, it also requires minor adjustments to physical facilities.

When the manager, who is in charge of selling this innovation, calls on the manufacturers and receivers, these customers acknowledge the benefits and agree that the new system is better, but often decline to implement it. This is what led to the frustrated e-mail I received.

When I discussed this with the manager, it turned out that his company had developed the innovation largely internally, and that he was selling it to his customers' transportation buyers. These transportation buyers were responsible for lowering the customers' freight bills, not for lowering the cost of handling the product. The problem was that the innovative new system reduced the handling costs, which were on the customers' operations managers' budgets. The transportation buyers incurred a higher freight cost, while the operations managers gained the benefits. Even though there was a strong net benefit to the customer company, the transportation buyers resisted the change.

Successfully selling paradigmatic change to a customer requires a very different process.

## Five steps to customer paradigmatic change

Unlike product sales, selling paradigmatic process improvements requires significant time, especially in customers who are early adopters. However, once a critical mass of early adopters accepts the innovation, the sales process becomes much easier and faster. Managers can systematically create paradigmatic change in customers through a five-step sequence.

**Early relationship building.** The most important first step for operations managers faced with the task of selling an operational innovation to a customer is to develop relationships with their *operations* counterparts in the customer companies well before they are needed.

This is very difficult for many operations managers, who are very busy and focused on internal day-to-day issues. However, the most productive changes generally come from a meeting of the minds among operations counterparts in customer and supplier organizations, who understand each other's business and are professionally motivated to increase their mutual efficiency and profitability. Through the process of relationship development, operations managers will naturally identify the counterparts in the customers who are most innovative and open to change.

**Channel mapping.** Systematic channel mapping with interested customers (analyzing the costs as products move through a supply chain from supplier to customer), described in chapter 16, is important for two reasons, one obvious, the other more subtle.

First, an intercompany channel map will allow managers to systematically identify the key points of potential value that process innovations can bring to both companies.

Second, the process of channel mapping itself is critical to the sales process. In order to develop an effective channel map, a team must conduct a broad set of interviews with all of the managers who are involved with product flow throughout supplier and customer companies. These interviews will allow the team to develop important cost information, but, critically, will also allow them to gauge each interviewee's interests and willingness to change. This information is very important in framing the change process, and in deciding how the change program should best be framed (who will champion the change, and who will resist it). Also, during the give and take of a lengthy interview, the interviewer can explain the mutual benefits in a way that lays the groundwork for the later sales process.

**Showcase project.** One of the core tenets of effective paradigmatic change is to develop a comprehensive new paradigm that is better than the old one, and is detailed enough to guide practical day-to-day activities. A showcase project, described earlier in this section, is extremely useful in demonstrating this.

**Customer road map.** Market mapping is very important in rolling out new products, with managers identifying and targeting early adopters and fast followers. It is just as important in intercompany process change. Here, operations managers can gain direct lessons from best practices in product sales and marketing. The objective is to create a road map to guide the sequence of customer targeting and acceptance.

In process innovations, however, customer targeting is more complicated than in product sales. Some innovations fit only certain customers, while others may require a critical mass of geographically clustered customers. For example, the transportation company described earlier decided to target customers with facilities that needed only minor physical changes to accommodate the new handling system. The company also identified high-volume customers that were located near one another, and that shipped products to customers who were relatively close by (here, handling costs were a relatively high proportion of the total cost). For this company, the customer road map had to reflect the customers' potential payoff, willingness to adopt early, and operating fit. The objective was to build customer acceptance and market momentum by starting with the open-minded customers who could reap the biggest payoff with the least disruption.

**Patience and diversification.** Paradigmatic change is political, not simply economic. Even when a supplier makes a convincing case, internal forces within the customer may offer resistance. This can occur even when a significant group of the customer's operating managers favor the change. But customers can unexpectedly change and become receptive to the innovation. Consequently, it is important to be moving several customers through the sales process simultaneously, and to maintain a diversified portfolio of customers in various stages of the sales process. The objective is to systematically build the momentum and critical mass that lead to broad market acceptance.

*Paradigmatic change is political, not simply economic.*

▼

## Benefits of customer paradigmatic change

It is indeed possible to systematically create paradigmatic change in your customers. The process is not widely understood, but it is very feasible. For those who master the process of customer paradigmatic change, the reward will be important profitability gains and formidable barriers to entry for years to come.

---

**THINGS TO THINK ABOUT**

**1.** Selling process innovations to your customers is completely different from selling innovative products.

**2.** Process innovations, such as customer operating partnerships, that integrate your company with your premier customers give you the best of all worlds—sales increases, cost reductions, and strong barriers to entry.

**3.** Like all successful change management, it is very important to develop relationships with your *customer* counterpart managers well before they are needed.

**4.** Think about your top twenty-five customers. How many of your operations managers have deep, long-standing relationships with their customer counterparts? How often in the past three months have they met with their counterparts or talked with them on the phone? How many of these communications concerned day-to-day problem solving, and how many were simply developing friendships and brainstorming?

---

## What's Next

This chapter explains how to sell process innovations to your key customers, and how to manage change within your customers. The next chapter tells you how to manage change in your key suppliers, and how you can utilize your suppliers as a very valuable resource.

*Here's how to invite your best suppliers to suggest innovative ways to develop new customer-supplier business efficiencies.*

## 30

# MANAGE YOUR SUPPLIERS AS A RESOURCE

▼

**A FEW YEARS** ago, I visited the major appliance company that pioneered the make-to-order manufacturing system profiled in an earlier chapter.

The manager of the manufacturing unit told me that their suppliers were one of their most valuable resources, but they had not realized it until they engaged them in the new system. The company's managers were surprised that their most important suppliers quickly adopted the company's new make-to-order system in their own businesses, significantly compressing cycle time and creating new sources of profitability throughout the channel. The suppliers also suggested a number of major improvements in the manufacturer's business processes.

This discussion came to mind when I met with the senior purchasing group of a major electronic equipment manufacturer. They had identified a number of opportunities to coordinate with their suppliers in mutually beneficial ways. They felt stuck, however, because they did not have the resources to develop these initiatives to the point where they felt they could engage the suppliers.

During the course of our meeting, the purchasing group realized that they were simply assuming that they would have to create projects for their suppliers, and then give the suppliers detailed instructions on how to execute them. By the end of the meeting, a much more powerful alternative became clear: rather than developing detailed project specifications for their suppliers, they could manage their suppliers as a resource.

This process involved two tasks for the company's managers: (1) defining their needs and determining the flexibility they had in their own internal processes, and (2) inviting their best suppliers to work with them. In a novel but logical move, they invited their key suppliers to take the lead: they asked the suppliers to analyze their joint business operations and suggest new efficiencies.

Most of the equipment manufacturer's suppliers viewed the manufacturer as a very important customer, and they were always looking for new ways to create value and in return get more of the manufacturer's business. After a little investigation, it became clear that the suppliers had ample willingness and resources to devote to working on creating joint supply chain efficiencies with the manufacturer in order to reduce the manufacturer's costs, and in return sell more products. But, importantly, most of them had simply assumed that the customer would not be receptive—and the manufacturer had simply assumed that the suppliers would not be interested. This big mistake is very common in supplier management. By deciding to use these suppliers as a resource, the company's managers created a powerful process to leverage its limited supplier management resources. Both the company and its suppliers gained new possibilities for large mutual profitability gains.

## From adversary to partner

Most customer companies have implicitly adversarial, zero-sum customer-supplier relationships. They charge their supplier management and purchasing personnel with reducing product prices and disciplining suppliers by assigning penalties for problems in operating areas like on-time deliveries and order-fill rate. But few companies have reached out to their suppliers and invited them to join in identifying and removing obstacles to efficient joint business processes on both sides of the relationship.

> Few companies have reached out to their suppliers
> and invited them to join in identifying and removing
> obstacles to efficient joint business processes
> on both sides of the relationship.

▼

Innovative supplier management, using your suppliers as a resource, allows both you and your suppliers to move past the traditional adversarial relationship toward a deep partnership that creates significant profitability gains for both parties.

In Japan, supplier management is viewed as an essential management function. Suppliers are viewed as the "hidden factory." This perspective is largely missing in all too many companies.

In many companies, the cost of purchased materials and components far exceeds the internal value added through manufacturing or assembly. Yet internal company projects almost always have much better staffing and resources than supplier-related projects, even if the latter offer much higher returns.

Internal company projects, like redesigning a factory floor to streamline product movement, are generally very disciplined and comprehensive. They feature management teams that develop systematic knowledge through techniques like process mapping. Supplier management projects, by contrast, tend to be inadequately staffed, somewhat ad hoc, and rife with assumptions (e.g., the supplier is an adversary that must be disciplined) rather than the systematically developed knowledge that leads to comprehensive win-win process redesign projects. (In contrast, see chapter 17, "Profit from Customer Operating Partnerships.")

In a few industries, including, importantly, those that provide consumer products to major retailers, innovative suppliers have stepped up to the challenge. These suppliers have even gone a step further, offering different levels of customer integration to different sets of accounts, depending on account importance and account willingness and ability to innovate, as described in chapter 19, "Supply Chain Management in a Wal-Mart World."

In these sophisticated operating partnerships, the best suppliers implicitly penalize accounts that are stuck in adversarial mode, and favor those that are adept at creating win-win relationships. The best suppliers seek situations where they can be managed as a resource, creating innovations that benefit both customer and supplier. They shun situations where supplier management is a one-sided affair.

## Key success factors

Three factors are especially important in developing an effective supplier management process: partner selection, relationship building, and contracting.

**Partner selection.** Many supplier management projects fail because managers do not take adequate care in selecting the right supplier partners. In order for a deep, innovative partnership to develop, five key factors must be present:

▸ *Real new value*—this value must be measured, observed by both companies, and fairly divided, a process that is essential to keep the partnership vital, even if the original sponsoring managers exit.
▸ *Complementary specialties and capabilities*—there must be a good fit and adequate flexibility that will endure over a considerable period of time.
▸ *Strategic alignment*—developing a deep partnership with a major supplier often changes a company's relationship with competing suppliers, and the converse is true for the supplier.
▸ *Willingness to partner*—there must be a lack of internal organizational conflict on both sides of the relationship.
▸ *Ability to implement*—both companies need to qualify each other to ensure that they both have the ability to follow through on their intentions over a significant period of time.

All too often, managers initiate supplier partnership programs with the first supplier that approaches them, whether or not the supplier fits and is well qualified to follow through. More often than not, this is a prelude to early failure, and a highly visible early failure can stop a supplier-partnership initiative dead in its tracks. Partner selection is far too important not to be managed thoughtfully and proactively.

**Relationship building.** Relationship building requires finesse and understanding. Often, it takes a few months to get past festering old issues. Here's what one senior vice president observed: "Patience and persistence are the cornerstones of building a relationship. Both companies have to learn each other's business."

Some managers assume that they have to create an atmosphere of mutual trust before these partnerships can be established. This is not necessarily the case. In customer-supplier relationships that have long been characterized by adversarial tensions, the companies may choose to enter into close, cooperative operating partnerships because they recognize the mutual benefits. They start with vigilant trust, and over time develop deeper trust as they recognize that nothing can be gained by taking advantage of each other.

**Contracting.** Once an innovative partnership is developed, contracting is very important. Developing an effective contract is as much an art as a science, because a productive relationship should and will evolve in new, mutually beneficial ways. Effective contracts are liberating, not confining.

This is a complex topic, but a few underlying principles provide directional guidance. A good contract will have effective incentives for both parties to continue to deepen the relationship and to find new ways to create mutual value over time. In addition, the contract should have a "migration out" provision that will specify how to restore the status quo if the relationship ends and a new partner needs to be obtained.

> Effective contracts are liberating, not confining.

▼

In many situations, it is especially fruitful to scan your suppliers' supply networks to see if there is an opportunity to get involved in raw material or component purchases for your suppliers in order to lower costs or ensure supply continuity and availability. For example, several manufacturers make agreements with key suppliers in which the manufacturer assumes the risk of the suppliers' advance purchase of certain costly materials. As another example, a producer of electronic devices included its suppliers on its plastics master contracts in certain cases where the suppliers alone did not have sufficient volume to secure low prices and responsive terms. The company noted that it was the ultimate purchaser of these materials, and the plastics supplier agreed to give the same low prices on all materials that ultimately fed into the company's products. This had a big impact on the company's costs and profitability.

## Hidden resource

Your suppliers can be your most valuable hidden resource. If your supplier management function is adversarial in tone, your suppliers will respond in kind. But if your supplier management function sets its sights on innovation and value creation, you can find a clear pathway to significant profit improvement and success.

■  ■  ■

**1.** The choice of which supplier to recruit as a partner is critical, especially for your early initiatives.

**2.** Contracts should be structured to build trust, and they should create a process that continually spawns innovative, mutually beneficial profitability improvements.

**3.** Are your supplier relationships basically adversarial or constructive? Do you have an explicit process to penalize your suppliers for deficient performance? Do you have a joint quality process with these same suppliers to work together to identify and eliminate the underlying causes of the problems?

**4.** Suppliers can be a great resource for insightful managers. In the past three months, how often did your company ask your key suppliers for help in improving your joint business processes, or in reducing your cost and improving your profitability? How often did you ask your key suppliers how you could improve *their* efficiency and profitability?

## What's Next

This chapter, along with the four chapters that preceded it, explains how to lead and manage paradigmatic change. The next three chapters describe how to build a high-performance organization that is tuned and conditioned to maximize your company's profitability.

*In many organizations, managers manage one level too low.*
*And this leads to organizational gridlock, making it difficult*
*to create paradigmatic change.*

# 31

# MANAGING AT THE RIGHT LEVEL

▼

**ARE YOU MANAGING** one level too low?

Many managers are frustrated by the difficulty of engaging their colleagues in the paradigmatic change that creates major profitability increases. Very often, the root problem is that they are managing one level too low.

Several years ago, the CEO of a major telecommunications company was disturbed by the seeming inability of his company's managers to initiate and manage renewing change. The company was facing new competitors and major market changes, and it was imperative to respond with major improvements in operational efficiency, market development, and competitive positioning.

Yet he perceived that his managers were mired in day-to-day operational details and didn't have time to conceive and manage fundamental change. Moreover, he felt that they had a "victim" mentality, in which they observed their organizational gridlock in the face of competitive encroachment and felt unable to break out of the bind.

When I looked at the organization and met with the managers, it was clear that they had a problem—a problem I've seen in many organizations, both before and since. Each manager was doing the job that should have been done by the manager below. The vice presidents were functioning as directors, the directors as managers, and the managers as supervisors.

Managers at multiple levels throughout the company were focused on the same set of work, and most did not trust their subordinates to perform without close supervision. When I looked closely, a surprisingly large proportion of the subordinates' work consisted of gathering information to answer managers' questions, not actually getting something done.

This was so pervasive that nobody saw it, and it was paralyzing the company.

## Managing effectively

It is surprisingly natural to manage one level too low. Managers are promoted because they are good at their jobs, so it is most comfortable to continue managing in the way that was successful in the past. Importantly, newly promoted managers are rarely explicitly retrained and reoriented to understand how to manage differently at the new level. Most often, it is simply assumed that they will figure it out.

> It is surprisingly natural to manage one level too low.

▼

Yet, managing appropriately at different levels of an organization requires very different skills, activities, and time horizons, because the objective of management changes radically. Managers who recognize these differences succeed in their new positions and rise rapidly in the organization. Those who do not remain mired in the day-to-day, often feeling victimized and helpless, and not really understanding why.

Managers at different levels of a company have fundamentally different jobs.

- ▶ **Managers** oversee and operate functional areas within departments. They are responsible for efficient execution and process improvements, and they generally operate in a relatively short-term time frame.
- ▶ **Directors** are department heads. They are responsible for overseeing the efficiency and development of the staff of their departments. But this is only half of their job. The other half is a

combination of restructuring their departments' work for major improvements, and coordinating with their counterparts in other departments to jointly improve the company's profitability. Note: *jointly improve* is very different from *jointly manage*. Here, the time frame of management is primarily medium-term.

▶ **Vice presidents** are responsible for the company's future. They should spend *most* of their time working with their counterparts to develop and oversee sweeping programs of profitability improvement and renewing change. This involves gauging and understanding profitability patterns, market opportunities, and management effectiveness. Vice presidents should not be focused on managing the company as it is today, but rather on creating a fundamentally new and better company. This involves close coordination and teamwork, and a long-run perspective.

Vice presidents should not be focused on managing the company as it is today, but rather on creating a fundamentally new and better company.

▼

This may sound obvious, but try a mental exercise. Imagine you have a video of the work each manager in your company performed last week. You give this video to an outside observer who simply counts the minutes each manager spent on each sort of activity described above.

What would the summary chart look like? How much time would managers at each level have spent on change initiatives aimed at major profitability improvement versus managing the day-to-day? This quick diagnostic will tell you whether they are managing at the right level.

Recently, I had dinner with a top manager of a well-known multibillion-dollar company. He shared his concerns about his company's managers. The company's operations department had a tradition of largely promoting from within. Many of the managers were very experienced at running their day-to-day operations, but they had difficulty focusing on process improvements that changed the basic nature of the business. In essence, he was describing an organization in which everyone managed one level too low.

Interestingly, in this company, this problem did not occur across the board. The sales and marketing managers were operating at the right levels and were being very effective. The prime problem lay in the operations department. In other companies, the situation is reversed. Often, the problem of managing one level too low can be found in some departments but not in others.

## Management-process quality

In just-in-time inventory systems, the objective is not merely to lower inventory levels per se, but rather to force the organization to stop using inventory to hide the underlying problems. Remove the inventory, and the quality problems become apparent. So do process-coordination problems. Drain the swamp, and the stumps appear.

Just as excess inventory can hide myriad process and coordination problems, managing one level too low can obscure many management-process problems. To drain the swamp, managers must refocus their attention on the level that is right for their job. Once this happens, it will be straightforward to see where corrections are needed to enable business processes to function well without higher-management intervention, and to institute lasting improvements.

If a manager is operating one level too low, the effects spread widely. Not only is the manager ineffective, so are all who must coordinate with that manager to create change. The organization quickly becomes gridlocked. And the problem is hidden: no one sees the opportunity cost of diverting management attention from new profit improvement initiatives and change management.

> If a manager is operating one level too low,
>
> the effects spread widely.
>
> ▼

This happens in company after company, and more often than not, no one realizes the tacit cause.

## Management imperatives

Throughout this book, I describe how successful managers in leading companies are surveying their markets and targeting certain accounts for the tightly coordinated relationships that rapidly increase revenues and profits, while they target other accounts for arm's-length relationships that incorporate carefully chosen profit levers.

This process requires a high degree of coordination at all levels of the company. Vice presidents have to work closely with one another to conceptualize and develop these new capabilities. Directors across the company have to work with one another to redefine market segments, target accounts, and create integrated processes for account development. Managers must become adept at working with colleagues from other departments in scatter-site operating teams.

Managing one level too low creates an insurmountable roadblock to succeeding in the new paradigm. When managers are preoccupied with the day-to-day, they lose the vision and capability to create this new way of doing business. Not only do they fail to create new efficiencies within the old way of doing business, but, more important, they lose the opportunity to succeed in the new. Their companies fall further and further behind.

## Managing management effectiveness

What can a manager do? Here are three action steps to secure your company's organizational effectiveness.

**Video** your managers, figuratively. Do this in two steps. First, have your managers list the components of their jobs and estimate the proportion of their time spent on each component. Second, have the managers actually keep time logs for a few weeks to check their perceptions.

Follow this with an assessment session, using an internal or third-party resource. Here, the managers look at their tasks and identify both those that could be done at a lower level and those critical tasks that they should do but which are falling between the cracks. It is important to have managers at different levels work on this together, as each manager's actions affect the others. The group can then make a process-improvement action plan and follow up with the same exercise six months later, and a year later. This will ensure that the change occurred, and that the new way of managing endured.

**Redefine** their jobs. Create a new set of job descriptions for managers at each level. These job descriptions should *explicitly state* the proportion of time to be spent on managing the day-to-day business versus creating change. This is critical. All job descriptions say that managers should improve the business, but unless you specify the *amount of time* to be spent changing things, the day-to-day will always crowd out the innovative.

Here's an issue: if a manager spends a lot of his or her time doing unproductive work, and a new lower-level associate would be needed to free up the manager, the cost of the new associate will count against budget while the incremental results of the manager's new activities will be hard to measure. But the results can be dramatic. For example, most companies can get the equivalent of a 25 to 35 percent increase in the size of their sales force by offloading administrative work onto a few new administrative personnel at headquarters.

**Institute** selective training. When managers move up a level, they need a brief, highly focused intervention to ensure that they understand the critical change in focus that the new position requires. As a manager moves up the organization, he or she not only becomes the top expert but, more important, also needs to shift focus from operating the current company to creating the future company. It is imperative to have a periodic third-party checkup on the mix of activities, using either an internal or an external resource, because it is very difficult for a manager to detect the natural drift toward managing one level too low.

## New productivity

As managers become more knowledgeable and disciplined about managing at the right level, their subordinates will become more capable, and performance will improve surprisingly quickly. The whole organization will become much more creative, productive, and profitable.

At the same time, the level of stress among managers will decline noticeably.

Stress is caused by two factors: the nature of a job, and an individual's feeling of lack of control. Of these, the latter is far more important. For example, an emergency room doctor has a difficult job, but lots of control. An assembly-line worker has a routine job, but little control. Most often, the doctor feels less stress than the assembly-line worker.

Managers who manage one level too low overmanage their subordinates. These subordinate managers feel a lack of control that they experience as stress, gridlock, victimization, and helplessness. This is what the CEO of the telecommunications company I described earlier saw in his company.

Top managers who guide their organizations so that everyone manages at the right level gain an enormous lever to improve their company's profitability and performance, both in the near term and for the future.

### THINGS TO THINK ABOUT

**1.** It is very natural to manage a level too low. Most managers instinctively continue the behavior that brought them success in the past. Yet this problem can paralyze your organization, halt your career progress, and impede profitability management.

**2.** Most companies do not have an explicit process to reorient promoted managers to their new jobs. This is especially problematic for new director-level managers (who are the key players in profitability management), and for new vice presidents (who are responsible for positioning their companies for the future).

**3.** Think about your actions over the last two months. What proportion of your time did you spend on managing the day-to-day business? Coordinating with your counterparts on profitability management? Repositioning your company for three to five years from now? What does this picture look like for your subordinates? Your bosses? Your peers? If you spend a few hours thinking systematically about this, you will get a 70 percent accurate view of your company's organizational effectiveness.

**4.** It is not uncommon in a company, that in some departments managers are managing at the right level, while in other departments managers are managing a level too low.

## What's Next

This chapter focuses on managing at the right level. The next chapter explains how to develop middle management excellence, a crucial component of organizational productivity and profitability.

*What is the single most important thing you can do*
*to maximize your company's performance? Build*
*the capabilities of middle management.*

## 32

---

# MIDDLE MANAGEMENT EXCELLENCE

▼

**WHAT IS THE** most important thing a CEO can do to maximize his or her company's profitability?

The answer is to creatively, systematically, and relentlessly build the capabilities of the company's middle management team: the vice presidents, directors, and managers. Middle management performance is the single most important element in corporate performance.

Regardless of what high-potential initiative the CEO chooses for the company, the middle management team's performance will determine whether it is a success or failure. And if the middle management team is performing in high gear, the managers will generate the right initiatives, and constantly adapt and improve them during implementation.

I recall reading a description of one major U.S. automobile company's middle management team. The phrase that stuck in my mind was "the frozen middle." The essential idea was that whatever initiative top management decided the company would pursue, it would be slowed to a standstill by the unwillingness and inability of the company's middle management team to carry it out. Ultimately, this company lost enormous market share to foreign competitors, and even now struggles to recover.

Middle management performance is the single most

important element in corporate performance.

▼

In education, it is well known that the quality of a school system is largely determined by the quality of the principals. If a school has a good principal, it will perform well. If the school has good teachers but a poor principal, performance will suffer. In all sectors, middle management makes all the difference.

## Initiatives or capabilities?

Try this mental exercise. Think about a typical three-month period for your company. What proportion of your company's top management time was spent on each of the following three activities: (1) developing new strategic initiatives, (2) managing the company's operations, and (3) building middle management capabilities? In most companies, the time spent on the first two dwarfs the time spent on the third.

Yet, building middle management capabilities is the most important key to succeeding in the other two activities. This is true for two reasons.

First, virtually all major strategic initiatives have to be carried out by the middle managers. Their flexibility and leadership skills will determine how effectively they tailor and adapt the initiatives to the company's changing circumstances.

Second, a strong middle management team will produce outstanding operational results and high sustained profitability, easing the temptation for top managers to manage one level too low and intervene excessively in day-to-day operations. A well-functioning middle management team also will proactively create a stream of new initiatives to improve profitability and seize new opportunities. Middle management excellence is the key leverage point for great performance.

The preceding chapter described the problems stemming from managing at the wrong level. The failure of many top managers to devote adequate time and attention to systematically developing middle management capabilities is one of the most severe consequences of managing one level too low.

# The problem

An important underlying problem is that middle management excellence, like leadership, is a difficult concept to pin down. Consequently, it is hard to specify a systematic program to build middle management capabilities.

In some companies, middle management development takes the form of disjointed short courses, either in-house or outside, that cover important aspects of management. These usually are helpful, but are not enough. Many managers find themselves too busy to dedicate much time to their personal development, especially if they regard the content as weakly relevant. A few fortunate managers get to attend lengthier, comprehensive executive education courses.

Mostly, it seems that top managers simply assume that management experience coupled with constructive management reviews will be enough for middle managers to figure out how to do their jobs well. While the most able managers can thrive in this situation, more simply settle into a routine of managing business as usual, accompanied by occasional initiatives when big problems arise.

It doesn't have to be this way. In the great companies of our day, middle management excellence is in fact one of top management's very highest priorities. Even after a manager leaves the company, he or she has the look and feel of the company's management team: a focus on systematically teaching his or her subordinates to analyze and improve the business, and on teaching them to pass this skill on to their own management teams. That's why the managers from these top companies are in such high demand.

## The core of middle management excellence

For many years, the late Professor C. Roland Christensen, Harvard Business School's legendary teacher of teachers, taught a doctoral course on teaching using the case method. In the course, he made a very powerful observation.

Professor Christensen noted that a great course is like a great musical. If the audience leaves a musical whistling two or three tunes for the rest of their lives, it is a great success. Similarly, if a class leaves a course with a deep understanding of the two or three most important ideas in the field, and with the ability to apply them capably for the rest of their lives, the course is a great success.

The biggest challenge in developing a course is always to identify clearly the two or three most important underlying concepts. With this understanding in mind, a teacher can organize all of the course material in a way that amplifies, explains, and enriches the students' understanding of these essential underlying ideas. At the end of a great course, the students will indeed whistle the course's two or three tunes for the rest of their lives.

The two-or-three-tunes principle applies to management as well. What are the most important two or three tunes that create middle management excellence? Here are my three candidates: (1) managing at the right level, (2) coordinated profitability management, and (3) managing as teaching.

## Managing at the right level

In most companies, the mix of business activities reflects a combination of what was needed three to five years ago, what is needed today, and what will be needed three to five years from now. In a surprising number of companies, the activity mix reflects perhaps 50 percent past needs, 30 percent present needs, and 20 percent future needs, at best. This is a critical problem, because it takes up to five years for managers to develop and implement the major initiatives needed to adapt a company to succeed in the future.

The primary cause of this problem is a lack of systematic middle management leadership, rooted in the problem of managing at the wrong level. As managers progress up the business hierarchy, their focus must increasingly shift from managing the company as it is (or as it was) to building the company of the future. At each level, middle managers must increasingly learn and practice change management and leadership, so that they are masterful by the time they reach the vice president level.

## Coordinated profitability management

There is a pervasive assumption in business that if each functional area of a company is well run, with sales maximizing revenues, operations minimizing costs, and so on, the company will be as profitable as possible. In fact, nothing could be further from the truth. This is the key theme of this book.

It is essential that middle managers, primarily at the director level, develop a broader view of the business. They must learn to coordinate with one another in order to understand which parts of the business are profitable, which are not, and, most important, *why* this is occurring.

This requires a high degree of interdepartmental coordination at the middle management level. As a company's markets change, profitability maximization becomes a moving target.

Profit mapping is critical to the success of this process for two reasons, one obvious, the other more subtle. First, profit mapping shows where a company's islands of profit are in its sea of red ink, and offers a process for creating a plan to systematically change this picture. Second, and just as important, the profit-mapping process gives a company's whole middle management team a shared perspective on how they can coordinate to affect profitability, an insight into how each manager's activities affect the others', and a foundation for creating a joint, apolitical action plan. The latter point is especially important.

In the absence of this shared view and shared agenda, the company's departments usually create competing initiatives, with all the counter-productive politics that this situation entails. And politically charged competing initiatives will indeed freeze a company's middle, bringing the company's progress to a dead stop.

## Managing as teaching

The essence of great management is great teaching. You can create new innovations and advance in the hierarchy only if your managers are capable of operating on their own. If you find yourself constantly pulled into day-to-day issues, the underlying problem probably is that you haven't succeeded in teaching your managers to manage.

The essence of great management is great teaching.

▼

As a manager ascends the company hierarchy, his or her manage-ment emphasis must shift from managing to teaching and develop-ing managers. The CEO typically doesn't do this, except in a few very successful companies, so it has to take place at the vice president level and below.

Great teaching doesn't happen overnight. Even at first-rate universities with engaged, capable students, it takes a semester or more for students to learn a subject. Here are some cornerstones to great teaching that apply to managers as well as professors.

- ▶ **Clarity on the essentials.** Like professors, managers must know not only their field but also how to *teach* it. The essential first step is identifying the two or three tunes that are the key to great performance. These generally are the *whys*, not the *hows*.
- ▶ **Enriching the understanding.** In a great course, the bulk of the course material is organized to amplify and illustrate the two or three underlying concepts. In this way, the more detailed knowledge enhances the learner's ability to work with the core ideas, while making the whole body of knowledge more memorable.
- ▶ **Active learning.** Productive learning often takes place in stages. First the learner is exposed to the core concepts, then tries to apply them and finds that he or she needs to understand them better. This makes the learner more receptive, and so the process repeats itself. Most effective courses are structured this way. Periodic tests help to highlight progress and areas where more work is needed. By contrast, all too often in business, subordinates are simply instructed and then left largely on their own.

## Teaching managers to manage

The highest calling in management is teaching your managers to manage. Middle management performance is the single most important element in corporate performance. Yet how many top management teams view this not only as a high priority but also as a core business process subject to careful measurement, rigorous analysis, and constant improvement?

Middle management excellence—resting on managing at the right level, coordinated profitability management, and managing as teaching—can be systematically developed and constantly improved. It is the ultimate point of leverage for all corporate performance.

**1.** Developing excellent middle managers is one of your most important profit levers. Yet in all too many companies, this process is not treated as a mission-critical top-management priority.

**2.** Middle management excellence does not result naturally as a byproduct of normal business processes, such as operating reviews and project milestone readouts.

**3.** Middle management excellence is critically intertwined with profitability management because the epicenter of profitability management is tight interdepartmental coordination by a company's director-level managers (who are the company's department heads).

**4.** The three cornerstones of middle management excellence are: managing at the right level, coordinated profitability management, and managing as teaching.

**5.** The key to great teaching is not just deep knowledge but the ability to join deep knowledge with a great teaching plan. In your company, is there a set of explicit teaching plans to guide your managers in mentoring their direct reports to become great managers? Do you have one?

## What's Next

This chapter continues the theme of organizational effectiveness. The next concludes this theme by explaining how to use action-training to change a company's culture. Culture change is one of the most difficult tasks a manager can face.

*Culture change presents a major obstacle to many executives seeking to unlock the latent profits inherent in their companies. Here's one company's action plan for improvement.*

## 33

# ACTION-TRAINING FOR CULTURE CHANGE

▼

**RECENTLY A VICE** president of a leading high-tech company asked me how a top manager could create a culture of growth. Her company was starting to emerge from a difficult period, and this thoughtful executive was wrestling with how to refocus her managers to achieve profitable growth.

The difficulty of changing a company's culture confronts many managers. I remember talking to the president of a major telecom company who said that the company needed to change its culture to succeed in the newly deregulating world. His management team would have to think and act very differently. What should he do? Send a memo to all managers? Give a speech?

The difficulty of managing culture change presents a major obstacle to many executives seeking to unlock their companies' large latent profits. Change management has many components, but one of the most intractable issues is changing the company's culture—the way a company's managers do business. This involves transforming what they focus on, how they go about their jobs, and how they work with one another. This is what the vice president called creating a culture of growth, and what the telecom company president saw as changing the company to succeed in a deregulating environment.

In successful culture change, a company's managers must do two things: (1) define and internalize new ways to work, and (2) become proficient at the new processes. They have to go through the process of culture change together. As the managers develop new ways to work together, they will change one another. This is a virtuous cycle.

As the managers develop new ways to work together,

they will change one another.

▼

The process of changing a company's culture takes time, and requires that the top manager be an effective teacher. And the key to being an effective teacher is developing an effective teaching plan.

## Training that works

The telecom president looked at how other companies managed change effectively, and decided to develop an action-training program centered on the profitability management process. This program had a well-crafted structure and a very specific action-objective, making it very different from general training programs that so often seem to lack payoff. Here's how it worked.

The president had recently reorganized the customer-facing functions of the company into geographic market areas. Each market area was headed by a group vice president and had about fifty marketing, operations, and finance managers. The challenge was to coalesce each market area's managers into a highly coordinated team, with appropriate plans for market development, competitive response, and profitability management.

The president structured a nine-month action-training program in which each market area's management team met off-site for monthly sessions of one to one and a half days. Each market area had its own set of sessions led by the area's group vice president. The sessions were co-led by an outside expert with a deep understanding of the company, industry, and management teaching process.

The sessions combined carefully chosen teaching cases, discussion, and a session-by-session buildup of each market area's plans for change and growth.

In each session, each group discussed teaching materials on an important area of business: first profitability, then competition, market development, strategy, etc. The discussions focused on the company's own business.

Between sessions each month, each group utilized what it had learned in the preceding session to develop the relevant portion of its new plans. In the following action-training session, the group devoted about half of the session to reviewing, discussing, and improving the planning work that they had just completed. The other half was devoted to new teaching materials and training for the next planning assignment.

> The sessions combined carefully chosen teaching cases,
>
> discussion, and a session-by-session buildup of each
>
> market area's plans for change and growth.

Importantly, the program's primary deliverable was a concrete set of new plans, created by the company's own managers, appropriate for the company's new situation. The president was clear that the objective of the action-training program was to create the new plans, but the critical byproduct was comprehensive culture change. This gave the whole process a cohesive goal, a strong sense of purpose, and a feeling of urgency that would not have been achieved if the stated goal was simply vague culture change.

The action-training program followed the outline of profitability management developed in this book. This is the session-by-session program that each group followed:

▶ **Month 1: Business blocks.** The group divided each market area into market segments, called business blocks, which were geographic clusters with similar characteristics, such as a group of suburbs or a city center. This was a new way of looking at the company, which formerly focused on broader entities like states or regions.

▶ **Month 2: Profitability baseline.** The group constructed a 70 percent accurate spreadsheet-based profitability analysis with return on invested assets for each business block. What did they see? Islands of profit in a sea of red ink.

- **Month 3: Competitive inroads.** The group looked carefully at competitors in each business block. They estimated where each competitor would try to make inroads and what business they might lose. They modeled this using the profitability spreadsheets. It became clear that a number of smart competitors were headed for the islands.
- **Month 4: Market development.** The group projected its market development plans for each business block, and estimated the profitability in light of competitor activities. The teams saw the wisdom of focusing their marketing resources where the payoff was greatest, instead of spreading them across broad areas.
- **Month 5: Strategic alternatives and resources.** In this critical segment, the group formulated strategic alternatives that reflected their understanding of competitive dynamics and market opportunities. They thought about alternative ways to focus their resources, crafting coordinated packages of new services and market development. They estimated the profitability impact and resource requirements of each alternative.
- **Month 6: Strategy selection.** The group decided which clusters of business to pursue aggressively, where to focus on improving marginal returns, and which clusters did not warrant aggressive investment (the company was committed to providing a strong baseline level of service everywhere). The group made detailed projections and developed a resource budget.
- **Month 7: Reconciliation with corporate needs.** The key managers in all of the market areas combined their projections and resource needs, and reconciled these with corporate requirements. Where necessary, they made adjustments to align their plans with corporate needs.
- **Month 8: Implementation.** The group determined the key implementation steps needed to achieve their objectives. They specifically identified how the functional managers would coordinate with one another, and developed a rough timetable with responsibilities.
- **Month 9: Final plans.** In the final session, each manager in each market area created a set of department plans within the framework of the group's plans. This concluded the planning cycle.

■  ■  ■

# Leadership and muscle memory

This action-training process was extremely effective on several levels: culture change, insightful planning, and coordinated implementation. The payoffs included a number of long-term capabilities.

**Effective leadership.** Each group vice president was in the room in every session with his or her key managers and staff. This was critical. Because the analysis was unfolding session by session, everyone had an opportunity to shape the group's views, and everyone was shaped by these views. As the months passed, the group developed new plans and, importantly, a deep understanding of how to work together in a new way. The group changed the views of those managers who were resistant at first. The group vice president gave the managers real-time coaching, feedback, and development, while at the same time listening to them and learning from their perspectives.

**Effective plans.** The teams pioneered fundamentally new ways to analyze their market areas, and developed powerful integrated plans. The new plans represented the best joint understanding and analysis of the market areas' best managers, and they far surpassed what could have been achieved by small groups of staff planners working alone. They were appropriate for the new era, and not just adapted from old plans from the old era. They embodied a deep understanding of the company's profit levers, and the profitability potential of every part of the business.

**Effective teamwork.** Beyond effective plans, all the managers in each group developed a detailed, shared understanding of their business, with all its potential and risks. Managers quickly began to coordinate with one another to improve the company's profitability.

**Muscle memory.** Over the sessions, each group developed muscle memory in their understanding of profitability management. Muscle memory is a term used in fields ranging from learning the piano to learning golf. It means that for continued effectiveness, one must go beyond an understanding of what to do, beyond getting it right a few times, and practice until one's muscles are trained to get it right all the time.

A classic problem with traditional company training is that it teaches techniques but fails to develop the muscle memory necessary for continued success. Action-training develops the deep understanding, teamwork, and muscle memory needed for effective change. It creates a permanent capability for profitability management, as well as a first set of highly effective plans. With the foundation of comprehensive analysis and understanding that an action-training program provides, planning cycles in subsequent years can go much more quickly while producing ever-more-effective results.

## Getting it

In my experience, four to five months is the time frame for cultural change under the best circumstances. In this period, a top manager with an effective change process can get his or her management team to do business in a new way.

In my experience, four to five months is the time frame

for cultural change under the best circumstances.

▼

Management of culture change is not necessarily more difficult than other aspects of management, but it is very different. It requires a different set of management tools and approaches. There are clear pathways to success and known time frames for effective change. Action-training is one of the most effective ways to accomplish transformational culture change, with both immediate and lasting benefits.

---

### THINGS TO THINK ABOUT

**1.** Changing a company's culture is one of the most difficult challenges a manager can face. At best, it is a four- to six-month process. But there is a known pathway to success.

**2.** Successful culture change involves two things: (1) imparting knowledge of a new way to do business, and (2) muscle memory. Action-training imparts the needed knowledge, and provides a structure to practice the new work processes to the point of proficiency.

**3.** It is critical to link the action-training to a concrete deliverable—like creating a new set of plans—in order to give the process focus, urgency, and a sense of reality.

**4.** The best results occur when top managers and their subordinates go through the process of culture change together. They form an extremely tight team with great alignment and flexibility.

---

# What's Next

The first five chapters of this section explain how to manage the process of paradigmatic change. The subsequent three chapters, including this one, describe how to develop a highly productive organization necessary for profitability management. The final three chapters of this section tell you how to be an effective manager and leader.

*Today's CIO has opportunities far beyond the hopes and dreams of twenty years ago. More than ever before, the CIO's effectiveness will determine the destiny of the company.*

## 34

# NEW CIO ROLE: CHANGE WARRIOR

(coauthored with Massimo Russo)

**WHAT SEPARATES EFFECTIVE** CIOs from ineffective ones?

The answer has changed dramatically in the last twenty years. Two decades ago, technical expertise was the critical variable. Today, it's whether the CIO can move the rest of the company to do things differently.

The problem is that many CIOs developed their management skills in the earlier era when technology assessment and implementation were the key issues. Now they need a completely new set of skills.

I recall reading an article a few years ago about why so many software implementations in areas like customer relationship management (CRM) were failing. In fact, virtually all of the systems had software that worked properly and users who understood how to use it. The problem was that the underlying business processes had not changed, so the software's capabilities were largely going to waste.

When top management asked whether the software was worthwhile, the answer was no. (Note: *worthwhile* is very different from *working*.) In many companies, this led to a pervasive feeling in upper management that software projects were oversold. The real issue was that many CIOs defined their jobs too narrowly, and did not take sufficient ownership for the whole change management process.

The consequence of this syndrome is that today in many companies, IT budgets are being squeezed. This leaves the CIOs with even fewer resources to manage change. There is a tremendous opportunity cost because well-implemented IT has the power to produce huge increases in profitability and other benefits.

> Twenty years ago, technical expertise was the critical
>
> variable. Today, it's whether the CIO can move the rest
>
> of the company to do things differently.

▼

Today, many CIOs are asking how they can turn this around.

## Corporate IT lifecycle

Over the past twenty years, the corporate IT function has fundamentally changed. Even as new technologies continually arise, the corporate IT function has moved from youth to maturity in its role within companies. This is manifested in three important ways.

**First.** IT applications have shifted from automating existing processes to enabling the creation of new ones. The older applications were chiefly in back-office areas like finance and human resources, while today's are often in front-end areas like customer management and in mission-critical areas like supply chain management.

Twenty years ago, remote order entry systems allowed companies to replace paper orders with online orders. This produced efficiencies and required new processes, but the organizational changes were incremental in nature.

Today's software enables managers to do fundamentally new things, like identify the best customers and sell to them differently. At the same time, they have to change the way they sell to other customers, or stop selling to them completely. This requires major changes in the way users structure and conduct their core business, along with parallel changes in critical related areas like planning, compensation, and resource allocation. Unless these occur, the software's capabilities will be underutilized.

**Second.** IT capabilities today are much more powerful, by orders of magnitude, than they ever were. Twenty years ago, when I developed my first analysis of a company's profitability, it took more than a month to construct and run the database on a PC-AT. Today, leading companies have data warehouses that allow managers to run their businesses with precision in real-time. It's almost like culture shock. Today's IT capabilities are far outrunning an organization's ability to utilize them.

**Third.** Software packages are proliferating more and more rapidly. Each software package may well show value in a business case analysis. The problem is that organizations can't possibly digest all the potentially useful software packages, even if they all have positive net benefits. As a result, in many companies, less than 10 percent of their software's capability is actually being utilized. In this context, it is critical to prioritize the software in order to create an integrated change process, rather than a seemingly endless series of independent projects. The CIO must carefully pace and manage the change.

## Technology lifecycles

In classic product lifecycles of technical products, the emphasis shifts from getting the technology to work, to using it to do existing things better, to doing new things because of it. In today's world of mature corporate IT, many users don't fully understand what new things their IT will enable them to do, and don't appreciate how differently they will have to manage in order to reap the benefits of these new capabilities.

Today's CIO must shift from managing activities within the IT department to managing change throughout the rest of the company. The problem is that the history of corporate IT has created a sea anchor on the ability of CIOs to make this shift.

In the mid-to-late 1990s, when CIOs were shifting focus from back-office automation to front-end systems that changed the way business could be conducted, they were hit by Y2K (concerns about computers failing at the start of the new millennium). Y2K forced CIOs to focus on ensuring that their core systems would not fail, reinforcing the role of the CIO as technologist.

The burst of the Internet bubble followed soon after. The Internet's promise was oversold, with business expectations far outrunning the technology's ability to deliver. When the bubble burst, many managers became very skeptical about the overall potential of IT, and a pervasive backlash resulted.

Many CIOs found themselves stuck in a very difficult position: they had primarily technical skills in an era when business change management was becoming critical, and their companies had lost faith in IT.

## How GE got it right

The case of GE is very instructive. After wandering through the desert for a while, the company created a new vision of a powerful, effective CIO.

Before 1997, the CIO function at GE was primarily oriented toward back-office applications, and these were not really on top management's radar screen as strategic capabilities.

When the Internet bubble developed, GE's top management moved strongly to change the company's culture. Their goal was to bring GE managers closer to the technology so that they would embrace the new possibilities. They even set up a program for what they called "e-mentoring," pairing experienced top managers with young, technology-savvy managers.

At the same time, GE established e-business groups in each business unit in order to develop new technology-enabled opportunities. The objective was to stimulate demand throughout the company for new IT, and to force the IT departments to change in response.

The problem was that these changes created tension between the e-business leaders, who were businesspeople, and the traditional IT executives. GE solved this by merging the two groups. The goal was to fulfill a new vision: a set of new business-minded CIOs.

In some divisions, e-business leaders replaced traditional CIOs, while in others, business-minded CIOs replaced the e-business leaders. The acid test was that a new CIO had to be a credible partner of the division's CEO, capable of strong business involvement. For example, the Six Sigma leader at NBC became the CIO of GE Aircraft Engines. This manager had strong process improvement skills, strong business leadership experience, and some IT experience.

This marked the end of the era of predominantly back-office, technology-oriented CIOs at GE.

Similar changes are occurring at other leading companies. A top executive at a large consumer products company stated that they would not hire a CIO who had not managed a P&L (profit-center) business unit or a major business operation. In these situations, the new CIO needs a capable chief technical officer or chief architect on staff. Unlike in the past, however, the technology role is decidedly supportive.

# Business-minded CIO leadership

How can a CIO make the transition to the new world of business-minded IT leadership? Two areas are particularly important: project selection and change management.

**Project selection.** I recall the CIO of a major company telling me years ago that IT priorities were set in a monthly meeting, and that if a business manager couldn't make the meeting to advocate for his or her projects, the projects were simply cut. In today's business world, the CIO has a completely different role: cocreator of IT opportunities to change the business, and comanager of these changes.

The CIO must be conversant with the strategic goals of the business and the alternative ways that the company can meet them. Armed with this knowledge, the CIO can partner with the operating managers to create more powerful ways to do business utilizing new IT capabilities. The CIO must go far beyond rank-ordering managers' requests, and often actually take the lead in redefining the business. This requires, first and foremost, that the CIO deeply understand the business, far beyond the day-to-day operations as currently conducted.

But simply identifying new value opportunities is not enough. The business-minded CIO also needs to assess the business units' attitudes toward change. This has two components: (1) determining how entrenched the current business processes are, and (2) analyzing how willing and able the business units are to make the business changes necessary to gain the full potential of new IT.

These two factors are crucial indicators of the likely success or failure of IT projects. They also tell you the magnitude and timing of the payoff. They enable the CIO to project the difficulty, speed, and nature of the business change management process that must accompany IT deployment.

With this view of the potential value of different projects, and an understanding of the nature and likely pace of actual change of each, the business-minded CIO can develop a set of strategic IT plans that addresses both system deployment and business change management.

Here, it is especially important to balance "quick hits," having fast payoff, with longer-term initiatives. This will motivate the business managers to see the whole change program through to its completion.

In many ways, the strategic IT plan is analogous to a company's strategic market management plan. In a good marketing plan, the company's marketing managers scan the current and potential customer base. They evaluate alternative programs of market development by assessing customers according to potential margin gain, willingness and ability to partner, and operating fit. A good strategic IT plan should do the same with respect to the company's business units.

**Change management.** In partnering with the business units to drive change, the CIO must engage at three levels: senior management, operating management, and project management.

At the senior management level, CIOs in several leading companies have found it effective to implement a senior executive IT council. This is a steering committee comprised jointly of top IT managers and top operating executives. The council develops a clear understanding of the company's strategic initiatives and the IT agenda that will enable them to succeed.

Director-level business advisers are crucial at the operating management level. These are experienced IT managers assigned to work with company business units. Their goal is to work with their counterpart business managers to develop a joint understanding of the value opportunities and change issues, and to create programs of linked IT deployment and business change management in order to realize the full promise of the IT investments. In a number of leading companies, these business advisers actually lead the change process in their business units.

Finding IT professionals with a strong knowledge of business issues can be difficult. In more and more leading companies, the business advisory role is recognized as a key leadership position, instrumental in driving business change.

At the project management level, the implementation process for applications that change the business must be completely different from traditional back-office implementations. Traditionally, implementations are sequential: software is developed and deployed, then people are trained to use it.

Today, there must be two parallel tracks in the implementation process: business change management and software deployment and training. In fact, the business change management process must *precede* the software deployment. Managers must understand the future process vision and begin the change process *before* a commitment is made to develop a new system.

■ ■ ■

> Today, there must be two parallel tracks in the
> implementation process: business change management,
> and software deployment and training.

▼

In a good change management process, business process change will create a groundswell of IT demand. The IT department can then engage the business units in joint programs of change management, with the ultimate deployment going much more smoothly. There is less resistance, and much fuller use of the new capabilities.

## The effective CIO

Here's how one very effective CIO summed up his experience: "The game is really won or lost before the project selection process. If the project is scoped too narrowly because of vision or budget constraints, you are in trouble even if it gets ranked to the top of the list. One of the key issues in my ten years as a CIO has been the need to respond appropriately to the many small projects generated by middle management. Some of these have to be done, but they should be fill-in work around the few strategic initiatives that will matter to the shareholders.

"Unfortunately, few senior business executives are skilled in leading all the major changes necessary to capture value from major IT-intensive initiatives. That is where the effective CIO comes in. The CIO can and should shape the vision with the senior executives, marshaling *all* the resources necessary to get the job done, including training, business process redesign, and new hires if needed."

Today's CIO has opportunities far beyond the hopes and dreams of twenty years ago. The key to success is actively engaging the business, partnering with counterpart business leaders throughout the company to drive paradigmatic change and major profit improvements. More than ever before, the CIO's effectiveness will determine the destiny of the company.

**1.** The role of the CIO has changed fundamentally over the past decade. It has evolved from chief technologist to change warrior.

**2.** Today, effective CIOs must understand how new technologies can enable their companies to change the way they do business. They also must be proficient at change management in order to help create the new business practices that the new technologies enable.

**3.** Project selection is critical to success. A company can't digest all the potential projects that have a positive business case ROI. The CIO must focus on accomplishing the few that really matter, managing them from conception to results.

**4.** For effective change management, a CIO has to integrate his or her organization into the company's ongoing work processes. Director-level business advisers are critical to this process.

## What's Next

This chapter describes the huge changes now occurring in the critical job of the CIO. The next two chapters explain how you can develop the essential attributes of a manager and leader, respectively.

*You don't have to complete a master's program to become a masterful manager. But understanding the process of obtaining a master's degree will help you think about how to improve your skills.*

## 35

---

# MASTERFUL MANAGEMENT

▼

**HOW CAN A** person become a great manager?

This question is particularly apt for the many young people who are completing their master's studies, and facing graduation and the prospect of entering the ranks of new managers. It also is crucial for experienced managers who want to remain in touch with the essence of their profession.

It is natural for a new graduate to focus on the process of completing a grueling program, to be relieved that it is over, and to be excited by the prospect of entering a new phase of life. But it is important not simply to rush into the next phase of life without reflecting on the meaning of achieving a master's degree.

A master's degree is very special. It marks a very important watershed in one's life. There is a great difference between what came before and what will come after. Understanding this is the key to starting to develop into a great manager.

### Levels of achievement

In order to appreciate the meaning of a master's degree, it is very helpful to understand its historical context. The early universities were established in the context of the guild system in the late Middle Ages. In the guild system, there were three levels of achievement.

The first level was apprentice. If a person wanted to learn a craft, he found an expert practitioner and worked in his house as an assistant for a number of years. In return for helping the head of the house, he was taught the fundamentals of the craft, and over time, he was increasingly allowed to practice the skills of the craft.

The second level was journeyman. After a number of years of apprenticeship, the young person became skilled at the craft, and was allowed to journey around practicing the craft on his own. Over time, he gained experience and perfected his skills, becoming more and more accomplished.

When the journeyman became extremely skilled, he could seek to attain the third, and highest, level of the craft. He could become a master. In order to become a master, the journeyman had to produce a work of superb refinement, his *masterpiece,* which met the highest standards of the guild. When he accomplished this, he was allowed to establish a house of his own and to teach apprentices.

## Becoming a master

For students achieving a master's degree, there are important parallels. Most master's students have progressed through career stages roughly analogous to the old guild system. Initially, they were undergraduates, and their primary task was to concentrate in a discipline and acquire a solid working knowledge of the foundations of the field.

After graduation, most moved into entry-level positions in which they could apply their expertise and continue to learn, somewhat like the journeyman stage.

When these individuals achieved a high level of experience and accomplishment in the practice of their field, they applied to a graduate program to learn to become a master. These master's programs offer a rigorous course of study that prepares the student to be certified as a master, much like the masters of old.

The master's thesis, which many students write, is the analog to the masterpiece of the old guild system. It is a student's masterpiece, a demonstration that the student has mastered the discipline and can produce an original work of rigor and insight that moves human knowledge forward.

Reflecting on the role of the masters of the old guild system offers important insights into masterful management. In the old guild system, a master craftsman had two essential tasks.

First, the master had an opportunity, and an obligation, to produce a series of ever better, continually refined masterpieces. These moved forward the state of the art of the craft. Many of these masterpieces are on display in great museums throughout the world today, and their makers' names are forever etched in history.

Second, the master had an opportunity, and an obligation, to take on apprentices and to teach them the craft, starting them on their journey toward mastery. Both of these essential tasks were necessary for the success and perpetuation of the craft.

Wandering through a museum today, it is easy to focus on the masterpieces—but it is just as easy to forget the guild-based career development process that produced them. Without the systematic process of training new masters, today's museums would be a shadow of what we see today.

## The masterful manager

Like the masters of old, today's masterful managers have two essential tasks, both equally important. First, they must develop rigorous, well-grounded strategies, initiatives, and programs that maximize their companies' profitability and move them forward into the future. Second, they must actively train and develop the next generation of managers who can accomplish their vision, and who someday can take their place as they move up the ranks.

Masterful management requires excellence in both parts of the duality. Unless both are done well, the company will not prosper over time.

The higher up a manager rises in an organization, the

more important the teaching becomes.

▼

There are many roads to becoming a masterful manager today, but they all require that at some point the manager shifts focus from learning and practicing to teaching and working through others. The higher up a manager rises in an organization, the more important the teaching becomes. This is the essential message of several of the preceding chapters in this section.

Similarly, the most effective consulting assistance involves teaching and working through a company's own managers, while ensuring creativity and discipline in the process. The ultimate measure of consulting success is building the company's own capability to succeed in new areas on its own.

I recently had dinner with a group of middle managers of a major company. We talked about the company and its management process. One of the managers commented, "It's okay to experiment, but you'd better not be wrong." In reality, learning by doing is necessary to developing thoughtful, creative managers, and a few mistakes along the way are a natural part of the process. That's why good showcase projects start with smaller customers or territories.

In the most effective companies, there is an extraordinary emphasis on developing managers. Higher-level executives create direction, and then focus most of their time and attention on coaching and teaching their subordinate managers, monitoring their results, and helping them understand how to improve their performance. In this way, the masterful organization continually renews itself.

This process is analogous to what happens at a great teaching hospital, where the master surgeons always have residents and interns at their sides. The master surgeons, like master managers, stay focused on the duality of creating new ways to do things and training the next generation.

## Masterful strategies

The strategies, initiatives, and programs developed by masterful managers working through their subordinates are almost always superior to those developed by managers working alone. This occurs for two reasons.

First, the best managers are attracted by companies that offer the opportunity for effective management development and learning by doing. Second, teaching is the most effective form of learning. A masterful manager has to have a rigorous and well-developed understanding of the business in order to coach the subordinate managers effectively.

In this way, the masterful organization

continually renews itself.

▼

When one reads through the business press and annual reports, it is like walking through a great museum. The successful strategies, initiatives, and programs are all on display, but there is much less mention of the underlying systematic process of developing the managers that produced them. Masterful managers understand both sides of management excellence.

## Successful implementation

Masterful managers, and those trained by them, are experts in developing and implementing new initiatives. They are oriented toward working through others, and are receptive to others' ideas. An organization characterized by master managers is very receptive to change because the managers are conditioned to be open-minded and inquisitive. They are used to trying out ideas on others, and have been taught to view management as a process of give and take, a marketplace of ideas in which real value wins.

In this process of idea development, younger managers develop relationships with one another well before they are needed. A cohort of effective young managers becomes comfortable working with one another, and they rise up in the organization together. The company with a critical mass of masterful managers thus becomes a self-perpetuating masterful organization—continually approaching its full profit potential, and continually changing and adapting as new opportunities evolve and develop.

An organization characterized by master managers
is very receptive to change because the managers are
conditioned to be open-minded and inquisitive.

▼

**1.** Masterful managers are great at two essential tasks: developing new ideas and initiatives that move their companies forward, and developing great subordinate managers who can grow to replace them as they move up in the organization.

**2.** Most company initiatives focus on the first task. In all too many companies, the second task is largely overlooked, to their serious detriment.

**3.** Great management development is a process that can be made explicit and subjected to constant improvement. Mentoring subordinate managers has a great positive impact on the mentors' knowledge and abilities. Today's leading companies place great emphasis on this process.

**4.** Learning by doing is an essential part of great teaching. Showcase projects provide a good opportunity to develop new ideas and new ways of doing business in a controlled, low-risk manner.

## What's Next

This chapter describes how to become a masterful manager. The concluding chapter explains how to become an effective leader.

*We know leadership when we see it. But just what*
*are the key ingredients of powerful leaders?*
*Can we learn to be great?*

# 36

## THE ESSENCE OF LEADERSHIP

▼

**WHAT ARE THE** essential qualities of an effective leader? Can they be recognized in young people? Can they be developed?

These questions were the topic of a meeting I recently had with a top admissions officer of a leading graduate school of business. This official was reflecting on the profile of applicants to be accepted into the school. She wanted to be sure that this profile was the most appropriate one, and not take anything for granted.

Great leadership seems to be easy to recognize, and you usually can tell when someone is lacking in leadership qualities. But how do you define it? This is a critical question both for selecting and developing your subordinates and for developing your own leadership capabilities.

Here's a definition of leadership that has stuck with me: leaders are "people who leave their footprints in their areas of passion."

Not surprisingly, I heard this definition in a presentation given by the admissions officer and a colleague of hers. In fact, this admissions officer was showing leadership by inviting me and others in to talk about admissions profiles: she was taking an already excellent process and, rather than being complacent about it, making it even better. She was leaving her footprints in her area of passion.

Some companies have a culture of relentless, almost compulsive improvement. No matter how good the company is, it should be doing better. It reminds me of a Smithsonian exhibit on American ingenuity called "If We're So Good, Why Aren't We Better?"

By contrast, other companies are smugly stuck in the past. I remember one vice president telling me that his company was doing everything right because "if there were a better way, we would have found it, and we'd be doing it."

The lesson: when you have the lead, step on the gas. After all, that's how you got there.

## Ambidextrous leadership

In a sense, great leaders have to be ambidextrous. On the one hand, they have to be able to execute capably within the current business paradigm, "the way we do business." On the other hand, they must be able to reflect on the current paradigm, find ways to fundamentally improve it, and manage the large-scale change to a successful conclusion. You need two hands, and a lot of commitment, to change the propeller on the airplane in midflight, but that capability is the essence of successful leadership.

Think of it this way: someday your current job will be a line entry on your résumé. Under the entry, you'll have two or three bullets to describe your major accomplishments. "Did a good job of doing what always was done" can't be one of them.

"Doing a good job of doing what always was done" is the ante; it's what you have to do to keep the job. The bullets, your major accomplishments, come on top. They are your successes at changing the current paradigm, and this is how you showcase your leadership.

By the way, there is a lot of power in reflecting at the beginning of a new job on what you want the two or three bullets to be, and deliberately setting about building them over the course of your job tenure. Otherwise, you run the risk of having them simply be the incidental byproducts of the opportunities that happened to come your way.

Most people can develop their leadership

skills by working at it

▼

Can you be a good leader without being a good manager? In my experience, the best leaders are also great managers, and the best managers have strong leadership capabilities. To be successful, you must have both a passion for improving your organization and the capability to drive your efforts through to completion.

It certainly is possible to team someone who likes to change things with someone who prefers to manage stability. In fact, the most effective teams have one person who constantly pushes the limits and another who constantly ensures that the organization doesn't blow up. The former winds up going slower than he or she would like to, the latter winds up going faster than is comfortable, and the compromise is great for the company. However, both members of the team need to have the full capability to manage ambidextrously. Otherwise, they will not have the common understanding and mutual respect to agree on the compromises necessary to create an effective course of action.

Managing the day-to-day, which is the core requirement of any position, is no small task. It requires that you produce consistently good results, meet profitability objectives, and constantly improve your business processes. Success involves competence, ability, and teamwork. You can and should derive a great deal of satisfaction from doing a good job at this, but don't mistake day-to-day management for leading paradigmatic change.

## Leading paradigmatic change

Quantum change management is very different from day-to-day management. It involves conceptualizing and creating fundamental improvements that change the way business is done.

In order to lead paradigmatic change, you need eight essential personal characteristics. These characteristics are above and beyond your day-to-day capabilities and the domain knowledge you need to analyze what to do.

▶ **Capacity for passion.** First and foremost, you need a burning drive to make things better. Change management is a grueling process, and passion will see you through it. Some managers just seem to have "fire in the belly."

▶ **Perspective.** In order to convert passion into action, you must be able to step back and view what you're doing even while you're doing it. This is what the admissions officer was doing when she was reflecting on whether the admissions profile was correct, even while she was busy with her day-to-day activities.

▶ **Creativity.** Once you have a perspective on your business process, it takes creativity to see fundamentally new and more-effective ways to do things. Some people are more naturally creative than others, but you can get your creative juices flowing by surveying a variety of business practices in a variety of companies. In good measure, business school case studies offer this perspective. So do business magazines and other publications.

▶ **Organization skills.** Leading major change requires both soaring creativity and mundane practicality. You have to translate a broad vision into a very-well-organized, practical step-by-step program. Otherwise, people won't have the confidence needed to let go of the old tried-and-true way of doing things.

▶ **Teamwork.** Virtually all major change involves engaging, persuading, and working with other people. You have to have the organization's best interests at heart, and really be motivated to make things better for those you seek to lead. With this attitude, and a good, practical plan, people will be inclined to follow you.

▶ **Persistence.** After passion gets you started, persistence is what carries you through. I can think of several brilliant, creative, passionate managers who came up with great ideas but lost interest when it was time to slog through the implementation. Ultimately, they designed great plays but never put the points on the scoreboard.

▶ **Open-mindedness.** Large-scale change necessarily involves a good measure of learning by doing. By definition, you're sailing into uncharted waters. A good leader needs a high level of tolerance for ambiguity.

▶ **Integrity.** Last, but by no means least, leaders need integrity. This doesn't just mean not breaking the law. That's honesty, which certainly is an important component of integrity. But integrity goes beyond that. It is a matter of being genuine, being motivated by your deeply held values to make your organization and your coworkers better off. This is where the passion, persistence, and teamwork come from. Without integrity, you're simply promoting yourself, and people will not follow your lead.

## Can leaders be developed?

Like anything else, leadership ability is distributed throughout a population. Some people are natural leaders, others are more comfortable with a well-defined context, and many people are somewhere in between.

Natural leaders have important abilities, but they often need careful training in the more practical aspects of converting a creative vision into a concrete program of action. They need to understand the length of the change life cycle so that they don't underestimate the importance of persistence.

Most people, however, can develop their leadership skills by working at it. The first step is recognizing that excellence at the day-to-day is critical, but it is not enough. The second is the need to look inside yourself and decide whether you are willing to be uncomfortable for a prolonged period while you conceptualize and lead the change. The ultimate reward is the deep satisfaction that comes from seeing something new that wouldn't have been there if you had not created it.

Once you decide to become a leader, you can develop the characteristics you'll need by being thoughtful about the accomplishments that you want on your résumé and deciding to devote the time and attention needed to achieve them. Like anything else, practice makes perfect.

To be a great leader, you need a certain level of intellect, but not necessarily great genius. You need a certain level of social skills, but not necessarily those of a great salesperson. However, you do need a compulsion to operate at two levels: to be a great doer, and a great reflector.

Most important, to be a great leader, you need to find what you really like. That's where the passion, commitment, and integrity come from. In my experience, the most important underlying factor in leadership is whether a person has searched out and found a great match between what's in his or her heart, which is what he or she really enjoys, and the work situation.

Think about the definition of leaders: "People who leave their footprints in their areas of passion." It's easy to focus on the first part, how to leave footprints. But the real power comes from the second, working in your area of passion.

If you're doing what you really like, you almost can't help

but feel passion toward making it better.

▼

How can you recognize leadership potential in a young person? The most important clue is whether the person has identified and sought out a work situation in which he or she feels real passion. If a person doesn't have the drive or ability to get his or her own situation right, how will he or she be able to do this for a company? If you're doing what you really like, you almost can't help but feel passion toward making it better.

---

## THINGS TO THINK ABOUT

**1.** Leaders are "people who leave their footprints in their areas of passion."

**2.** Most people focus on the first aspect of leadership—how to leave footprints. However, the second aspect—working in your area of passion—is the real key to success.

**3.** How can one tell who will be an effective leader? For a start, look at whether the person is working in an area that he or she really enjoys.

**4.** Think about your own job and career. Are you working in an area that you really enjoy and find fulfilling? If so, consider how to improve your leadership techniques. If not, think hard about how to move toward what you really would love to do.

---

# EPILOGUE

# WHAT'S NEXT . . . FOR YOU?

**EACH YEAR, I** talk to my class at MIT about careers. I tell my students to consider the "$10 million test." Imagine that you just inherited $10 million, and you no longer *have* to work. I know . . . you would spend two months on the beach . . . but then you would get bored. And you would start thinking about what you really *want* to do. After you did a lot of soul-searching, you would settle on an understanding of what you really *would like* to do.

My advice to them, and to you, is to spend the time to figure this out *now*, and to do what you really want to do *now*. The world has an enormous amount of variety, and whatever situation fits you best is either out there or you can create it. Your prime job is to understand what it is you really want, and to be creative and energetic about finding or creating it. This process, after all, is what leadership is all about.

If you spend your life doing what you really want to do—the job that gives you real satisfaction and pleasure—you will be much happier and much more effective. And much more materially successful.

If you work in an area you really like, you will be naturally inclined to make it better, and your colleagues will be drawn to work with you by your selfless affinity to your work. Great results will naturally follow.

This is the essence of leadership. It is the ultimate key to success in profitability management, and in all other aspects of business.

Thank you for reading this book. I wish you good luck, and I hope that you let me know about your experiences leading your company's profitability management initiatives to a successful outcome.

Jonathan Byrnes
Cambridge, Massachusetts
jlbyrnes@mit.edu
October 2010

# ACKNOWLEDGMENTS

**I AM VERY** grateful to a number of people who have helped me along the way. First and foremost, I want to thank the managers with whom I've worked in my consulting and research, who enabled me to develop the concepts in this book. I also want to thank my students at MIT over the years for analyzing and challenging these ideas in class, and for staying in touch to discuss their experiences in applying these ideas in their jobs.

I'm especially grateful to Gerry Allan. Gerry was a classmate in the Harvard Business School doctoral program, and we worked together on many of the projects in which these ideas were developed. He also read and commented on early drafts of most of the columns, as well as this book.

Sean Silverthorne, Editor of *Working Knowledge*, was tremendously helpful, and I'm grateful for the opportunity he gave me to write for the publication.

MIT's Yossi Sheffi, Chris Caplice, Jim Rice, Hank Marcus, and Don Rosenfield have been great friends and colleagues for many years, and I appreciate the help that they have given me in my teaching and research at MIT. Harvard Business School professors Ben Shapiro, Roy Shapiro, and Jan Hammond have been terrific mentors, friends, and colleagues for a long time.

Bill Copacino discussed a number of these columns with me, and read and commented on a draft of this book. He also has generously shared many of the experiences he had when he was CEO of Accenture's Business Consulting Practice, and as a top manager in several leading companies. Dan Furman, GE vice president, was very helpful in discussing the concepts in several columns. Joseph Bode, who has served as a top executive at Firestone, Revco Drugs, Black & Decker, and Keystone Automotive, generously discussed the material in this book with me, and reviewed the manuscript. Ciji Ware was a wonderful guide to the publishing process, and is a great friend.

My wife, Marsha, has been tremendously helpful in all phases of the book, from the original articles to the final proofreading.

I would like to thank and acknowledge Stuart Smith, former vice president of Dell, for his important contributions to chapter 7, "Dell Manages Profitability, Not Inventory," and Steve Doyle, my Harvard classmate and president of SXD Associates, for his important contributions to chapter 11, "Account Management: Art or Science?" Mike Duffy, executive vice president of operations at Cardinal Health's Medical Segment, made many crucial contributions to chapter 19, "Supply Chain Management in a Wal-Mart World."

Massimo Russo, vice president of the Boston Consulting Group, coauthored chapter 34, "New CIO Role: Change Warrior." I am grateful for his intellectual partnership and friendship.

My literary agent, Eric Lupfer, of WME Entertainment, was a terrific source of wisdom, experience, and guidance throughout the whole process.

David Moldawer, my editor at Penguin's Portfolio imprint, provided enormous help and patience in shaping this book. He is a true professional, and it is a special pleasure to work with him.

Most important, I'm tremendously grateful to my family—my wife, Marsha, and my sons, Steve and Dan (and daughter-in-law, Kristin). They have been at the center of everything wonderful in my life, and this book would not have been possible without their love and support.

Needless to say, I share credit for all of the helpful concepts and ideas in this book, and I take sole responsibility for any and all errors.

# INDEX

# ABOUT THE AUTHOR

**JONATHAN L. S. BYRNES** is a senior lecturer at MIT, where he has taught at the graduate level and in executive programs for nearly twenty years. The courses he has taught, Case Studies in Logistics and Supply Chain Management and Integrated Account Management, together cover all strategic and operational aspects of customer-supplier relationships.

He has authored more than one hundred books, articles, cases, notes, and expert submissions. He wrote a monthly column on managing profitability, called "The Bottom Line," in Harvard Business School's *Working Knowledge* e-newsletter for four years. Dr. Byrnes has supervised thesis research projects in a number of organizations, including ABB, C&S Wholesale Grocers, Cardinal Health, Cisco, Dell, Flextronics, Honeywell, iRobot, Lahey Clinic, Nebraska Medical Center, Northrop Grumman, Philips, Procter & Gamble, Raytheon, SanDisk, and United Technologies.

Dr. Byrnes earned a DBA from Harvard University in 1980, and has served as president of the Harvard Alumni Association. He also served for five years on the board of directors of the Harvard Business School Alumni Association, and for two years on Harvard's Committee on Shareholder Responsibility.

He is president of Jonathan Byrnes & Co., a focused consulting company that he founded in 1976. He has advised more than fifty major companies and industry associations. Dr. Byrnes serves on the board of directors of MSC Industrial Direct, a New York Stock Exchange company. He has served on the advisory boards of Objectiva Software and Autopart International, two companies that were acquired at a substantial gain, and he currently serves on the advisory boards of OCO, RMG Networks, and WaveMark, all early-stage companies.

For more information, his Web site is http://mit.edu/jlbyrnes. He can be reached at jlbyrnes@mit.edu.